A HANDBOOK
for
SEMINARY PRESIDENTS

 *This book is published in cooperation with the*
ASSOCIATION OF THEOLOGICAL SCHOOLS
IN THE UNITED STATES AND CANADA

A HANDBOOK
for
SEMINARY PRESIDENTS

G. Douglass Lewis, *editor*

Lovett H. Weems Jr., *associate editor*

WILLIAM B. EERDMANS PUBLISHING COMPANY

GRAND RAPIDS, MICHIGAN / CAMBRIDGE, U.K.

Wm. B. Eerdmans Publishing Co.
255 Jefferson Ave. S.E., Grand Rapids, Michigan 49503 /
P.O. Box 163, Cambridge CB3 9PU U.K.

Printed in the United States of America

11 10 09 08 07 06   7 6 5 4 3 2 1

Library of Congress Cataloging-in-Publication Data

A handbook for seminary presidents /
edited by G. Douglass Lewis and Lovett H. Weems Jr.
p.   cm.
Includes bibliographical references.
ISBN-10: 0-8028-3397-7 / ISBN-13: 978-0-8028-3397-6 (cloth: alk. paper)
1. Theological seminary presidents.
I. Lewis, G. Douglass (Granville Douglass), 1934-
II. Weems, Lovett H. (Lovett Hayes)

BV4166.5.H36   2006
230.071′1 — dc22

2006008542

www.eerdmans.com

Contents

v

115297

Contents

Acknowledgments

This handbook is a project of the Association of Theological Schools in the United States and Canada (ATS). It involved the full, diverse spectrum of schools from across the Association, which now consists of more than two hundred fifty theological schools representing Roman Catholic, Orthodox, evangelical, and mainline Protestant seminaries, spread geographically across the United States and Canada. More than one hundred individuals, most of them seminary presidents, were involved in the project as writers, editors, critics, or advisers. It is truly a book written by seminary presidents for seminary presidents.

The project emerged out of the desire to provide a resource for presidents that would enable them to do their work better and, in turn, develop more effective seminaries that are better able to serve churches and communities across North America. Our research showed that no comparable resource is available for seminary presidents. We hope this handbook conveys both a depth of understanding about the nature and role of a seminary president and practical information that enables a president to do a better job.

We have never worked on a project like this that had such enthusiastic involvement from so many people. They all know theological education from the inside and are committed to its mission. They not only contributed from their experience and knowledge but also testified to how much they learned from engaging in the project. Current and future generations of seminary presidents owe all of them a great debt. The repayment of the debt will come, we hope, in the form of higher quality and more effective presidential leadership in theological schools across our countries. What a long-term gift that will be to churches and society as a whole.

A special word of thanks must go to three key staff members at ATS: Daniel Aleshire, Nancy Merrill, and Bill Myers. They encouraged and supported the project from beginning to end. They also contributed as writers, editors, advisers, and critics. Thanks also go to the Religion Division of Lilly Endowment Inc., which funded the Leadership Education program of ATS. The Handbook for Seminary Presidents project is a key part of that program's work with seminary presidents. Craig Dykstra, Vice President, Religion, and John Wimmer, Program Director, affirmed and supported the project. Joe Arnold, Executive Assistant, Lewis Center for Church Leadership, Wesley Theological Seminary, provided administrative support for the project.

Each chapter had a team of three persons who designed and created it. The writer/editor had primary responsibility for constructing the chapter. His or her name is listed first under each chapter heading. The other two persons were designated as contributing writers. A list of all the contributors and the institutions they served is included at the end of the book. Listed below are members of the Advisory Committee who thought through the early design of the project and a group of outside readers who critiqued a first draft of each chapter. We thank all these individuals for their valuable input.

One further note of thanks must go to ATS and its staff, who continue to create and deliver a variety of resources to support theological education. ATS will continue to develop its Website and will there provide a section of resources for seminary presidents. The resources listed at the end of each chapter of this handbook will be on the Website, and as new resources helpful to presidents appear they will be added to the list. We invite presidents who discover particularly helpful materials to make ATS aware of them for addition to the Website. By that means the community of presidents can continue to contribute to one another's learning, growth, and practice.

G. DOUGLASS LEWIS, *Editor*
LOVETT H. WEEMS JR., *Associate Editor*

ACKNOWLEDGMENTS

Advisory Committee

Daniel Aleshire   The Association of Theological Schools in the United States and Canada

Charles Bouchard   Aquinas Institute for Theology

Myron McCoy   Saint Paul School of Theology

William Myers   The Association of Theological Schools in the United States and Canada

David Neelands   Trinity College Faculty of Divinity

Cornelius Plantinga Jr.   Calvin Theological Seminary

Louis B. Weeks   Union Theological Seminary and Presbyterian School of Christian Education

Barbara Wheeler   Auburn Theological Seminary

Outside Readers

Bruce Birch   Wesley Theological Seminary

Michael Cooper-White   Lutheran Theological Seminary at Gettysburg

Scott Cormode   Claremont School of Theology

Norman Dewire   Methodist Theological School in Ohio

David Greenhaw   Eden Theological Seminary

Philip Krey   Lutheran Theological Seminary at Philadelphia

Myron McCoy   Saint Paul School of Theology

John Phelan Jr.   North Park Theological Seminary

Reiss Potterveld   Lancaster Theological Seminary

Russell Richey   Candler School of Theology of Emory University

June Stowe   Wesley Theological Seminary

Barbara Brown Zikmund   Hartford Seminary

Introduction

G. Douglass Lewis and Lovett H. Weems Jr.

What's So Special about Seminary Presidents?

Another book about presidents and what they do? Aren't there already enough books on presidents, leadership, and management? True, the shelves of bookstores and libraries, the Web, and thousands of articles lie in wait to inform us about leaders — what they should do and how they should do it. The author of every book or article believes his or her words contain something a little different and unique. We, however, want to claim some distinction for this book.

Only those who have occupied the office of a seminary president know the special demands, challenges, opportunities, stresses, and joys of the job. It is not a job for everyone. At its heart it is a vocation, a calling. Those deciding to apply for or accepting an invitation to serve in such a position usually have been through a serious process of discernment. A commitment to service and response to a call usually characterize those who wear the mantle of seminary president most easily and successfully.

A president stands at the center point of an institution. He or she is on the "hot seat" of a daily struggle to understand and fulfill the seminary's mission while maintaining its economic vitality. No president can have the detailed knowledge required to make each and every component of a seminary run smoothly and effectively. Nevertheless, a president remains ultimately responsible for the effectiveness of each component and for integrating the parts into the whole of the institution. Such overarching responsibility requires knowledge and skill in multiple areas. But more importantly, it requires the ability to choose, support, and hold accountable those who have the specific abilities needed for the institution to work effectively.

There is a hard-to-define, almost mysterious, dimension of presidential leadership. No one chapter in this handbook addresses it specifically, but many allude to it. Who the president is personally and how he or she functions, even in small matters, deeply influence how others in the institution perceive what is possible for the organization. It is more than knowledge and skill. It is "persona" — the depth of a person, one's spirituality, one's interaction with others. It is saying the right words on critical occasions, being courageous and confident in the midst of crisis and conflict, conveying hope, and enabling others to become more than they thought they could be. There is no one pattern or prescription for how a president performs this mysterious dimension of leadership, but people in the community know when it is present or absent. A president can manage an institution with specific knowledge and skills; but without this more elusive dimension of leadership, success is unlikely.

The contributors to and supporters of this book maintain that presidents are key to whether their institutions succeed or falter. Obviously a president alone does not wholly determine the health and well-being of a seminary. But how a president functions, manages, and leads provides the linchpin that holds the other components of the institution together. Does this lofty claim overstate the role of president? We invite you to read these chapters and comprehend the range of things a president must know and do and how these in turn affect and shape their institutions.

What Does It Take to Be a Successful President?

As we noted, a seminary president's role is best grounded in a sense of vocation or call. Without a call, it can become a mere "job," and the intense demands of the position feel weightier and more energy-consuming. But call alone does not ensure success. It also requires individual gifts and graces. One can catalog the desirable attributes for presidents, but the exact combination of personal gifts obviously varies and "one size does not fit all." Many different personalities can succeed in the role of president.

The particular context and culture of the seminary are another variable. Certain personalities match one setting and not another. No formula can guarantee a successful match. A seminary president needs insight to recognize the unique culture of the school and the ability to adapt to that culture while at the same time transforming the institution and its culture to fulfill more effectively a mission unique in time and place.

No president, no matter how personally gifted or culturally attuned, can succeed without a body of knowledge and a set of skills. The position is demanding because it requires such a broad range of knowledge and skills. The president does not need to know all the details but must at least ask the right questions and pick people who have the skills to manage each area.

This book provides the framework and some of the specific information a president needs to survey the major tasks of the job. The various chapters in this handbook cover the major areas of a seminary that demand presidential attention. Each chapter defines a particular area of responsibility and the unique role of the president in it. An analysis and discussion of the area identify many of the critical issues likely to confront a president, suggest some best practices for dealing with these issues, and pose some of the questions a president should be asking. Finally, each chapter includes a section that suggests additional resources for those who want or need to explore the area more deeply.

Why Do We Need Successful Seminaries?

The logic behind this handbook project goes something like this: The ultimate goal is to affect the quality and depth of religious life in America. The primary institutions that affect religious life are the many and diverse local congregations in communities across North America. The quality of the ministry in these congregations is greatly shaped by their pastoral leadership. Pastors who are clear about their vocation, well trained, and well sustained are more likely to develop effective ministries. Seminaries are a key link in the chain of calling, preparing, and sustaining pastoral leaders. Thus, we are back to the need for effective seminaries and the role that a president plays in developing and leading a theological school to fulfill its mission and also maintain economic vitality.

Within the larger context of higher education in North America, seminaries are admittedly very small educational institutions. How can they be so influential? First, they are a primary theological resource, sustaining and interpreting the historic faith in the contemporary context. Second, they are the primary educational resource for preparing pastoral leaders for the churches of the continent. Seminaries have a tremendous multiplier effect. By a conservative estimate, a pastor who spends thirty years in congregational ministry will likely touch and variously influence one hundred thousand individuals and numerous community groups. No other channel has such direct impact on the religious life of cultures and nations. A positive intervention in this chain of religious influence can achieve a tremendous payoff. Our intervention focus is on the seminary president and the key role he or she plays in the chain.

The Association of Theological Schools, through its accrediting and programmatic roles, and the generous funding of the Religion Division of Lilly Endowment Inc. have helped to develop this fundamental logic. They have invested substantially in the encouragement and support of seminary presidents in the belief that they are key actors in shaping and leading theological education and thereby affect the chain of religious influence in North America.

To our knowledge, there is no other resource like this *Handbook for Seminary Presidents* that is so specifically focused on this critical leadership group. Our hope is that in some small but influential way it will contribute to the greater effectiveness of seminary presidents, their schools, the leaders they educate, and the congregations and communities they serve.

CHAPTER 1

The President's Vocation and Leadership

DANIEL ALESHIRE, The Association of Theological Schools
CYNTHIA CAMPBELL, McCormick Theological Seminary
KEVIN MANNOIA, Azusa Pacific University

Introduction

Samuel heard a voice in the night. He was attending to the needs of an aging Eli and assumed the voice was Eli's, so he went to the old priest, only to hear Eli say that he had not called. Samuel went back to his cot and, once again, heard the voice calling him. He went to Eli and discovered that Eli had not called this time either. Samuel returned to bed for what was left of the night and, a third time, heard a voice. A third time Samuel went to Eli, and a third time Eli said he had not called. There is no reason why Samuel should have thought the voice in the night belonged to someone other than Eli, for, as the text notes, "the word of the LORD was rare in those days" (1 Sam. 3:1), and "Samuel did not yet know the LORD, and the word of the LORD had not yet been revealed to him" (v. 7). Eli was very old, and no doubt wounded from watching his sons sin themselves into faithlessness. After the third time that Samuel came to him, Eli's sadness lifted. He began to suspect that Samuel was hearing the voice of Yahweh. So Eli told Samuel that, if he heard the voice again, he should answer, "Speak, LORD, for your servant is listening" (v. 9). The voice came, and Samuel responded as instructed. The Lord spoke, but it was a word of such judgment on Eli's house that Samuel was afraid to tell Eli. Eli insisted that Samuel tell him, and the priest recognized that these painful words were surely from the Lord.

Most seminary presidents have heard this story told tenderly and have studied it critically. The tender hearing is in the authentic piety that brings students to theological schools, as year after year they indicate that their most compelling motivation to undertake theological study was a sense of God's call.[1] The tender hearing continues in the hopeful sermons preached at graduates' ordination services, often using this text. The critical study struggles with the judgment that is the reason for the call. There has been sin and faithlessness, and the word that Samuel hears is worrisome and troubling. Stories of divine judgment, if not subjected to critical study, can too easily become a cover for human judgments that are inevitably more harsh and less just than the judgment of God.

Leading a seminary gives a president more than the occasional opportunity to wake in the night and hear voices. It may be the voices of

---

1. ATS Student Information Program, "Entering Student Questionnaire."

the funds that are needed but not yet raised, the voices of students who have left the relative prosperity of other careers for the relative poverty of seminary study, the voices of donors who have given sacrificially, the voices of more needs than a school can ever hope to meet, the voices of deep religious need in the culture, or the voices of divisive struggles in the church. There are many voices, enough to fill the day and the night. Some are tender and reassuring. Others are shrill, even intimidating. Like Samuel's call, these callings invite presidents to action — presidential work is about getting up and doing things. Unlike Samuel, who heard the multiple callings of God to do one thing, the leader of a theological school receives one calling that involves doing many things.

We use the word *calling* in many ways, most of which do not resemble Samuel's experience. Seminary students, for example, say that they come to seminary because they have experienced a "call." The seminary admitted them, but the seminary did not call them. It is different with presidents. They should undertake this work only with a deep sense of calling, but that calling is like Samuel's. It is not a "calling" to which one aspires; it is a calling that one experiences in the context of a board or religious superior's summons to this work.

In this chapter, we identify several issues related to vocation and leadership. Vocation, or calling, has many facets, but we will mention only a few. Leadership has even more, but once again, we have chosen to address only a few of them.

Vocation

Presidential leadership in a theological school can be a source of both deep satisfaction and exceptionally hard work. The satisfactions of guiding an institution that forms religious leaders and informs thoughtful theological discourse are many. The presidency grants access to privileged moments as donors translate their faith commitments into funding for programs, students, and the future of the school. It often provides opportunities to participate in significant denominational decision-making and ecumenical engagement. But presidential leadership can also be difficult work — finding and managing the necessary resources, dealing with difficult personnel issues, navigating the sometimes complex terrain of academic governance, and attending thoughtfully to multiple constituencies. It is difficult because institutional leadership always is exercised in a world of competing demands and loyalties, where a greater number of important things need to be done than can be done. Religious work that is bound on the one hand by deep satisfactions and on the other by persistent difficulties is best accomplished with a deep sense of calling, of vocation.

The vocation of the presidency of a theological school, of course, begins with the discipleship that all Christians share, and it typically continues with the broad tasks of vocational ministry, because most seminary presidents are ordained. Whether a president is ordained or not, the calling of the seminary presidency goes further; it involves the leadership of a theological school. The call to leadership in a theological school is similar in many ways to the call to leadership in other institutions. Leadership of a theological school differs from leadership in congregations, however, because schools do not have the volunteer culture that dominates parishes and congregations, even though those congregations may have large ministerial and program staff structures. Leadership of a theological school differs from a denominational agency because a seminary tends to have more diffused and shared patterns of governance than the more corporate structures of most denominational agencies. The call to leadership of a theological school is different only to the extent that the culture, ethos, and structure of a seminary tend to be somewhat unique. Rather than rehearse the more generic issues of the call to leadership, we have chosen to explore facets of that call where personal identity interacts with presidential work. In this way, "vocation" refers to the interior sense of commitment that interacts with the institution's call to exercise presidential leadership.

Personal Faith and Faithful Work

In an interview with three seminary presidents who were about to retire, former *In Trust* editor William MacKaye asked what had nourished them and sustained them in their work.[2] Bill Lesher, retiring after presidencies at the Lutheran School of Theology in Chicago and Pacific Lu-

2. William MacKaye, "Describing the New Leader: What's Needed in a Theological School President Today," *In Trust* (Summer 1997): 20-23.

theran in Berkeley, said that he didn't know how anyone got through this work without an active life of devotion. The other interviewees were quick to concur. Maintaining a life of faith is as overwhelmingly obvious as it is devastatingly difficult. Ministers who handle the holy for a living can become oblivious to its drama in their own lives. Seminaries are seedbeds, at least that is what the name implies, and presidents can spend so much time hoeing and weeding the seedbed that they fail to cultivate the faith that is central to the first calling — the call to Christian discipleship. Seminary life can be spiritually enriching. Seminary worship, preaching, and Eucharistic celebrations can be powerful moments — privileges to which few other Christians have access. The work and worry load, however, can render them ineffective. So presidents need to remind themselves of the obvious and take seriously their vocation of personal faith. The rhythms of prayer and worship, and study and service, however they are defined and practiced in the schools' religious communities, are crucial for sustaining believers who are seminary presidents. They provide the personal foundation and integrity that hard work requires, and leading a theological school is hard work.

Religious callings are often associated with difficult tasks, like leaving Ur of the Chaldees, or taking up a cross, or getting into a shaky boat and heading toward Rome. Leadership, by definition, is hard work. If a seminary could go where it needs to go with little effort, if its various constituencies agreed without fail on its directions and best course of action, if the money just floated down from heaven, then leadership would be easy and, probably, unnecessary. James Dittes, in a book several decades old now, reminded pastors that those troubling moments when the people in the congregation say no, or break their promises, or resist the gospel's claim on their lives are the very moments that define the pastoral vocation.[3] It is precisely because people in congregations do these kinds of things from time to time that they need pastors and seminaries need leaders. Seminary leadership is not always hard; it is often far more rewarding than it is demanding. However, there are moments of great difficulty in almost every presidency, moments of stress and anxiety, moments of unrelenting complexity. A personal sense of

3. James Dittes, *When the People Say No: Conflict and the Call to Ministry* (San Francisco: Harper & Row, 1979).

vocation can sustain presidents in these moments. Theological schools need leaders who understand that the personal price is worth paying and that the Bible's image of the "yoke" demonstrates that the burden is bearable.

Privileged Work with Peers

Presidential work is privileged work and, as such, involves the vocational understanding of this privilege and its proper stewardship. The privilege is, first of all, one of perspective. While presidents bear the burdens of leadership and the ever-present needs of the school, the president is often the only individual who sees the broad landscape of success painted by the seminary's many efforts over time. Presidents see accomplishments in a school that few others can see because few others have the privilege of perspective. This perspective is an institutional necessity. Someone needs to be able to see the cumulative accomplishments of a school and be able to talk about them to people who care for the school and its mission. Perceiving institutional accomplishment requires both the platform that the presidency provides and time to devote to thoughtful viewing. Institutional successes emerge only over prolonged periods of time, and seeing them requires someone whose job entails carrying the institutional memory, continuing to tell the story of what was accomplished in past administrations as well as the accomplishments that are currently accruing to that story. The role of principal teller of the story is a second aspect of presidential privilege. While it is at times fatiguing to welcome guests, visitors, new students, and prospective donors, the president engages in these rituals not because the office represents power or authority but because it represents the legacy of the school. In many ways, presidential work is privileged work, and privilege is best exercised under the discipline of faithfulness to a calling.

Privilege also requires patterns of interactions with others who share similar privileges in other settings. On the campuses of most theological schools, presidential work is lonely. A new president soon learns not to think out loud on campus because people invariably hear presidential musings as if they were proposals. Presidents need peers with whom they can think out loud without repercussions in their own schools. They need peers with whom they can share frustrations, tensions, and personal stresses. Vincent Cushing, who retired after almost two decades as president at Washington Theological Union, spoke in an Association of Theological Schools (ATS) meeting about what he thought contributed to his development as a president. He and David Hubbard, long-time president of Fuller Theological Seminary, agreed to meet one weekend a year and continued to do so for many years. Thus a Roman Catholic and an evangelical Protestant became conversation partners. They found that their common vocation transcended the differences in their religious communions. Two distinguished careers were supported by finding peers and committing to the discipline of periodic, informal conversations. Presidencies are buoyed and energized by conversations with trusted peers, by the shared discovery that the burdens of the office are more a function of the office than a president's particular style of work or personality. Presidents benefit from having partners with whom they can have soul-bound, honest conversations, where real worries can be spoken out loud, and where threatening questions can be raised. Finding these partners, for many presidents, is a vocational expression.

Institutional Mission and Scholarly Administration

The mission of a theological school is the goal toward which the school orients its resources and effort, and the vocation of missional leadership is the process of keeping the institution's energy and resources focused on that goal. Mission is not just a statement for recitation to prospective donors or for "branding" on institutional publications. Mission is the school's central and primary purpose. A president cannot lead without an institutional mission because there would be no direction for leadership. A president cannot serve well over time without a sense of shared calling with the school's mission.

Focusing on the missional goals of a theological school is seldom a straightforward process. A theological school progresses toward its goals somewhat like a sailboat reaching its destination when the wind is blowing the wrong way. Leadership typically advances a school by tacking against the wind, not by assuming that the wind will blow in the direction of the goals. Tacking requires the ability to locate the goal from a variety of angles, the confidence to sail in directions that can appear contrary to the goal, and the capacity to determine progress when the wind requires sailing sideways. A sense of vocational mission is not enough — leadership requires and consumes a great range of skills — but all the skill in the world won't be effective if there is no clear sense of what needs to be accomplished and why. In the necessary meanderings of presidential work, institutional mission forms part of the vocation of presidential leadership.

Mission not only directs and stabilizes the work of a school; it also grounds the president's work and provides renewal along the way. Many seminary presidents have described how important the mission of the school has been as both guide for their work and support for their soul. When the work is going well, the mission provides confidence and a sense of accomplishment. When the work is going poorly, commitment to the mission provides stamina to endure the stress.

The mission of a theological school is served as presidents follow the call of scholarly administration. In seminaries, scholarship is not only the work of the faculty; it is also the work of faithful presidents. For several years, a group of seminary leaders met for a weekend each summer to discuss their work. Each was in a senior administrative position; most held PhDs and had imagined that they would have careers in teaching and research. The purpose of their meetings was to think about their administrative work and to pursue what it meant to do this kind of work as a form of scholarship. Max De Pree, former chair of the Herman Miller Corporation, long-time board member of and donor to Fuller Theological Seminary, and thoughtful author on leadership, met with the group one year. He observed that seminary presidents tend to think a lot about the book they want to write or the pastoral work that they will do again in the future, but they tend not to spend as much time as they should engaging in the intellectual dimensions of the administrative work they are currently doing. It was an informal discussion, and different participants took home different memories of the observations that were made. But several of them recall that statement. De Pree was suggesting that seminary leadership requires serious intellectual energy, and if senior administrators spent their intellectual energy on the things they would be doing if they were not administrators, they would give insufficient intellectual energy to their administrative leadership.

Theological schools need intellectually engaged leadership, and one aspect of presidential leadership is accepting the call to scholarly administration. This kind of scholarship may not result in books as much as it results in institutional work well done. Senior administrative work requires different patterns of intellectual work than faculty scholarship requires. Building, motivating, and sustaining senior management teams; constructing development plans and matching those plans with donors' interests and commitments; and providing institutional guidance in the context of highly educated and often independent thinking colleagues require intellectual effort. Good presidential work may be the most intellectually challenging work in a theological school, and presidents need to focus their intellectual attention on the diversity and complexity of their tasks.

Leadership

We have focused on understanding the vocational dimensions of seminary leadership. Vocation forms the environment in which this work is done, but it does not define the tasks of leadership. Leadership in complex environments has many dimensions and requires many abilities. Like our reflection on vocation, our list here is more instructive than exhaustive, and it makes sense only in the context of understanding that seminary leadership is vocational work in a religious context.

Leading a Community

The fundamental nature of leadership is embedded in community. Leadership is not the private exercise of gifts for the gratification of the leader. If there is no community, there is no reason for a leader. A soloist doesn't need a director; a choir does, and only a choir can make music that involves the complexity and beauty of multiple parts sung by multiple voices. A choir leader is needed because a choir has a musical goal that only a choir can attain. A theological school has a mission that only a community of people working together can accomplish. It takes students, faculty, administrators, contributors, trustees, and congregational and denominational constituents. The vocation of leadership in a theological school involves the efforts necessary to help a community accomplish the mission that only a community can accomplish.

Because leadership is a function of the work and needs of the community, one of the first requirements of a leader is a reasonable "fit" with the community. That fit has to do with the affinity a leader feels for the mission and work of the school, the constituency it serves, and the legacy it bears. The person who is an ideal and effective president of one school may be totally ineffective in another. Leadership in theological schools is more than the exercise of certain gifts and abilities. It is the use of those gifts and abilities within a particular community with its unique ethos and culture, at a particular time in the community's history. Ethos and culture change over time, the needs of the community and its mission change over time, and the effectiveness of a leader will be as much a function of fit with the school's identity as it is a result of the competent use of skills, abilities, and leadership capacity.

Because leadership is one of the many gifts needed by communities with work to do, it is never a function of an individual's desire or ability to lead. Leadership is necessary because the community can't do its job if it does not have someone who provides three critical resources for its work: maintaining focus on the mission, coordinating and guiding the efforts necessary to accomplish the mission, and securing and managing the resources that the mission requires. Presidents do not choose to work in these areas; they are the tasks that go with the job. These are not tasks that impose on the president's "real" work — these tasks *are* the real work. Rather than an unwanted burden, these tasks are the means by which presidents engage their fundamental calling.

Central to the president's job is maintaining the school's focus on its mission. An organization has a way of forgetting its primary goals and investing resources and time in activities that are not central to that mission. Different people in a community have different ideas about what the organization should do or the ways in which it should be done. Leadership involves providing the community with the direction and discipline necessary for its mission. At times, the mission needs to be reconceptualized; at other times, it needs to be refocused; and at still other times, it simply needs to be faithfully and effectively implemented. Communities seldom are able to stay focused without someone whose job is to help it stay focused on its primary mission. Leadership helps the community stay focused on its mission.

Schools, like all communities with a mission, need someone who will provide overall guidance and coordination. Schools, even small theological schools, are complex organizations, and while each serves a common mission, their individual units have a way of going in different directions unless there is someone whose job is to see that tasks are coordinated and integrated and serve the organization's purpose. The president is often the only person in the organization who is formally held responsible for the work of the organization as a whole, so presidential leadership involves the guidance necessary to keep that work coordinated and integrated.

Theological schools need someone to find and manage the resources that are needed for their work. These resources include money, facilities, and personnel. Presidential leadership typically involves a close relationship with securing the needed funds and facilities, oversight of the processes related to managing those funds and facilities, and participation in the processes that secure the personnel. These areas of work go together, and the president cannot be responsible for obtaining money while others decide how to spend or manage it. Effective presidential leadership is typically not dictatorial, but it does require ownership of these principal tasks and the capacity to support the community by finding and securing the necessary resources.

These three principal tasks are not necessarily the work of a single individual. In many ways, it is most helpful to understand the presidency as a function, not just as an individual's job. One individual can't raise the money, keep the books, speak to the constituency, coordinate the overall mission of the school, and attend to the supervision of its people. It almost always takes more than one person to do all of this. In many schools, the job of the individual called president is to supervise and coordinate the work of several individuals who, together, serve the presidential function.

Leadership of a community is not only an institutional necessity; it is also a requirement for the function of the presidency. For the presidency to work, the seminary needs capable people who form a leadership team, who are empowered and entrusted by the president to do their work, and who are held accountable for getting it done.

Leading with Awareness

Leadership of a theological school is always situational and relational, and this requires presidents to be aware of the context, of their position in relationship to others, and of themselves.

A theological school has a culture — a set of customs, values, and typical approaches to its work — and the president needs to be aware of this culture in order to be able to work effectively in it, to be able to determine what needs to be changed in it, to identify the most effective strategies for change, and to understand the resistance that will greet change. All leadership is contextual, but the diffuse and shared patterns of governance in theological schools make it especially important for a president to be sensitive to the school's culture. Culture and custom are more than potential threats to needed change. All communities need customary ways of doing things because the work is complex and customs make the work more predictable and less complex. The culture of a typical theological school reflects accrued wisdom about the community's work; and, to the extent possible, the president needs to embrace the culture, understand and affirm its enduring value, use it as a resource for the work that needs to be done, and not see it as a roadblock to that work.

A president functions in a particular position in a school, and effective leadership requires an awareness of this position. Presidents bring their own personal identity to their work, and good leadership is impossible apart from the authentic personhood of the leader. Presidents do not function, however, as just one of many persons in the school. They occupy a certain position, and that position causes them to be heard and experienced by others differently than would be the case if they were not in that position. A thought voiced by a president can be heard as the announcement of a new initiative, and it can invite a range of responses that the president never anticipated. The president's role attracts the suspicions and recalls negative experiences that individuals may have had with others in similar roles, and the effective leader is aware that these are functions of the position and not the person. Being aware of position also means understanding where the leader is in the context of other stakeholders in the institution. On a given issue, the president might be positioned with the board but distant from the faculty. Leadership in that situation involves an awareness of where the leader is relative to both faculty and board. Seldom is leadership exercised when all the stakeholders in a school are of the same opinion as the president, and awareness of where the president is in relation to others in the institution is crucial for identifying the pace and trajectory for change.

A president also needs to be self-aware. Personhood and role are so intricately mixed in leadership that good leaders are, as best they can, seeking to separate their personal reactions from the reactions that would best serve the institution. This is never easy and, probably, never completely possible, but leadership requires the discipline of trying. Leadership requires the kind of self-awareness that contributes to confidence in a proposed course of action, even when others disagree. It requires an awareness of what precipitates anger or frustration and being willing to manage those feelings to the benefit of the leadership agenda, and not to personal agenda; such self-control is a critical asset to institutional leadership. There are lonely moments in the leadership of a theological school, and those moments require a self-awareness that is honest in ways that are able both to critique the leader's personal agenda and to affirm the leader's correct assessment of a situation and the response it requires.

Leading with Institutional Will and Personal Humility

In the book *Good to Great,* Jim Collins and his team of young researchers studied companies in a variety of segments of the U.S. economy that had broken ahead of other companies in the same segment and had maintained their leadership position for fifteen years.[4] Their research is intriguing because culture can be much too interested in short-term results. Theological schools need to build for the long term. Everything that they are about — from the commitments they promote to the graduates they educate — is needed for the long term.

What kind of leadership contributed to these companies becoming "great" and sustaining their greatness over the long term? The researchers interviewed the senior executives who were active with these

---

4. James C. Collins, *Good to Great: Why Some Companies Make the Leap ... and Others Don't* (New York: HarperCollins, 2001).

companies as they "broke ahead" and as they worked to maintain their relative position over the years. The interviews revealed that these leaders did not define themselves by the perks of their jobs or use their positions to promote personal fame. They were personally humble and professionally passionate about their companies and determined on their behalf. Collins describes them as people of intense professional will. There could not be a healthier or more virtuous pair of leadership qualities for presidents of ATS schools than *personal humility* and *strong professional will*. Humility is necessary because the successes of a company or a theological school are always the work of the community, never of an individual. Presidential leadership makes huge demands and requires considerable effort. This demand and effort may seduce a president into thinking that the school's successes are somehow uniquely related to the president's work. Humility is a necessary reminder that the accomplishments of a community are always the results of many people's efforts. Professional will is the intense commitment to see that the organization achieves its goals. A leader who pushes an organization primarily because he or she is a demanding person can be troubling, but it is another matter to push toward the maximum organizational achievement. Professional will involves tenacity for the organization's mission and the efforts necessary to attain it.

Leading through Change

One way of understanding leadership is that it is not necessary unless the institution needs to move from one place to another. If an institution doesn't want any improvement, expansion, or redirection of its work, it doesn't need much leadership. Competent management can oversee an organization that seeks only to do what it has done in the way it has done it before. However, in this era, simple management will not be needed for long. Organizations that do not change have a way of ceasing to meet their missions, even if those missions themselves do not change. Leadership in a theological school is an exercise in the art of discerning what should change, what must change, what should not change, and for what purposes appropriate change should be undertaken. Change is always complex, it is typically resisted, and its outcome is never obvious at the start. It is as difficult as it is necessary. Leadership involves helping the school discern when change is needed, identifying the trajectory the change should take, and guiding the community across the uncharted terrain that characterizes any change.

Change is not limited to the school. David Tiede, who retired after twenty years as president at Luther Seminary, talked with a group of seminary presidents about the several jobs he had had during those twenty years. He concluded about halfway through his tenure that he was already on his second job, and if he were to stay, his job would continue to change. Leadership is like that. As the community accomplishes certain goals and faces new and different challenges, the work required from the president changes. The skills and commitments that led the school well as it addressed issues that are now resolved are of considerably less value when the school is facing other issues and agendas. The Luther Seminary board formalized this perception by determining that it would reexamine the president's job description every five years to identify what most needed to be done and the presidential skills most needed to help the institution accomplish these tasks.

In an important book on leadership, Ronald A. Heifetz and his colleagues examined the kinds of changes that institutions face and that, correspondingly, often form the primary agenda for leadership.[5] He classified two fundamentally different kinds of change: technical and adaptive.

Technical changes are those that are made to move the organization along its orderly path toward increased capacity. Changes in the administrative computing system, for example, can make a school more efficient in its operations, and such a change can consume a massive amount of energy while it is being considered, implemented, and accepted. In the end, however, the change is a technical change. The work is improved; the coordination is strengthened; perhaps some money is saved in the long run. Technical change may make an organization's work fundamentally better, but it does not make it fundamentally different.

Adaptive change is of a different order. It is often imposed by the changing context in which an organization does its work and the resulting requirement for change in the organization. Religion in North

---

5. Ronald Heifetz and Martin Linsky, *Leadership on the Line: Staying Alive through the Dangers of Leading* (Boston: Harvard Business School Press, 2002).

America is changing; it is reconstituting itself in ways different from earlier expressions. It will be impossible for a theological school to do business as it always has in the context of these changes. Theological schools that are related to rapidly growing constituencies must change to meet the theological education needs of those constituencies. Theological schools related to constituencies that have experienced significant numerical decline are faced with a very different set of factors as they seek to respond to the theological education needs of the increasing number of part-time and bi-vocational pastors. These changes are not so much technical adjustments as they are fundamental adaptations of the school's patterns of work — perhaps even its mission.

Both kinds of change can be difficult for a theological school, but both are necessary. A part of the work of the president is to help the institution figure out what change is needed, to help the community of individuals who form the institution to understand why the change is necessary or advantageous, and to oversee the efforts that the change requires.

Leading by Telling the Story

Another central feature of leadership in a theological school is telling the school's story. We mentioned earlier that the president has the privilege of perspective. Most others in a school see only part of the whole story of the school because that is their perspective. Faculty see the school one way, students see it another, and the board sees it still another way. The president has a perspective, by virtue of office, which both includes and transcends these more limited perspectives. Presidents exercise their leadership by telling the school's story from this privileged perspective. The story needs to be told to faculty and students so they can place their perceptions in a broader framework. The story needs to be told to the board so they have a perspective about the impact of their governance. The story needs to be told to prospective donors and to major givers so they know why they should support the school with their gifts. All theological schools have good stories to tell, and telling the story is one way in which leadership is exercised.

The president is often the only individual who relates to all the constituencies of a school. While this means that the president has the difficult task of interpreting the constituencies to one another, and sometimes mediating among them, it also means that the president is the one person in the institution who can share a common story with all the constituencies. While this sometimes puts the president in the difficult position of being the person in the middle, it also provides the arena in which leadership *in a community* is exercised.

Additional Resources

Collins, James C. *Good to Great: Why Some Companies Make the Leap . . . and Others Don't.* New York: HarperCollins, 2001.

This book, based on research with multiple organizations, discusses the principles necessary to transform an institution from a good organization into a great organization. Each of these principles has direct implications for a leader's role and function in bringing about this transformation.

Dittes, James. *When the People Say No: Conflict and the Call to Ministry.* San Francisco: Harper & Row, 1979.

This book is a classic work that recognizes the inevitability of conflict in human institutions. Focusing on ministry in the church, it discusses how to survive and lead in a community of people who differ from and battle with one another and the leaders.

Heifetz, Ronald A., and Martin Linsky. *Leadership on the Line: Staying Alive through the Dangers of Leading.* Boston: Harvard Business School Press, 2002.

Building on the principles developed in Heifetz's earlier book, *Leadership without Easy Answers,* this book discusses how leaders can survive and succeed in difficult and challenging situations.

The resources identified in this handbook are listed on the ATS Website where the list will continue to be updated as new resources become available: www.ats.edu > Leadership Education > Presidents.

CHAPTER 2

The President's Role in Administration and Personnel Management

ADOLF HANSEN, Garrett-Evangelical Theological Seminary

JEAN STAIRS, Queen's Theological College

KENT M. WEEKS, Senior Attorney, Weeks, Anderson, and Baker

Introduction

A theological school has many institutional matters to manage and many individuals through whom this is done. Finding the most efficient and effective ways to carry out these responsibilities is the function of administration and personnel management.

In most theological schools the president is the chief administrator, having been hired by a governing board and authorized to hire all other people in the institution in accordance with institutional guidelines. He or she oversees the management of the school, sometimes through direct involvement and at other times through delegation of authority. Knowing when and how to employ each of these approaches is a sign of wisdom.

Administration

Organizational Design

Although theological schools differ in the way they are organized, all have senior administrators who commonly report directly to the president: an academic officer, an administrative and/or fiscal officer, and an institutional advancement officer. To whom a student affairs officer reports varies considerably, depending in part on how the student affairs area is defined.

The president can provide direct supervision for only a limited number of people. Four to six individuals, including the assistant to the president (commonly one person with both administrative and secretarial responsibilities), is the most desirable number.

Individuals who have institutional responsibilities in functional areas (such as information technology, marketing/communications, or church relations) do not easily fit within most institutional structures. Therefore, alignments based on institutional mission, particular personnel strengths, and available resources need to be worked out in creative and productive ways.

Questions the president needs to consider and reconsider on an ongoing basis in this regard are: Who needs to be at the table? Who does not? When does a particular group need to remain the same? When does it not?

Shared governance, the delegation of authority, is a desirable quality of leadership. Customarily, the faculty in theological schools have authority over designated academic areas (such as curriculum design and implementation) that they carry out in a manner consistent with the institution's governance structure and mission. The president participates in this process without determining its outcome.

Many theological schools find it valuable to develop an organizational chart, which gives each employee a framework for understanding the institution: who does what, who is related to whom, and who is accountable to whom.

Management

It is important for the president to be aware of his or her own style of functioning, to reflect on that awareness, and to grow in self-understanding as well as in the understanding of others. Sometimes an instrument that provides categories for organizing one's thinking (such as the Myers-Briggs Type Indicator) is helpful. Such an instrument may also be useful in team-building if each member of the team completes it and participates in a process in which all members learn about one another's style of functioning.

For time management, the president needs to set parameters for the number of hours he or she spends in reading/reflection/writing, in dealing with office matters, in group meetings, in individual conversations, and in activities outside the institution. Sharing those parameters with others and asking them to respect them can often be helpful, yet a president must also maintain some degree of flexibility.

Furthermore, the president needs to determine major goals in light of the school's strategic plan and the time allotted for their accomplishment. One way to do this is to identify six goals for a six-month period (known as 6 by 6), discuss them with others on the leadership team, focus on carrying them out, evaluate their status at the end of six months, and then identify six goals for the next six months (all new or a mixture of old and new).

To manage meetings, the president needs to determine which ones to attend, what role to assume in those meetings, and which personal views to express or not express at certain points in the process. Giving the president's view too early in a process will often limit discussion. Furthermore, if it is not clear if the president is giving a personal view or an institutional view, this may also limit discussion by creating ambiguity and confusion.

The president has the unique opportunity to develop a vision by keeping in mind what he or she believes is best for the whole institution and to express that in a manner that enables others to participate in and share the vision. This is not an easy task. In order to maintain such a focus, the president needs to ask continually: Where are my personal interests and perspectives affecting my responsibility to represent the whole institution in fulfilling its vision?

To manage his or her office, the president needs to depend on a trustworthy, competent, and prudent assistant to carry out numerous administrative and secretarial tasks, including receiving incoming calls as well as visitors, taking and sharing pertinent messages, opening and sorting mail, responding to routine correspondence, filing materials that need to be kept, setting appointments appropriately, and protecting the president's time prudently. The president may save considerable time simply by having his or her assistant ask an inquirer, "Is this something I can help you with?"

In addition, a president can accomplish considerable work by being a "one-minute manager," walking in hallways and offices (covering all of them eventually), interacting informally with employees, sometimes asking deliberate questions and listening to responses, sometimes letting others ask the questions, and sometimes just being present. Developing such a style can often foster effective communication.

Decision-Making

It is crucial for the president to understand which decisions he or she needs to make and which can be delegated to others. The "old-fashioned" management language said, "Push the decision down" or "Let the person at the lowest possible level make the decision." The newer language says, "Let the person in closest proximity to the matter make the decision"; then, if necessary, "widen the circle." The operative principle in each approach is for the president not to become involved in decision-making that trusted colleagues can carry out on their own.

At the same time, it is important for the president to identify the strategic decisions that move the institution forward and to ensure that they are made in a timely fashion by appropriate persons and processes.

The president should also understand the time by which a decision needs to be made. If it is important, but not urgent, the decision can often wait. If it is urgent, however — whether important or not — it needs to be made accordingly. Postponing important decisions that are not urgent is not desirable but may at times be necessary.

Follow-up on decisions is essential. Letting those involved know who is responsible for taking the next steps, by what date they need to be taken, and to whom the results need to be reported will enable decisions to make a difference in the institution. The president by his or her own follow-up has the opportunity to set the example for the entire institution.

Negotiating Differences

The question at the heart of any negotiation is, "What do you want?" If the individuals or groups expressing their differences can articulate this, the possibility for a resolution is much more likely. This question can also be stated as: "What are you seeking?" or "What objective do you have in mind?" or "What are you trying to accomplish?"

Once the president has asked the question and the differing parties have given a preliminary response, everyone can consider options to reach that goal. An individual, either speaking personally or as a representative for a group, may have a particular option in mind, or the individual may not have thought of any specific options.

The president will often hear both a request (that is, what someone wants) and a particular way to fulfill the request, stated explicitly or implicitly. If the president doesn't think that the request is a realistic possibility, he or she can say no in a gracious manner. However, if the president is thinking no but doesn't want to be directive, he or she can say, "Let's look at the options for accomplishing what you have proposed."

After as many options as possible have been enumerated, including those whose implementation may be quite unlikely, the discussion can proceed in a way that narrows the options. Sometimes an option will emerge that is mutually satisfactory. Sometimes it will not. At other times, there may need to be ongoing reflection regarding the two or three options that remain.

Using such an approach will not only help the president's own discussions to be more effective but will also provide a model for others to use in their own interactions.

Policies

It is prudent for any theological school to set forth in writing the policies that govern its administration. The more significant ones, particularly those of legal consequence, are customarily approved by the governing board. The others are often left to the president, who affirms current policies or sets in motion a process to establish new ones.

All employees must be aware of, and must follow, institutional policies. Although such policies are often shared orally, they also need to be written in a clear, concise, and legally sound manner. They should be organized in one or more handbooks (one governing all employees or governing each specific class of employees such as administration, faculty, and staff) and should be given to each employee when he or she is hired.

Presidents also need to understand government policies that apply to a theological school and to carry them out in ways that fulfill the regulations appropriately. The president needs to see that this is done, though he or she can delegate that task to an institutional colleague.

This also applies to church policies that pertain to a theological school, though the extent varies to which a theological school is an independent entity with its own governing board or is controlled legally, politically, and/or financially by a given ecclesiastical body. The president needs to articulate a point of view that is approved by the governing board and that fully recognizes both institutional and ecclesiastical interests.

Procedures

The president must distinguish between policies and procedures (the latter being ways to carry out the former). He or she needs to integrate the implementation of both.

Because details of institutional procedures are usually not understood quickly, the institution should have a manual that explains procedures that are applicable to all employees (such as scheduling, purchasing, printing, and mailing). Although the president customarily delegates the tasks that relate to procedures, he or she must still be informed in order to follow them in an exemplary manner.

Preventive Legal Planning and Management

Compliance with federal, state, provincial, and local laws is critical if the theological school is to reduce risk and meet its institutional objectives. One way to monitor compliance is to undertake periodic reviews of major institutional legal documents, including the charter or constitution, bylaws, handbook policies, employment practices, and important procedures. The president has the responsibility for delegating or monitoring such compliance reviews.

The president needs to ensure that policies and practices are consistent and, if they are not, to determine why not. Some schools develop practices that vary from their policies. If a dispute arises, this dichotomy can create enormous problems for theological schools.

Preventive strategies also need to include an assessment of the purpose and mission of the institution as they relate to statutory exemptions for theological schools. Both in the United States and in Canada, theological schools may be exempt from compliance with certain laws, such as those related to employment, when the position in question involves a religious component. It is best to identify from the outset which positions are exempt, in order to forestall challenges to decisions allegedly made on discriminatory grounds when in fact the alleged preference is protected by statutory law and is required by mission mandates.

An increasing source of conflict for theological schools relates to institutional requirements of students that fall outside the normally accepted domain of "academic" requirements. The institution needs to state clearly what personal competencies and skills students need so that students are aware that passing courses and obtaining credits are not the only requirements for graduation or certification.

The president must also manage his or her relationship with legal counsel. Commonly, a theological school will retain a law firm. If a lawyer who is a board member represents a school, the practice needs to be carefully examined because of potential conflicts of interest. The president must know when to consult counsel in order to obtain adequate advice, but he or she also must control costs of legal services. Preventive practice suggests that it is far better to consult a lawyer at the beginning of what may become a legal problem than after the problem has occurred, at which time advice tends to focus on how to clean up the mess.

Prudent judgment, good faith, and professionalism will go a long way toward the prevention of legal conflicts and will aid the president's focus on the mission of the theological school.

Information Technology

It is essential for a president to be reasonably competent and comfortable using a personal computer. He or she should be able to use it for personal e-mail (that is, receiving his or her own e-mail, though using filters to screen and/or sort mail), for institutional Listservs (employees, employee groups, students, trustees, alumni), and for Internet searches. In addition, it is increasingly necessary to be able to think in computerization categories such as database management, spreadsheet analysis, encryption security, and hyperlink connectivity. A president who is not proficient in such areas needs to find someone who can help him or her learn these skills.

The president customarily delegates the authority to manage institutional technology, including the design and implementation of security measures, to an institutional colleague who oversees both administrative and academic computing. To divide these tasks is less and less desirable, because system integration is increasingly important.

Helpful practices include requiring that all employees and all students have an institutional e-mail address and that each address follow a uniform pattern, creating an intranet for institutional communication (installed as the home page on each institutional computer), developing an institutional database for all employees to access and a student database for students and designated employees to access, and designing a user-friendly Website for the public to access.

A president who regularly uses these resources sets the example for all in the theological school to follow. However, he or she needs to thoughtfully and deliberately monitor time spent with the computer.

Personnel Management

Building a Leadership Team

The administrative work of the theological school will flow more efficiently and effectively if the president establishes a strong, respectful, mutually supportive, and trusting leadership team. Building such a team calls for competent, self-initiating team players with effective communication skills. Within the first year of office, the president should receive a thorough review and analysis of the staffing structure and existing personnel to help in assessing whether change is necessary. A strategic plan for staffing, developed in consultation with senior administrators and in relationship to the long-range goals and financial capacities of the theological school, will provide the basis for such an evaluation. Everyone, from support staff to senior administrators, needs to be committed to working together for the well-being of the school and to supporting the vision of the governing board and the president.

The president should select individuals for employment on the basis of their qualifications, skills, and abilities for particular positions. The president needs to evaluate candidates' qualifications in light of the specific requirements of the theological school and the description of the position. Commitment to equality in the workplace and adherence to ATS standards and government regulations (such as the Employment Standards Act, Human Rights Code, and Employment Equity Legislation in Canada; and Title VII of the Civil Rights Act of 1964, the Age Discrimination in Employment Act of 1967, and the Americans with Disabilities Act of 1990 in the United States) is essential. The theological school's employment policies and procedures need to guide the president in developing an appropriate definition for the position, choosing a means for advertising or posting the position (internally and/or externally), and determining his or her direct involvement in the hiring process versus delegating it to another senior administrator.

Offers of appointment must be made by a formal letter of agreement setting forth terms of employment, starting date, length of probationary period (if any), commencing salary, fringe benefits, and other applicable matters. A job description is often enclosed. Also, an announcement of the person hired to fill the position must wait until the institution receives a signed and dated copy of the letter of agreement. Any subsequent changes in assignment need to be discussed with the employee, communicated in writing, and placed in the employee's personnel file.

Throughout this ongoing process of building a team, the president needs to be precise in any and all commitments made. Putting them in writing is a way to clarify details and recall them later. It is also a way of following through with consistency and fairness.

Supervision and Performance Appraisal

Providing an effective orientation is the first step in fostering a good working relationship and producing a well-informed employee. Offering general information about the institution, its organizational structure and flow of authority, and the place of the new employee within it (including a review of the job description) can provide a helpful context of understanding. Introducing a new hire to employees beyond his or her immediate colleagues can also be valuable. A handbook pertaining to the particular employee can provide additional information that can encourage a fulfilling employee/employer relationship.

The president should ensure that daily supervision and annual performance reviews occur in a healthy and constructive manner. This may mean, for example, that the president assumes the role of coaching other senior administrators in their supervisory tasks or in ensuring that those who supervise have access to training or development opportunities in human resources. One coaching method that may be helpful in supervision is known by the acronym GROW:

G = Goals   What do you want to achieve?
R = Reality   What is happening now?
O = Options   What could you do?
W = Will   What will you do?

The president ensures that senior administrators conduct periodic appraisals (at least annually, and more often during the probationary period), to foster positive supervisory relations, promote effective communication, identify organizational or individual strengths and weaknesses, agree upon a course for improvement (if required), develop future career goals and job-related objectives, and identify training opportunities. The performance appraisal needs to be put in writing, appropriately signed and dated, and placed in the employee's personnel file. In some theological schools, an employee has the right to review his or her own file under supervision, if arrangements are made in advance and appropriate authorization is given.[1]

Promotion

Even though most theological schools have rather limited opportunities for promotion, they do occur when the administration reevaluates a position and assigns increased responsibilities to it or when an employee is a successful applicant for a vacancy. Whether or not an employee is promoted or remains in a particular position, salary increases are commonly provided on the basis of annual performance appraisals and the institution's policies regarding merit. The president reviews all consequential promotions in light of available resources and overall staffing needs.

Termination

Disciplinary action normally follows a progressive model; that is, under usual circumstances, discipline progresses from verbal to written repri-

---

1. See John Whitmore, *Coaching for Performance: Guiding People, Performance, and Purpose,* 3rd ed. (London: Nicholas Brealey, 2002).

mands, to suspension of employment, to final discharge. However, some situations are so serious that strictly adhering to the progressive discipline model is inappropriate, and more serious disciplinary action up to and including termination is warranted at the first offense. Examples of such situations include, but are not limited to, insubordination, assault, theft, or fraud.

The president has the responsibility to ensure that disciplinary actions are based upon transparent guidelines and principles. Before taking any disciplinary action or enacting termination, the president or a senior administrator needs to solicit appropriate advice to ensure that the institution is meeting the legal and practical requirements of the process. Notice of dismissal must be given in accordance with fair process within the theological school and must be consistent with the provisions contained in applicable laws. Compensation may be granted at the discretion of the theological school.

The termination of a faculty member is governed by procedures set forth by each theological school.

Compensation

The categories that commonly comprise a compensation package include salary, fringe benefits, and perquisites that pertain to one or more classes of employees (such as tuition reimbursement for a family member who attends the institution). Compensation package details are included in a letter of employment, or in documents that accompany such a letter, and the president reviews such packages each year when making plans for the new fiscal year.

The frames of reference the president uses for increases, particularly salary, include the salaries of other employees at one's own institution, the salaries of colleagues in similar theological schools, and the salaries of people in the geographical region in which the institution is located.

The president reviews current salaries, fringe benefits, and perquisites of all employees, receives recommendations for increases (as appropriate) from other senior-level administrators, and finalizes all figures in accordance with available resources.

Conflict Management

If a theological school is committed to implementing its mission and strategic goals, over time the organizational structure, faculty, administration, and staff will probably undergo change. This may precipitate conflicts between various parties, including faculty, administrators, staff, and the president. In inter-group relations (for instance, between faculty disciplines), conflict is often ideological. It may develop when various factions disagree about what constitutes the proper methodology of a discipline, or the rationale for initiating or terminating a particular program.

Conflict also occurs when groups do not receive clear messages about roles, responsibilities, and expectations, or when they sense a lack of transparency about, and commitment to, the school's mission, strategic plan, and established benchmarks for institutional well-being. In some cases, conflict results from a clash between individual personalities or working styles. In other cases, conflict centers on diversity of gender, race, or ethnicity.

Attitudes about conflict will vary considerably from person to person. Theological schools themselves may have particular "attitudes" toward conflict and these will be represented in institutional policies and procedures.

Presidents must recognize the relationship between the degree of conflict in an institution and the level of morale. The president who learns to promote good morale and diagnose conflict at an early stage, and who helps faculty, administrators, and staff deal with it effectively, fulfills one of the most difficult requirements of the role.

A trustworthy president first and foremost will model open and effective methods for dealing with personal, interpersonal, and systemic conflict. Offering a personal or public apology, when appropriate, can model a way forward that is helpful for others in similar circumstances. Clarifying misconceptions that may cause conflict and being willing to enter a mediated process also demonstrates the president's commitment to a healthy and effective administration. Encouraging open debate and free expression can ensure a fair hearing for diverse viewpoints about significant issues and can enable people to deal with conflicts before they become critical. Discussion and broad, creative development and evaluation of options will lead to resolution of complex and sensitive situations.

The institution needs to establish formal procedures for an employee to file a grievance and needs to review grievances regularly with personnel. Such procedures normally emphasize that it is the responsibility of the employee to bring to the supervisor's attention problems or perceived problems dealing with policy or procedural issues. In the case of a complaint that may lead to a formal grievance, it is in the best interest of both parties to attempt to resolve the issue in as informal a manner as possible. If the complaint cannot be settled by this means and within a short period of time, then the formal grievance procedure may be invoked. The president needs to retain an impartial stance in order to respond justly to all conflicted parties. If the process does not result in a satisfactory resolution, then parties involved should follow the appeal process defined by a particular theological school.

Questions

Clearly, a focus on what is right (strengths) is more productive than a focus on what is wrong (weaknesses). Therefore, a president may find it useful to ask the following questions concerning administration:

1. How can I, as president, celebrate what is right with the administration of the institution?
2. How can I enlist others on the leadership team to do likewise?
3. How can I and others use the energy that we generate in this process to deal with what is not right?

It may also be useful to ask the same questions concerning personnel.[2]

2. See DeWitt Jones, *Celebrate What's Right with the World* (Star Thrower Distribution Corporation, 2001).

Additional Resources

Bennis, Warren, and Patricia Ward Biederman. *Organizing Genius: The Secrets of Creative Collaboration.* Reading, MA: Addison-Wesley, 1997.

This book captures the spirit of discovery that pervades great groups. It describes the free-form organization of teams that are more interested in mission than in hierarchy. It offers a challenge, even to theological seminaries, to capture this spirit and to encourage the leader to be a gatherer of talent, a source of inspiration, and a bridge to the world.

Cleary, Patrick J. *The Negotiation Handbook.* Armonk, NY: M. E. Sharpe, 2001.

The author walks readers through the dynamic process of negotiation, including preparation for it and the rules by which it is carried out. He does this in a step-by-step fashion that translates his substantial professional experience into very practical applications.

Costa, Arthur L., and Robert J. Garmston. *Cognitive Coaching: A Foundation for Renaissance Schools.* 2nd ed. Norwood, MA: Christopher-Gordon, 2002.

This is a book written by educators for educators. It sets forth the principles and practices of coaching gleaned from corporate settings and modifies them so that they can be integrated into the life of institutions such as theological seminaries.

Fisher, Kimball. *Leading Self-Directed Work Teams: A Guide to Developing New Team Leadership Skills.* New York: McGraw-Hill, 1993.

This volume focuses on the development of self-directed work teams (SDWTs) that have a supervisor who empowers them through example and commitment rather than through agreement and control. The author delineates five stages of implementing empowerment, together with the leadership roles needed during each of these stages.

Goleman, Daniel, Richard Boyatzis, and Annie McKee. *Primal Leadership: Realizing the Power of Emotional Intelligence.* Cambridge: Harvard Business School, 2002.

Predecessors to this volume were Goleman's *Emotional Intelligence* (an international bestseller) and *Working with Emotional Intelligence.* In these, as well as in this latest volume, Goleman and his colleagues explore the role of emotional intelligence in relation to leadership, both in personal competence (self-awareness and self-management) and social competence (social awareness and relationship management).

Heifetz, Ronald A. *Leadership without Easy Answers.* Cambridge: Belknap Press of Harvard University Press, 1994.

The author understands leadership as mobilizing people to tackle tough problems. He moves beyond technical change (focusing on the same, but doing it better) to adaptive change (focusing on something different). In doing so he identifies strategic principles: identifying the adaptive challenge, regulating distress, directing disciplined attention to the issues, and giving the work back to the people.

Jones, DeWitt. *Celebrate What's Right with the World.* Star Thrower Distribution Corporation, 2001.

This is a twenty-two-minute video, with leader's guide, participant workbook, PowerPoint presentation CD, and reminder cards (www .starthrower.com or 800-242-3220). It teaches what a powerful force having a vision of possibilities can be, particularly when an organization (and its leadership) focuses on what's right, is energized by it, and thereby has energy remaining to deal with what's not right.

Katzenbach, Jon R., and Douglas K. Smith. *The Wisdom of Teams: Creating the High-Performance Organization.* Boston: Harvard Business School Press, 1993.

The authors believe that teams are the key to improving the performance of organizations, including theological seminaries. Yet leaders often overlook opportunities to maximize their potential, confusing teams with teamwork, empowerment, or participative management. The book's thesis is that teams can turn organizations around.

Weeks, Kent M., and Derek Davis, eds. *Legal Deskbook for Administrators of Independent Colleges and Universities.* Revised 2nd ed. Waco, TX: Baylor University Press, 1999.

This loose-leaf volume is updated annually. It analyzes key legal issues that independent institutions encounter, including matters related to student governance, faculty, compliance requirements, treatment of religious institutions, and taxation.

Whitmore, John. *Coaching for Performance: Guiding People, Performance, and Purpose.* 3rd ed. London: Nicholas Brealey, 2002.

This book further develops what the author initially delineated in his earlier work (1992) under the same title, though with a different subtitle *(A Practical Guide to Growing Your Own Skills)*. It delineates performance coaching that is based on context (awareness and responsibility), skill (effective questioning), and sequence (G: goals, R: reality, O: options, and W: will).

The resources identified in this handbook are listed on the ATS Website where the list will continue to be updated as new resources become available: www.ats.edu > Leadership Education > Presidents.

CHAPTER 3

The President's Role in Governance

ROBERT COOLEY, Gordon-Conwell Theological Seminary
CHRISTA KLEIN, In Trust, Inc.
LOUIS WEEKS, Union Theological Seminary and Presbyterian
School of Christian Education

OVERVIEW

Six Areas for Effective Presidential Leadership

Institutional Ethos

Community Building and Shared Vision

Formation of Databases and Institutional Research Systems

Strategic Planning and Casting a Vision of Success

Constituency and Public Relationships

Creating a Learning Environment

What Is Governance?

Definition and Key Elements of a Shared Governance System

The System Is Designed, Built, and Maintained by Institutional Leaders

The System Is Self-Correcting

The System Encourages Shared Responsibility and Joint Effort

The System Provides Flow of Information and Transparency
of Communication

The System Safeguards the Educational Task with Economic Vitality

Six Areas for Effective Presidential Leadership

The president of a theological school is the "gatekeeper" of its governance process and also the guardian of its mission. Historically, gatekeepers safeguarded the movement of people or commerce in or out of the fortress or citadel. In theological education, presidential "gatekeepers" have the added role to protect the seminary's educational mission from internal or external incursions and, at the same time, to safeguard the final authority, most usually, of a governing board in its broad policy-making and fiduciary responsibilities. Neither a board nor an academic faculty can do its work without this presidential gatekeeping. The effectiveness of presidential leadership will be determined by how well the president exercises the legitimate authority of gatekeeping, because it is through the governance process that the president inspires the necessary trust, confidence, and respect to lead.

Effective presidential leadership will give attention to six areas of the seminary's life and practice, and governance is essential to all areas.

Institutional Ethos

The institution's culture is the context in which the governance system operates. The president has unique opportunities to safeguard the institutional heritage, core mission values, theological tradition, and spiritual character. The president leads sacred and community activities, gives speeches and public addresses, pursues caring consultation in decision-making, and invites people who represent the institutional past for anniversary celebrations and current events.

Community Building and Shared Vision

Governance is a joint effort and calls for a shared response from several individuals and groups within the seminary. Group dynamics and participation, driven by a shared vision of the school's mission, are essential ingredients in successful governance. Community-building efforts lead to improved decision-making, and the president is central to building these human relationships and capacities. Participation around a shared vision leads to wider satisfaction and greater effectiveness.

Formation of Databases and Institutional Research Systems

All units within the governance system need adequate and accurate information. Institutional truth statements are constructed upon such reality. This necessity requires the president to be certain that such databases and systems are in place and are prepared to provide the board, administrators, and faculty with information that enables planning and policy formation for considering the pros and cons of possible strategies. Good governance is built on good information.

Strategic Planning and Casting a Vision of Success

One of the primary responsibilities of gatekeeping is to focus the institution's energies upon the future. This responsibility requires patience, listening skills, and a proper sense of timing. The president can use a strategic planning process, integrated with the governance calendar, to implement the statement of mission in such a way that it becomes a vision for success. The president is always reading the landscape and restating the vision for achieving the mission in order to absorb the reality of new circumstances. At the center of this presidential capacity is theological discernment that will form Christian community. The school's future is among the highest priorities for an effective president.

Constituency and Public Relationships

Relationships among stakeholders, constituencies, judicatories, and regulatory agencies are fundamental to the well-being of the institution. The president leads in strengthening these relationships, serving at all times as a bridge and a buffer. In classical terms, the president functions pastorally in pastoral care. He or she must devote much time to consulting, listening, and understanding concerns.

Creating a Learning Environment

Gatekeeping provides the president with ample opportunities to serve as educator. The governance units (board, administration, faculty, judicatories, etc.) provide a platform for the president to educate members about theological education, the church, and educational issues. Such times provide opportunities to capitalize on the intelligence of the members and to influence strategic decisions and complex policy formation. The president leads the way for the seminary to become a learning community.

The presidential gatekeeper shapes the governance landscape, and this directly correlates to the kind and quality of the school's graduates. Presidential leadership in governance is a true calling.

What Is Governance?

The concept of shared governance has become the established framework for the making of institutional decisions in American higher education. Generally speaking, the concept has become well-established in the world of theological education as boards, administrators, and faculties have worked together in joint efforts toward decisive policy and planning issues. As a system, it has the power to enable presidential leadership; it also has the potential to create adversarial relationships and weaken presidential authority. And so it is important to understand what governance is and what it is not.

Governance must be distinguished from authority. Authority is the mandated power to make decisions that impact the policies and planning of the institution. This power is derived from the institution's charter, bylaws, and other legal mandates. In practice, boards of directors or trustees are usually recognized as having "final or complete" authority for the development and control of the institution. Board governance gains its legitimacy from this formal authority.

At the same time, as an agent of the board, the president is seen as having a "delegated" authority. The delegation of executive authority by the board to the president legitimizes the president to lead the institution. The faculty is granted a "functional" authority to enable it to be responsible in the curriculum and educational policies and plans for the institution. This shared authority, properly exercised, can strengthen the leadership role of a competent president. Effective governance is founded in joint effort, and this foundation is the essential platform for meaningful presidential leadership.

Governance also differs from both leadership and management. Leadership is manifested when influence or power is properly and effectively exercised. It is courage to act for the advancement of the institution. Management is the exercise of competencies to control the institution's resources and operations in an effective manner and in accordance with the executive and governing policies. These policies are legitimized through the shared governance process.

Definition and Key Elements
of a Shared Governance System

If governance is distinct from authority, leadership, and management, then what is it? *Shared governance is the self-correcting system we design, build, and maintain to balance and direct the legitimate interests of an insti-*

tution's policy-making and decision-making structures toward fulfilling the seminary's mission within sustainable economic vitality. Shared governance includes collaboration, information sharing, interpretation, and decision-making. In the context of various constituencies and stakeholders, shared governance is a system open to the participation of students and staff.

The above definition of shared governance employs five elements to describe the system.

The System Is Designed, Built, and Maintained by Institutional Leaders

There is no one right way to design a shared governance system. The history, culture, and operational circumstances of the school need to be taken into account. The governance design will depend upon the structural nature of the school. Attributes of governance will vary depending, for example, on whether the school is a freestanding institution, a denominational seminary, or a university divinity school. Information on the best practices and experience of others can be a valuable resource in the design of an institutional system. Bylaws, board handbooks, and faculty manuals are excellent instruments for communicating the authorized design.

The System Is Self-Correcting

The system is a self-correcting mechanism that gauges the various decision-making functions and provides feedback that permits corrective actions to be instituted. When one policy or planning unit moves the seminary in an undesirable direction, some other element in the governance system rights the course. Effective presidential leaders can assess the cause and make necessary adjustments. This awareness permits solutions that are mutually satisfactory.

The System Encourages Shared Responsibility and Joint Effort

A well-designed governance system for making decisions and developing policies seeks to balance the legitimate interests of the board, the administration, and the faculty. The clarification of governance responsibilities reduces the conflict of roles and the tension that often results from shared authority. A balance can be struck between the board and administration on the one hand, and the faculty on the other hand. Boards and presidents must focus their energies on fiduciary responsibilities that will enable the institution to remain stable and responsive to changing environmental circumstances. The faculty must focus on students, educational programs, and the world of ideas emerging in theological education. These contrasting roles are necessary if the seminary is to fulfill its reason for being. Therefore, a shared governance process can balance the legitimate concerns about leadership of the board and the president with the professional concerns of the faculty.

The System Provides Flow of Information and Transparency of Communication

The system provides a mechanism for the formal flow of information and for transparency in communication and interaction. Information is the lifeblood of the governance system. The president is responsible for the information system that links the components of the governance system. Effective governance requires regular and formal meetings of the board, the administration, and the faculty. The content of these meetings should be institutional data that provide the basis for group interaction and decision-making. For broader consultation, matters of importance can then be communicated with other authority structures. This pattern creates the opportunity for useful feedback and demonstrates the openness of the system of governance in the theological school environment.

The System Safeguards the Educational Task
with Economic Vitality

The system's purpose is to safeguard the educational mission with economic vitality. Board members and institutional administrators can easily be distracted from the central mission of the seminary when they concentrate on finances and operations. After all, the financial strength of the school is critical to its sustainability. The centrality of the educational mission then becomes the faculty's fundamental focus, and their role in the governance system is to sustain and monitor institutional purpose and fulfilled mission. Through shared governance, this joint effort secures the twin bottom lines of institutional purpose: mission fulfilled with economic vitality.

Shared governance works best when other players in the governance process — namely constituencies, stakeholders, staff, and students — have their own prescribed methods for significant participation in institutional decision-making. Effective shared governance should be seen as an open system. These diverse voices can be heard through ad hoc groups, task forces, committees, and open forum sessions. The wise president will find ways for the board and faculty to hear these desired voices and to invite their participation in the affairs of the seminary.

A final word needs to be said about joint effort. Most seminaries are small institutions and focus on few academic programs and students. They may be small, but this does not mean that their operational infrastructure is simple. Quite to the contrary, they can be as intricate and complex as many large schools or small universities. Therefore, the variety of governance tasks produces an inescapable interdependence for the board, the president, and the faculty. This relationship calls for the fullest communication and flow of information between structures and a governance system carefully designed to ensure joint effort. The enjoyment of reaching resolution on institutional challenges grows out of the increased capacity for governance achieved through joint effort. The president can make the governance system work well by giving close attention to each entity that formally participates in the shared governance system: the board, the faculty, and the office of the president.

Governance and the Board

The governing board of a seminary is that group of people with the legal and ethical responsibility to develop and control an institution managed by a president and a faculty. Their role is to legitimize the institution and to see that it functions responsibly and effectively. They fulfill this role by safeguarding the statement of institutional mission and purpose, employing the president, and providing adequate fiscal, physical, and human resources to meet the needs of the school. The board also serves as a bridge and a buffer to the school's constituency and the public. The selection of board members, and a president's influence in that process, will vary according to institutional type. University divinity schools and denominational seminaries will have a greater dependency upon external forces than a freestanding institution. In either case, presidents must use their influence in the process so that individuals are selected who have great passion for theological education.

Effective boards seek members who can provide the board with a blend of people who have the competence for work, the capacity to secure wealth, and the ability to share wisdom. Candidates for board membership may wish to join the board for several reasons. They may be looking for opportunities to serve in a larger arena than the one provided by their local congregations. They may also be attracted by a desire for community recognition, social relationships, or loyalty to an institution. Presidents can assist in the selection process by encouraging the board to establish a board profile of desired demographics and skills and to work toward achieving that ideal. Other useful ways to exercise influence include encouraging the board to form a nomination or membership group charged with identifying prospective members and recommending such candidates to the board to fill vacancies. Presidents can assist such groups in their tasks by cultivating qualified prospects and acquainting them with the institution, its mission, and its personnel.

Boards depend upon presidents to assist them in their work. Typically, this assistance takes the form of providing reliable information, nurturing the members through a board education program, and inspiring the board through the exercise of visionary leadership.

The wise president will design and lead an ongoing board education program that involves assessment and evaluation processes. These processes may include the appraisal of "dashboard indicators" established to monitor varying attributes of the institution or to evaluate the achievement of goals established by the board to determine its own success or failure. Evaluation may also include a process of reflection upon past or present efforts to determine the reasons for success or failure. Such evaluations and reflections are an excellent way to examine board life, and the results can be a basis for an ongoing board development program.

Board self-study is another essential form of evaluation. Standardized board assessment instruments are available for seminary boards, and they should be used every three or four years to measure progress and board quality. A board retreat is the ideal time to learn from such assessment instruments, and it gives the president ample time to raise and discuss with the board its strengths and weaknesses. Improving the quality of the board must be central to the president's leadership, and board self-study and awareness are the surest way to improve the quality of the board and its governance work. In the case of boards with no mandated length of term, individual assessment of a member's participation in the work of the board is essential to the determination of whether that member's service should continue. This assessment should be under the direction of the board, either directly or through one of its committees, such as the executive committee or trustee/nomination committee.

The work of the board is precise, formal, and legislative; therefore, it must have the competent input of the president and the faculty if it is to fulfill its full responsibilities. It is for this reason that the board's authority to govern is shared with the president and faculty. It would be dangerous to forget that board members serve the school as laypersons and with part-time, volunteer involvement. Therefore, board members depend on assistance to do their work and on the fullest disclosure of information possible to make their efforts productive. The expertise and competencies of the president and the faculty are necessary to enable lay members to be knowledgeable about the demands and achievements of theological education. A harmonious relationship between the board and the president builds trust and faithful support.

Legally a board exists only when it is in session as a quorum; yet boards and board members have continuing roles and responsibilities. Endowment funds, even with money managers, require oversight; fundraising is an ongoing activity; campus representations and advocacy are requested from time to time; presidential searches must be conducted; and special crises and opportunities demand immediate attention. How a board organizes itself to complete its work determines the manner in which these continuous functions are addressed. Seminary boards have usually followed the pattern of setting up committees to give oversight to the normal categories of institutional organization: academic affairs, student affairs, finance, development, and buildings and grounds. In addition, committees are assigned to special tasks such as board affairs, audits, and investments, as well as a committee on the president.

In recent years, as institutional systems have tended to replace distinct functions, boards have been learning to reorganize around centers of action instead of committees. These board groups find focus in current strategic issues, and these may change from year to year, shifting the nature of group work within the board. This flexible board organization keeps the work of the board in a dynamic state, eliminating the turf protection and stagnation that often accompanies committee formats. Accordingly, presidential engagement can shift from the routine of supporting and maintaining committees to giving greater attention to institutional issues and strategic planning.

The greatest gift an effective president can give to a board is to foster an infectious group spirit. This spirit is achieved through personal relationships and interactions; the casting of vision with inspiration, prayer, and enthusiasm; and the reliable and disciplined manner of board work at its meetings. Group bonding grows out of this sense of the board's importance and unique role. It is this group spirit that attracts new members and motivates all members to greater involvement as they hold the seminary in trust with passion and dedication. The president needs a mutual partnership with the board chair in order to instill this group spirit. The quality of their relationship determines the success of the board's work and cohesiveness.

Strong governing boards also have well-designed plans for their annual work. A master schedule can be built around the rhythmic seasonal cycles of institutional requirements, such as fall enrollments and final budget approval, faculty agreements and long-range educational program plans, and year-end fundraising to achieve development goals and a balanced budget. As the president and the chair of the board guide the board in the framing of its work schedule, members become engaged in the anticipation of what is needed and required for a successful completion of the annual workload.

The regular meetings of the board can be planned and executed against this backdrop of the annual work schedule. The president, along with the board chair, must with vigilance prevent meetings from becoming dull events, filled with routine business and discussion. Reports and documents should be distributed prior to meetings so that basic information is known beforehand and the board can concentrate its attention and energy on the most important institutional issues.

A dynamic board meeting will have at least five elements.

1. The *spiritual dimension.* A meditation, a personal presentation of a spiritual journey, a faculty-led exposition of Scripture, a prayer session — any of these establishes a meaningful context for the work of the board and reminds each member that his or her work is theological. Often this offering will have a more significant impact on a member than any other part of the meeting.

2. The *interpersonal dimension.* Good fellowship creates a bond, a sense of group well-being that unites the board around its work. The president can be strategic in providing the social glue that produces fellowship. Special social events, including dinners, lunches, receptions, concerts, lectures, or even group travel, draw members together and increase their sense of belonging.

3. *Board education.* Every meeting should have at least an hour-long educational session to explore some aspect of the board's role, responsibilities, and performance. Board members can learn from feedback about their performance as a body and about the meaning of trusteeship. Effective presidents are always educators of their boards.

4. *Action assignments.* When issues are presented to the board, the variety of responses invites research and study. Items may be referred to special groups, the president, or other centers of expertise. The board benefits from well-researched options and recommendations.

5. *Decision.* Each meeting will have studies, recommendations, or policy statements requiring the formal decision of the governing board. The plan for the meeting must include the time necessary to arrive at a formal decision.

Board meetings can be productive, interesting, and engaging if these five elements are present and if presidents are responsible for attentively supervising their format and for providing the appropriate supportive resources and materials.

The governance system rests firmly upon the mandates that establish authority, roles, and duties. The constitution and bylaws are the major mandates; they state the general purpose of the institution and outline the general conditions and procedures that guide board operations. More and more, boards are designing manuals that serve as a ready reference to board information, such as bylaws, statements of policies, meeting minutes, member personal data, institutional programs, annual work plans, committee descriptions, an organizational chart of the institution, the current budget, and so on. If the manual is loose-leaf in format, it can be updated easily with annual information and current documents. New board members find such manuals extremely helpful in understanding their roles and responsibilities. Presidents can use such documents as a basis for new member orientation.

Governance and the President

The president's central role in a shared governance system is to serve as the gatekeeper of the decision-making processes and the formation of institutional policies. Such a shared system must be viewed as a single governance community bonded together by several elements. These elements may include denominational identity, theological views, jurisdictional expectations, or requirements of a constituency, but the strongest element will be the mission of the institution. Other elements will also have an influence on the governance community: civil regulatory agencies, some employees, professional associations, and accrediting bodies, among others. But the president stands at the center of this institutional life, guiding the work of the board and faculty, and at the same time giving attention to all of the vital relationships required by the institution's public.

President/Board Partnership

No constituent relationship is more important for the president than his or her partnership with the governing board. This partnership depends on mutual reciprocity. It is for this reason that an effective president will spend considerable time with the board and its members and devote great energy to the work of the board. This relationship of mutual exchange requires the president to define his or her responsibilities in ways that address the context of the relationship. Bear in mind that the board is a group with final authority and the president is an individual with delegated authority; the board consists of part-time volunteers and the president is full-time; the board has a continuous endurance and the president is usually limited by a term appointment or by his or her own sense of calling; and the board membership is made up of laypersons and the president is a competent professional. These contrasting characteristics call for the president to give priority to four ways in particular for relating to the board: gatekeeping, leadership style, board education, and reliable information.

Understanding the Role of the Gatekeeper

The effective president will value the influence of the presidential position. The president has the authority to advance the institution and to see to it that the institutional goals are achieved, and he or she must be willing to exercise influence in support of the institution's mission. Such a role requires the best possible self-understanding and a leadership style that acts on informed intuition. Presidents who value their influence and make strategic decisions also have little difficulty in empowering others in shared governance. In fact, such presidents expect participants to ask difficult questions and draw upon their own insights and creativity. This display of empowerment enhances the confidence level of those with whom the work of governance is shared. It encourages board or faculty discussion, and it helps board and faculty members to realize the power of ideas and dreams. Above all else, the president's control over his or her emotions, words, and actions is absolutely necessary in the role of gatekeeper. Respect is more important than popularity.

Giving Attention to Leadership Style

Leadership is the ability to influence others toward a common mission. Most people selected by boards for the presidency are known for their capacity to exercise influence, be it in the academic community, with donors, or with prospective students. Presidents who pay attention to leadership style know the importance of articulating a vision for success and of having the courage to act. Undergirding both will be a passion fed by faith-filled inspiration. The effective president has a clear vision of a future in which others participate; this vision puts the mission of the institution into operation and empowers shared governance. Shared vision fuels the intellectual and practical needs of governance. It is in this context of shared vision that a president can take risks with courage to act upon ideas, dreams, and intuition. Without this quality of visionary leadership, a president may exhibit courage but is doomed to adversarial encounters and a breakdown in shared governance. A great president has the capacity to inspire the school community to go where it needs to go with courage and passion. A great president needs courage to establish institutional direction and passion to influence the minds and hearts of those who share in governance responsibilities. In the end, the style of leadership must win hearts and minds. No member of a board or of a faculty will follow a presidential leader who does not lead with vision, courage, and passion.

Making Board Education a Priority

A wise president will recognize that the board does have continuous endurance in its institutional roles and must be continually enabled to fulfill its responsibilities with knowledge and understanding. Furthermore, board members can benefit from learning the ways of theological education, theology, and the nature and place of the church in society. An ongoing program of education for trustees is an effective way for the president to ensure that members develop their capacity to govern and to hold the institution in trust. In this fashion, the president becomes the educator of the board.

Every board meeting should have a formal learning opportunity that will increase the trustees' role in fulfilling the institutional mission.

Other special times and events should be designed to provide extended learning opportunities. All-day seminars designed around the expertise of the faculty are an excellent means of bringing the trustees into the world of theology and the church. Two- or three-day retreats provide the luxury of ample time for exploring and discussing issues of trusteeship and institutional governance. Governance mentors and consultants can be secured who will present the current best practices and insights on particular institutional needs and trends. Exchange visits between partner seminary boards can be a useful way to learn through comparison and contrast. And reading programs in which books, articles, and brochures are circulated to board members can reinforce group learning and provide individual stimulation toward learning the ways of effective trusteeship.

The president, as board educator, can influence the quality of the governance process through a formal and continuous program of board development, and this program must be a high priority in the leadership of the president.

Defining Institutional Reality through Reliable Information

It is the responsibility of the president to see that his or her governance partners, the board and the faculty, have reliable information that will enable them to do their work. This can be done through ensuring the availability of information, providing channels for communication, creating an environment for openness, and scheduling forums for interaction.

The quality and integrity of the information must be the responsibility of the president. Wise presidents avoid information overload and inappropriate detail that creates confusion, causes frustration, and misleads others. Above all else, attention must be paid to the accuracy and reliability of the information presented. The president's integrity in the governance process is at stake. The most useful information is that which brings focus and understanding to the issues that are strategic to the governance process and to the realization of the institutional mission.

Boards and faculties need reliable data in several areas to do their own work responsibly:

1. Analysis of student enrollment will shape academic plans, tuition pricing, and financial aid leverage.
2. Reviewing trends in ministry and tracking graduate placements inform curricular planning and student services and are necessary for building bridges with the school's public.
3. Exploring performance in resource development and fundraising helps to determine the course of institutional advancement.
4. Facilities audits create opportunities for scheduled maintenance and renewal and replacement projects.
5. Reports on financial performance of all seminary funds enable financial planning and decision making.

The governance process is energized when a president can add meaning and an interpretive context to the information presented. It is the president's responsibility to see that all available channels are open for information flow between governance partners and those in management who produce the data. Breakdowns in the flow of information undermine the quality of the governance process. Good governance depends upon good information, and that requires an environment conducive to openness. Secrecy should be the exception, limited to sensitive issues and matters of privacy. Presidential leadership requires public settings or forums for the purpose of shared information and feedback. Such interactions can inform the president on current concerns and viewpoints. Reliable information can go a long way toward creating a healthy climate for good governance.

In addition to the hallmarks of the president's engagement in the governance process listed above, two other features enhance the president's leadership: the relationship between the board chair and president, and the evaluation of the president.

Understanding the Relationship of the Board Chair and the President

The mutual reciprocity between the board and the president is best symbolized in the exchange of authority and professional competence between the board chair and president. This relationship is personal and more; it must be grounded in a constant concern for the work and role of the board in governance and for the general advancement of the institution. An open and sturdy relationship makes it possible to handle the difficult issues and perplexing questions faced by the president. The president's leadership is enhanced through the thoughtful and supportive contributions of an understanding board chair. Beyond the personal benefits, a good relationship creates opportunities for planning and directing the work of the board. Dual leadership with mutual consultation enhances wisdom about board organization, group and individual assignments, the discipline necessary for member participation, and the selection of candidates for board membership. The most obvious outcome of this relationship is well-planned board meetings keyed to strategic issues, with supportive data, energizing and anticipatory agendas, and the capacity for board self-assessment. A joint chair-president engagement in the structuring and resourcing of all plans to advance the institution is foundational to the board's contribution to institutional governance. A wise president will nurture the chair-president relationship.

Evaluating the President

The practice of evaluating the president begins during the period of candidacy and continues throughout the life of a given presidency. Presidential leadership often results in accumulated grievances, a sense of loneliness, and weariness with the responsibility of initiative. One president has called the experience "splendid agony." The board-president exchange inevitably leads to judgments of presidential effectiveness. At the same time, comments and judgments are made by others inside and outside the institutional community. It is the board's responsibility to implement a process of evaluation of the president. If the board fails to do so, then the president should request that such an assessment be instituted. At the very least, a formal conversation between the board chair and the president should take place. This conversation should be summarized in writing and filed in the institution's confidential files, recording the major themes of discussion and the proposed action plans to be implemented. A formal evaluation should be regularized by the board about every four to five years. Such an assessment should be handled by a consultant or a third party and not by members of the board, faculty, staff, or students. The most effective presidential review can be done in the context of an institutional audit, in which the evaluation is of the institutional condition and the relationship of the president's leadership to that condition. A formal evaluation should always begin with a self-assessment by the president.

Some institutions have found the informal evaluation of the president to be more effective and meaningful to all parties. These informal evaluations are based on a plan for continuous evaluation through a specially assigned trustee committee on the president. This committee meets during the course of each board meeting with the president, establishes goals and assessment criteria to be discussed at each meeting of the committee, and forms action plans to correct weaknesses or to recognize achievements. Matters of communal judgments and conversations can be assessed at these meetings. Meeting results can then be reported to the board in executive session. This regular process of informal evaluation greatly benefits the president by enhancing his or her self-understanding and confidence.

In either case, formal or informal, the board and the president should agree on the preferred method of evaluation and should insist that it be kept confidential. The goal of presidential evaluations is to further legitimize the presidential office and to strengthen presidential leadership, not to demean or diminish it. If the leadership of the president is ineffective, most presidents will know that their time is completed, and they can initiate proper action through resignation or retirement. Otherwise, the board must act in the best interest of the institution and have departure policies in place to guide the inevitable change in presidential leadership.

The president who practices effective leadership in governance is one who knows the rewards of being a "gatekeeper," the satisfaction of a full professional life, and the joy of building a successful institution that has realized its mission with economic vitality.

Governance and the Faculty

The fundamental role of the faculty in the shared governance process is to safeguard the centrality of the educational mission. How the president relates to the faculty and enables it to realize its governing role determines the nature of the president-faculty relationship. Experience shows that this is a most demanding expectation. Oftentimes, the vision of the faculty for theological education is in conflict with the board's and the president's vision. These conflicting visions can create tension in matters of institutional procedures, allocation of resources, and the governance process.

The historical development of governance systems has allotted to the faculty a dual role in the life of the institution. On the one hand, faculty members are professional educators, acting in accordance with professional authority and in ways accountable to their guilds and their consciences. On the other hand, faculty members are mandated with a functional authority for the curriculum and for the professoriate. This latter role positions the faculty within the institutional governance system and requires a measure of institutional commitment and involvement.

Unless the president and academic administrators can engage the faculty fully in the decision-making ethos of the institution, the faculty will function begrudgingly on governance issues and display an attitude of ambivalence. Presidents who wish to keep conflict to a minimum and to empower faculty roles in governance will give attention to keeping the faculty fully informed, will consult with the faculty on all strategic issues of mission and financial viability, and will utilize faculty expertise in the formation of strategic plans.

Keeping the Faculty Informed

It is the responsibility of the president, along with the academic administrators, to see that the faculty have reliable and significant information that will enable them to do their work in governance. The same communication guidelines that characterize the president's information system for the board apply to faculty communications. Faculties need strategic and reliable data-sets to make judgments on educational programs and policies. Formal channels of communication need to be in place so that the faculty need not wonder if information is trustworthy and meaningful. Openness among the faculty, the administration, and the president is essential to creating an attitude of trust and confidence in leadership. Regular forums for interaction with the faculty on institutional issues will go a long way toward creating a common vision to fulfill the institutional mission and achieve economic vitality. Good faculty governance depends upon good information.

Consulting with the Faculty on Institutional Issues

A wise president will take the necessary time and energy to confer with the faculty on issues that are strategic to the institution's well-being. This is especially true in times of institutional stress or complex change. The president's capacity to listen to the suggestions and comments of faculty before reaching a decision will ensure respect and appreciation for the president's role and authority. Such a practice creates a climate of shared vision and collegiality. This presidential practice will not guarantee consensus on all issues, but it will assure the faculty of their role in the shared governance process. They will respect the fact that the president has the ultimate responsibility for the decisions that impact the institution. In fact, they may even support conclusions that differ from their own.

Consultation with the faculty may take several forms. Regular meetings with elected faculty leaders create a steady stream of communication and generate creative and responsive interaction. Occasional faculty luncheons are appreciated, as are selected faculty conversations in the president's office. Orientation sessions with new faculty inaugurate good faculty-president conversations and focus attention on the president's vision for the institution. Walking the campus can be an excellent way to drop in a faculty member's office and to engage in informal conversation. Finally, the formal faculty meeting is the supreme opportunity to consult and listen to faculty opinion and counsel on institutional direction, although such meetings are not the appropriate setting for conflict resolution or addressing complex fiscal or resource issues.

Using Faculty Expertise in Strategic Planning

When the president engages the faculty to identify key institutional issues and draws upon their expertise in planning a strategic response, the president demonstrates the basic pattern of shared governance. This practice fosters a shared vision within the institution and develops a spirit of collective leadership and responsibility throughout the entire system. Faculty members represent a reservoir of intellectual capacity and expertise that a president cannot afford to ignore. Rather, these skills and knowledge need to be invested in the institution's future and will become building blocks in the president's articulation of the vision for success. Since the seminary is primarily a knowledge-driven organization, it depends for its success on the ideas and wise insights of the professors and administrators involved. Presidents are involved with numerous nonacademic matters; therefore, the faculty's role in strategic thinking and response buttresses and contributes to the leadership of the president. If faculty expertise is utilized in the strategic planning process, the board and president can be assured that the educational mission of the institution is central and is being monitored for effectiveness. Finally, faculty participation in the institution's planning ensures that crucial issues will be effectively addressed. As the winds of change continue to blow across theological schools, it is more important than ever that the faculty be utilized in the governance process through strategic planning.

The faculty has a recognized and mandated role in the governance process, and this status dare not be ignored by the president or the board. Effective presidential leadership will win the respect and admiration of the faculty and will gain the faculty's willingness to participate in the governance process. Shared governance, properly exercised, is the basis for presidential leadership.

A Final Word

The most common design for institutional governance is the tripartite system — board, president, and faculty. In this system, the president stands central and serves as the gatekeeper to its processes. In some instances, other parties have roles in the making of institutional decisions. Denominational judicatories, alumni organizations, the student body, and even staff employees may have representation. As institutions become complex and extend their educational services to branch campuses or extension programs, it is not unusual to have such activities under the governance leadership of a board of advisors. These additional partners in the governance system call for the same presidential attention as the standard structures of board or faculty.

A wise and effective president will understand the intricacies of the institutional governance design and seek to balance the legitimate interests of all parties. Remember, it is through the governance system that presidential leadership is deemed effective when the educational mission is sustained with economic vitality. The president's role in governance is pivotal.

Additional Resources

Chait, Richard P., Thomas P. Holland, and Barbara E. Taylor. *The Effective Board of Trustees*. Phoenix: The Oryx Press, 1993.

Chait, Richard P., Thomas P. Holland, and Barbara E. Taylor. *Improving the Performance of Governing Boards*. Phoenix: The Oryx Press, 1996.

Chait, Richard P., William P. Ryan, and Barbara E. Taylor. *Governance as Leadership*. Hoboken: John Wiley & Sons, 2005.

Fisher, James L. *The Board and the President*. New York: Macmillan Publishing Co., 1991.

Hesselbein, Frances, Marshall Goldsmith, and Richard Beckhard, editors. *The Organization of the Future*. San Francisco: Jossey-Bass Publishers, 1997.

Holland, Thomas P., and David C. Hester, editors. *Building Effective Boards for Religious Organizations*. San Francisco: Jossey-Bass Publishers, 2000.

Houle, Cyril O. *Governing Boards*. San Francisco: Jossey-Bass Publishers, 1989.

Ingram, Richard T., et al. *Governing Independent Colleges and Universities*. San Francisco: Jossey-Bass Publishers, 1993.

In Trust Magazine. www.intrust.org.

McCarter, Neely Dixon. *The President as Educator*. Atlanta: Scholars Press, 1996.

Schein, Edgar H. *Organizational Culture and Leadership*. San Francisco: Jossey-Bass Publishers, 1985.

Useful Websites

Association of Governing Boards (www.agb.org)
The Association of Theological Schools in the United States and Canada
     (www.ats.edu)
BoardSource (www.boardsource.org)
Council for the Advancement and Support of Education (www.case.org)
In Trust Inc. (www.intrust.org/resources)

The resources identified in this handbook are listed on the ATS Website
where the list will continue to be updated as new resources become
available: www.ats.edu > Leadership Education > Presidents.

CHAPTER 4

The President's Role in Defining Mission and Strategic Planning

DAVID L. TIEDE, Luther Seminary
DAVID DRAPER, Winebrenner Theological Seminary
WILSON YATES, United Theological Seminary
of the Twin Cities

Why Presidents Invest Leadership in Listening: The Listening Post

The new president has just been elected with applause for an inspiring vision. Faculty prepare to head back to their offices, and board members are checking their departure times. Then a business leader declares, "This school needs a strategic plan!" The room falls silent. Is this mere corporate talk? Or is it an oracle to the school? How will the president respond?

Leadership Begins with Listening

We all want our institutions to be excellent. For some that means improving what the school is doing or recovering a remembered past. Faculty want time for scholarship. Perhaps the president is only being asked to be effective in raising more support, pursuing what David H. Kelsey has called a "problem-solving approach."[1] "If we just stay on the road, we will surely arrive where we are going."

But what if the preferred future requires a new direction? Who would know? How will the school rally to its mission and realign its strengths to make it happen? Perhaps the very criteria of quality will be challenged. It is risky to put new wine in old wineskins.[2]

Listening Before Planning

Listening is an active part of leadership, preparing the way for planning.

Wherever the president came from, now everyone wants to be heard. The president's socialization and loneliness begin with listening to people other than personal friends. Students, faculty, board members, donors, and academic and church leaders have valid stakes in the

1. David H. Kelsey, *To Understand God Truly: What's Theological about a Theological School* (Louisville: Westminster, 1992), p. 25.

2. For two excellent assessments of the risks of leadership, see Robert Terry, *The Seven Zones for Leadership: Acting Authentically in Stability and Chaos* (Palo Alto: Davies-Black, 2001); and Ronald A. Heifetz and Martin Linsky, *Leadership on the Line: Staying Alive through the Dangers of Leading* (Boston: Harvard Business School Press, 2002).

school's future, but their concerns and wisdoms differ. The president's leadership begins with sorting out the interests and wisdom of various groups, even mapping them. What does each voice have to say to the whole school?

A wise consultant appeared at the door of a new president, inquired about the president's hopes, and attended to institutional realities. Then she met with the faculty. Her first question was, "Who is your customer?" The groan was audible. How crass! "OK!" she said. "Let me rephrase the question. Who depends on you to do a good job?"

The first response was both profound and cynical: "God!"

"Wow!" said the consultant. "I've never heard that answer. I'll accept it. But do you have a more proximate customer?"

When the laughter subsided, the discussion began. The first answer was "the students." But the conversation continued. The answer was, "The communities that call our graduates to lead them!" Then the question came, "How well are you serving them?"

To hear the answer, the seminary's listening post had to be set up outside the school. Careful listening to the answer had to take place before a mission and plan could be formulated, let alone adopted.

An alumnus wrote to the president, "Quit preparing your graduates for a church that no longer exists." The president reported this sharp word to faculty and board. Everyone first nodded, and then wondered. "For what church should we prepare our graduates?"

This listening is both practical and theological. It is practical, even political (your title, after all, is "president"), because schools are held in trust. As Yogi said, "You hear a lot just listening!" But the president begins to differentiate the voices, asking each group for the counsel they can best bring, and always listening for their sense of the institution's core purpose and how this calling can be best exercised. Listening gains power when the stakeholders hear one another, when faculty members overhear the president reciting their concerns, or when the seminary community hears the voices of those who call its graduates. Until the varied groups hear one another, the school and its president are talking to themselves.

Knowing Whom You Serve

A theological school becomes a lively enterprise when it knows whom it serves, what they need from the school, and how well they are being served by everyone's effort.

Peter F. Drucker is a great teacher of this lesson — specifically for seminaries. "A mission statement has to be operational, otherwise it's just good intentions. A mission statement has to focus on what the institution really tries to do and then do it so that everybody in the organization can say: This is *my* contribution to the goal."[3]

These practical concerns require theological wisdom, especially in time of crisis, to discern "What is the real threat and opportunity?" or "What in the world is happening?" or "What are we called to be about in the name of God?" Listening is theological because the seminary will embody its understanding of God. For better or worse, the answers will express the witness of a tradition. It is not about the president's private vision but about leadership in a community. The convictions vary from Roman Catholics, to academics, to evangelicals, to confessional Christians, to liberal Protestants, to Pentecostals. The president of a seminary must ask questions in such a way that the tradition can hear its answers.

A presidency then becomes a "bully pulpit": echoing and focusing the distinctive witness of a theological heritage and articulating the benefits of the school's mission. Planning, in turn, becomes a venture of mobilizing the promise of this enterprise.[4]

How Presidents Authorize Others: The Bully Pulpit

No leader has a "bully pulpit" without a message, an audience, and a context. As the president gains authority in defining the institution's vocation and action plan, members of the community pay attention in hope (and fear) that the plan is more than talk.

The president's role in strategic planning and mission gains and

3. Peter F. Drucker, *Managing the Nonprofit Organization* (New York: HarperCollins, 1990), p. 4.

4. Among the many methods for "strategic planning," Bryan R. Barry has written a concise book titled *Strategic Planning Workbook for Nonprofit Organizations* (St. Paul: Amherst H. Wilder Foundation, 1997).

loses strength by who is invited into the effort. A president lamented, "Our faculty and board genuinely want to move ahead, but we have a few torpedo artists in both places so eager to assert their power that they will stop the ship, even against their best interests." A counselor advised, "Remember the rule of five! Five people of integrity and courage can move any organization if they are engaged, never co-opted, but called upon for their wisdom."

Who knows whether the number is five? But it certainly isn't one, and it's not twenty. When presidents write strategic plans on their own, no matter how aspiring and professional their consultants make them sound, the plans go on the shelf until key legitimators assent. The engagement of others is not simply a function of their offices or community clout.

One of the president's most critical moments is discerning who will be engaged from varied constituencies in the planning. In some contexts, the president is required to rely on the people sent to the effort by the faculty, university, or church. At a school where church officials ran almost everything, they still demanded a strategic plan. The president's weary frustration was expressed in the title: "Memories of Excellence."

If they want their president to lead, communities will find their own ways to extend trust to the president so that able people who will help are in on the planning. This is a shared task of prayer and calling, not personal power or alliances. It is worthy of care.

Preparing the Way for a Mission Statement

The president represents, articulates, and advocates the mission long before a mission statement is formally adopted. The seminary's calling is the mantle of leadership, and the president soon feels its weight. The lonely, risky, and inspiring venture of stating and restating what has been and needs to be heard never ends. No mission statement can guarantee engagement. But when an institution adopts a formal mission statement, it has given itself a mandate to move toward a preferred future and has authorized the president and others to lead. A viable mission statement announces what the institution promises to do, for whom, and to what benefit. It is a common ground for planning what to do and when.

From the moment of its adoption, the president constantly and persistently recites the mission statement, then listens for others to appeal to it in critical discussions and welcomes their appeals to it. Its value is first tested in the clarity it expresses about the seminary's core work as this work affects varied constituencies. Its durability is proved in its coherence in helping to guide, prioritize, and justify the seminary's strategic decisions.

Adopting a plan to accomplish the mission is also a moment for thanksgiving, as a prayer at the beginning of the day, not its end. The plan is dynamic and incomplete. It does not give a map to perfection, but a compass and mileposts for a sustained journey.

When the journey has been launched, what leadership is needed from the president?

Measuring and Reporting Results

Many seminary presidents invest deeply in helping their schools to listen and in framing statements of shared conviction, even aspiration. They are often chosen for their gifts of articulating, inspiring, and communicating the heart of the matter. These abilities are crucial, lest seminaries lose their way. But presidents also must measure and report the results. "I know what counts," said one president; "now I need to learn how to count."

A new vice president for administration and finance read his seminary's strategic plan. "This is amazing," he said. "In many years of business strategy, I have never seen such a rich plan, so inspired with the educational task. Where is the operational section?"

The strategic plan is the institution's lesson plan, defining the president's homework. The president must be a continual learner, modeling inquiry for the community and teaching the seminary how to learn.[5] Theological schools are often superb at teaching, but challenged when it comes to learning together.[6] Faculty seldom think they "report

5. Presidents will do well to become acquainted with the excellent learning resources designed for them by the Association of Theological Schools (www.ats.edu) and for the good governance of their schools by In Trust Inc. (www.intrust.org).

6. See Peter M. Senge, *The Fifth Discipline: The Art and Practice of the Learning Or-*

to" anyone, and some board members can't understand why the president doesn't either manage people better or replace them. Old jokes about "herding cats" will persist. As a board member said, "How can so many smart people be so organizationally naïve?" Another noted, "I hope to see our academic experts bring their powers to this mission."

Presidents lead by teaching the board, faculty, staff, and constituency the lessons the school must learn to steward its resources and relationships to accomplish the desired results.[7] A plan that identifies real work to be done gives administrators, board leaders, faculty, and consultants opportunities to collaborate toward institutional effectiveness.

In a consultation with seminary presidents and board leaders, Max De Pree[8] once said, "No one can accomplish more than about five major things in a given year. When someone comes to me with an idea, I take out my list and ask, 'Which of these five things should I replace on my list, or is this something you should do?'" His stunning comment struck home with several new presidents. Most were trying to do too much.

Again, five may not be the right number, but what things will require focused attention from the president in the coming year? Without simply becoming the manager, one of the president's leadership tasks will surely be to identify who is responsible for accomplishing which goals and how the human and financial resources will be tracked.

---

ganization (New York: Doubleday, 1990); *The Fifth Discipline Fieldbook: Strategies and Tools for Building a Learning Organization* (New York: Doubleday, 1994).

7. See Chapter Five, "The President's Role as Academic Leader." The point in this chapter, however, is that the president's role in defining mission and strategic planning is a form of educational leadership. In his study *The President as Educator* (Atlanta: Scholars Press, 1996), Neely Dixon McCarter observed how the compounding of expectations on the presidency have reached the point that "most people, including many presidents, think presidents are involved in almost every conceivable activity except education" (p. 32). Presidents who have been professional educators may also grieve the loss of their classrooms and the expertise of their academic "work." But a seminary with a clear educational mission and a plan to move toward a preferred future gives its president not only a "bully pulpit" but also a public classroom where teaching involves good content, sound methods, and energized engagement by learners.

8. Max De Pree has been the CEO of Herman Miller Furniture Company and chair of the board at Hope College and a board leader at Fuller Theological Seminary. Seminary presidents will do well to read his book, *Leadership Is an Art* (New York: Dell, 1989).

How Presidents Lead for Results:
The Learning Laboratory

In 1994, the Association of Theological Schools concluded its "quality and accreditation project" with the adoption of new standards for "the good theological school."[9] These standards accommodate the remarkable diversity of theological schools and traditions that have emerged as major forces in the past half century, rivaling the earlier establishment of the eastern Protestant divinity schools.[10] Instead of measuring all of the theological schools in the United States and Canada by one tradition of quality, the new standards challenge every school to be clear about the benefits of its mission, accountable for its effectiveness in accomplishing its mission, and efficient in its work.

Focus on Performance

Institutions of higher education often resist efforts to measure their own performance. They grade their students and count all the publications of every tenure candidate. When asked for their institutional report card, however, seminaries often appeal to broad claims of academic excellence and spiritual integrity. But with a clear mission and a strategic plan to accomplish identified goals in stated time frames, a school has the ingredients for accountability, and the president can develop annual "dashboards" to measure results.

As an actionable plan develops, the president's message becomes, "Our mission statement promises benefits to others. Our plan will authorize leaders and hold them accountable to our *faithfulness* to our promise, our *effectiveness,* and our *efficiency.*"

---

9. See the collection of essays interpreting the new standards in the ATS publication *Theological Education* 30, no. 2 (Spring 1994).

10. H. Richard Niebuhr's classic study *The Purpose of the Church and Its Ministry* (New York: Harper, 1956) identified "the idea of a theological school" as "an intellectual center of the Church's life" (p. 107). The quality of a theological school was then assessed in accord with this "idea" by its being "that place or occasion where the Church exercises its intellectual love of God and the neighbor" and "by bringing reflection and criticism to bear on worship, preaching, teaching and the care of souls" (p. 110).

Faithfulness

Faithfulness means at least two things: (1) fidelity to the tradition and (2) keeping the promise made in the mission statement and plan. The deep measure of the fidelity to the faith itself undergirds the authenticity and credibility of everything the school does. Presidents must know, defend, and testify to this faithfulness with their minds, hearts, and strength. Still, such faithfulness is not readily measured in institutional "dashboards."

The school owes it to its stakeholders to measure its faithfulness in doing what it promised in its mission and plan. How will the world know you are doing your job? Did you promise to educate leaders? How many did you produce on what schedule? Is your purpose to provide scholars for the theological faculties of the twenty-first century? Where have you placed your graduates in the past five years? What are the results of your efforts? In the real world of performance, if it is worth doing, it is worth counting, at least annually.

Many donors are impressed by the superb teaching and publications of faculty, but they will make financial investments when they see results that make a public difference. The clearer the accountability for results, the more persuasive is the case for development.

Effectiveness

Effectiveness is now the primary standard for accreditation. The number of books in the library and ratio of earned research doctorates are still meaningful measures. This is graduate education, after all. But accreditation now presses the schools for measurements of what has been learned. Visiting committees want to see the institution's strategic plan, particularly the educational strategies or curricula by which schools intend to accomplish learning goals. Then the accreditors ask, "By what measures do you track effectiveness?"

Strategic plans that only define advancement goals for new construction or funding endowments have rudimentary measures of effectiveness. "How much did we raise?"

If the plan promises to advance the educational mission of the seminary, the academic leaders of the institution are accountable, at least annually. "What is being taught and learned that will strengthen the effectiveness of our educational mission? Are our courses and requirements serving this mission or some other agenda? What are our learning goals (cognitive, affective, relational, practical, contextual, etc.)?" Faculty development is key. A school reveals its strategic commitments in faculty hiring, promotion, and support of study, research, and writing.[11]

Efficiency

Efficiency is the institutional stewardship of surviving and thriving. This concern is addressed more thoroughly in Chapter Six, "The President's Role in Financial Management." The president's unique leadership is best exercised on the revenue side of the budget, making the case for the mission and plan, rallying support within and beyond the school. Presidents must be unfailingly hopeful, but they must also be honest.[12] If a seminary's mission and plan are not undergirded by a sound finan-

11. Daniel Aleshire, executive director of the Association of Theological Schools, recently made the remarkable proposal that "At its best, *theological* education is *leadership* education." See "What Is the Value of Seminary-Educated Religious Leaders?" presented at the Presidential Leadership Intensive Week, December 2002, available at the ATS Website (www.ats.edu). As varied traditions enter this venture with care for the leadership their communities need, the differences among the traditions and their schools will appear in their definitions of what the graduates will be expected to have learned concerning (1) their knowledge of the Christian story; (2) their understanding of how this faith will be persuasively communicated or proclaimed in various contexts; (3) their competence to lead these communities with deep respect for their local knowledge; and (4) their identity as Christian disciples who are called to make disciples. Each of these kinds of "learning" is subject to distinct measures.

12. In *Good to Great: Why Some Companies Make the Leap . . . and Others Don't* (New York: HarperCollins, 2001), his study of good organizations that became great ones, Jim Collins identified seven concepts at work in the organizations that made the leap to great performance. His account of "the Stockdale paradox" illustrated the importance of confronting the brutal facts, yet never losing faith. A prisoner of war in the Hanoi Hilton, Admiral Jim Stockdale endured years of torture and humiliation in the confidence of seeing his family again. Collins asked, "Who didn't survive?" Stockdale replied, "The optimists . . . they were the ones who said, 'We're going to be out by Christmas.' . . . You must never confuse faith that you will prevail in the end — which you can never afford to lose — with the discipline to confront the most brutal facts of your current reality, whatever they might be" (p. 85).

cial model, tracked with business plans, the school risks making promises without knowing the truth. When the president has not invested due diligence in financial planning, the hazards of institutional exigency can overshadow all planning, and the auditors will rule.

A president and school who have an able vice president for administration and finance are blessed. "Able" does not mean rigid or controlling, trying to run the school by the financial faucets. "Able" means managing the costs of personnel, finances, and facilities in service of the educational mission. It also means having the financial intelligence to alert the president to early financial signs of difficulty and opportunity. In an ideal world, it means having a financial officer who can build an economic model that the president understands of the future of the seminary's revenues and expenses.

Once a year, the president will present an analysis of "the state of the seminary" with primary reference to the seminary's competence and capacity to achieve the goals of its mission and strategic plan. For the first year or two, it may be difficult to gain much attention for this presentation, but over time, by whatever "dashboards" or measurements the school is tracking its faithfulness, effectiveness, and efficiency, the results become clear and comparable. Then the institution's strategic intelligence matures, illuminating the consequences of critical decisions and revealing the president's strategic leadership.

Why Presidents Thrive When the Vision Is Shared

The president's role in defining mission and strategic planning is played on the stages of the listening post (listening and differentiating), the bully pulpit (articulating and communicating), and the learning laboratory (teaching and tracking). On every stage, the president bears the seminary's hope. Presidents thrive when the vision is shared.

Presidents often wonder how they got themselves on these stages and how they can get out alive. Was this just ego need or a calling? The vision can blur, especially when a respected faculty member attacks the president's integrity or a massive setback intrudes.

New presidents will find consolation in asking those who have survived and thrived in the role, "How did you make it this far?" The stories are inspired and humble.

One president tells of speaking in dismay to a board chair only to be interrupted in a direct tone of voice, "Remember, it is still God's church. You are not alone in this." Another recounts agonizing about what to say to the community in the financial strains that followed the destruction of September 11, 2001. Then he stopped. For the first time he saw what was happening in the school: people were pulling together, engaged in exciting education; he saw new programs, the celebration of achievements by faculty, the presence of supportive donors, a new chapel going up. His words began to flow in a stream of consciousness that simply told the story of what this school was doing and why it was an important school and what it meant to the church and its relationship to God.

Peter Senge's term for this confidence is "shared vision." "A shared vision is not an idea. It is, rather, a force in people's hearts, a force of impressive power. At its simplest level, a shared vision is the answer to the question, 'What do we want to create?' Shared visions derive their power from a common caring."[13]

The apostle Paul testified to "a still more excellent way" beyond human virtues or powers (1 Cor. 12:31). Because the mission is God's, the president finally bears God's faith and hope and even God's love in the imperfect instrument of this school and this servant leader. No matter what, this faith, hope, and love are enough for the president to thrive and seek to advance the seminary's calling and strategic commitments.

Additional Resources

Barry, Bryan R. *Strategic Planning Workbook for Nonprofit Organizations.* St. Paul: Amherst H. Wilder Foundation, 1997.

Blackaby, Henry T. and Richard. *Spiritual Leadership: Moving People on to God's Agenda.* Nashville: Broadman & Holman, 2001.

Collins, James C. *Good to Great: Why Some Companies Make the Leap . . . and Others Don't.* New York: HarperCollins, 2001.

De Pree, Max. *Leadership Is an Art.* New York: Dell, 1989.

13. Senge, *The Fifth Discipline,* p. 206.

Drucker, Peter F. *Managing the Nonprofit Organization.* New York: HarperCollins, 1990.

Heifetz, Ronald A., and Martin Linsky. *Leadership on the Line: Staying Alive through the Dangers of Leading.* Boston: Harvard Business School Press, 2002.

Kelsey, David H. *To Understand God Truly: What's Theological about a Theological School.* Louisville: Westminster, 1992.

McCarter, Neely Dixon. *The President as Educator.* Atlanta: Scholars Press, 1996.

Nouwen, Henri J. M. *In the Name of Jesus: Reflections on Christian Leadership.* New York: Crossroad, 1989.

Senge, Peter M. *The Fifth Discipline: The Art and Practice of the Learning Organization.* New York: Doubleday, 1990.

————. *The Fifth Discipline Fieldbook: Strategies and Tools for Building a Learning Organization.* New York: Doubleday, 1994.

Terry, Robert. *The Seven Zones for Leadership: Acting Authentically in Stability and Chaos.* Palo Alto: Davies-Black, 2001.

The resources identified in this handbook are listed on the ATS Website where the list will continue to be updated as new resources become available: www.ats.edu > Leadership Education > Presidents.

CHAPTER 5

The President's Role as Academic Leader

CHARLES E. BOUCHARD, Aquinas Institute of Theology
SUSAN THISTLETHWAITE, Chicago Theological Seminary
TIMOTHY WEBER, Memphis Theological Seminary

The Evolution of Academic Leadership

The evolution of the university presidency has been amply documented. In the eighteenth century, the office of the president was more pastoral and spiritual; later its duties became administrative; in our own day, it has become primarily concerned with fundraising.[1] The seminary presidency, on the other hand, has absorbed all these tasks and more. In the midst of this rapidly expanding job description, how does the seminary president find time to be an academic leader? The president must avoid two extremes: becoming an academic micro-manager (coercing the faculty and rendering the academic dean superfluous) and becoming an absentee landlord of the seminary's academic mission.

Key Issues in the President's Role as Academic Leader

The President's Relationship with the Dean

The president's responsibility to create an effective relationship with the dean is the most crucial and the most delicate of his or her responsibilities as an academic leader.[2] It begins with hiring, which because of the dean's unique role in the seminary must be done with wide consultation of faculty, trustees, administrators, and students. The process should be guided by the president, and he or she must make the final decision. The president must select someone with proper credentials and experience, but also someone with whom the right "chemistry" exists. This is a highly prudential judgment, and the factors that lead to the final choice may or may not be recognized and affirmed by other constituencies. In the end, the president must often rely on instinct and experience, informed by consultation, in making the final choice.

---

1. See, for example, Judith A. Rile, "The Changing Role of the President in Higher Education" (http://www.newfoundations.com/OrgTheory/Rile721.html). She quotes G. Schmidt, *The Old Time College President* (New York: Columbia University Press, 1930).

2. See Leo I. Higdon Jr., "Making the Team: One of the Best Legacies That a President Can Leave Is a Strong Management Team," *Chronicle of Higher Education*, December 5, 2003, pp. C1 and C4. Creating this team starts with the president/dean relationship.

Many presidents inherit deans from their predecessors. Even if the president is certain that he or she can establish a strong working relationship with the dean, it is still prudent to build in a six- or twelve-month evaluation period and let the dean know that at the end of that period they will assess their working relationship and their ability to form an effective team. If the president has doubts from the start, or if problems emerge early on, he or she should not assume that the situation will improve with time. The president should discuss any concerns immediately and explicitly, and, if necessary, move to replace the dean no later than the end of year one. This will be especially awkward if the dean is tenured and will remain on the faculty. If both dean and president are truly committed to the school, however, they should be able to reach an acceptable solution.

The dean, as Jeanne McLean has pointed out, is "middle" management — in the middle between the president and the faculty and sometimes in the middle between the faculty and the board.[3] Sometimes the board wants the dean to run interference for it or to make the faculty "play ball" in order to achieve certain business-like goals, while the faculty wants the dean to act as advocate, especially with regard to salary, promotions, and benefits. Because the president is usually the board's primary contact, it can be difficult for a dean to know exactly where he or she fits in. Even simple logistics can be problematic: Does the dean attend board sessions or only committee meetings? Does the dean sit "at the table" with voice or only observe? How autonomous is the dean's relationship with the committee he or she chairs? Must the dean always voice the president's view, or can he or she speak from his or her own experience and priorities?

Trust and mutual respect are essential. It is important for dean and president clearly to delineate authority, to decide which decisions will be made by consensus and which will be solely the responsibility of just one of them. If they agree at the outset that the dean will be responsible for some decisions, then that authority should remain with the dean, and the president should be very careful not to undermine or second-

---

3. See Jeanne McLean's book, *Leading from the Center: The Emerging Role of the Chief Academic Officer in Theological Schools* (Atlanta: Scholars Press, 1999). This book is required reading for any president who wants to understand the stresses of the dean's job.

guess the dean. "Good boundaries make for good administration," as one president put it. (Above all, presidents should avoid letting themselves become the middleman between the dean and the faculty. A president should never allow individual faculty members or sub-groups to make end-runs around the dean. This is a fatal mistake that can be made despite the best intentions, especially because new presidents may be naïve or too willing to make a good initial impression by being helpful.) It is important that, in their dealings with one another, they make differences explicit. While these differences should not ordinarily become public, the president and dean need to know what they "agree to disagree about." This can be difficult, but it is vastly preferable to hidden agendas or unspoken resistance that interferes with every decision and that can ultimately ruin the relationship.

Administratively and symbolically, it is important to discuss who will chair faculty meetings. This can be a touchy issue, because even though the president is the chief executive officer, the faculty reports to the dean, and the dean has a specific responsibility to lead and form the faculty as a whole. If the president does not chair the meeting, he or she should remember that he or she is never *not* the president; therefore, any interventions should be prudent and well considered so that the president does not unwittingly preempt the conversation and stifle expression of views that are essential for good policy making.

Faculty Recruitment and Development

Recruiting and hiring faculty is fraught with difficulties. One president reports that in fifteen years he has had only one stress-free hiring: "Even though I thought we had developed a solid hiring policy, every single time some crack appeared that created suspicion and disappointment." Hiring is difficult for a number of reasons. First, department members do not always agree on what the department needs, and sometimes they are in total disagreement. Second, there is often tension about the relative priority of pastoral presence, academic scholarship, and teaching ability. Third, in schools that have strong denominational ties there is often pressure, or even policy, that limits the number of candidates who may be considered. Finally, faculty priorities may be in tension with strategic priorities established by the board or the president.

Hiring processes vary widely. In some schools, the president is a member of the search committee; in others, the president has a very circumscribed role. (One president laments, "In my seminary, the president gets the last word, literally yes or no, and not much else.")

Institutional practice for hiring faculty should be consistent. The president should avoid at all cost the impression that the process changes from one search to the next. The bias should be toward having a written policy that spells out the process and can be a point of reference for all involved. This may be in the faculty manual or simply an administrative policy, but it should be available to all and observed scrupulously unless formally amended.

The president may or may not be actively involved in specific faculty searches, but the president's vision for the school must influence hiring from beginning to end. He or she must always direct the strategic priorities — flowing from the strategic plan — that shape the search. The president's role in deciding who to hire is not just a question of how many faculty or of which departments get new members first. It requires a clear vision of what the institution is to be in five or ten years — "hiring for mission" so that the vision becomes reality. The president's vision and the basis upon which the final decision will be made should be clear to everyone before the search begins. A good example of this would be an institution's commitment to diversity. A search may yield a good candidate and yet fail to advance the institutional commitment to diversity. The president must be the one to continue to lift up the institution's overall commitment, even to the point of reconstituting or extending the search. The alternative is what we might describe as a form of institutional "impulse buying" — acquiring an attractive candidate even though he or she is not what the institution needs to meet its strategic goals. Like an artist before a canvas, the president must view the institution and its future from a distance in order to know just what shade and what shape will complete the picture.

As in many other areas, the best way to assure a successful search rests on two things: consultation and clarity. The search should begin broadly, with consultation with students, program directors, individual faculty (especially those who will be most affected by the hiring), the appropriate trustee committee, and the faculty *as a whole*. This last point may seem obvious, but even the best-intentioned president can unconsciously adopt a "divide and conquer" approach in hiring.

In some institutions, the president serves as a member of the search committee; this allows the president to signal a no on a particular candidate early in the process. If the president is going to say no, the earlier this is done the better for all. If the president is not on the committee, he or she should reserve the right to veto certain candidates early in the process. The president must also take care to specify, if it does not already appear in written policy, exactly what his or her role will be. Does the president merely rubber stamp the decision of the search committee, or is their work consultative? Can they submit a divided vote, or are they to achieve consensus on their recommendation? Do they rank candidates or submit one name only? Is the president free to choose none of the candidates they recommend? If the rules are clear from the start, it is much more likely that the final decision will be accepted (even if not fully supported) by everyone.

Program Development

The Master of Divinity program will remain the heart of the seminary curriculum, yet there are pressures that will make it necessary for seminaries to engage in ongoing program assessment and planning in order to remain not only solvent but responsive to the needs of the church.

The first pressure is that in many denominations there are too many seminaries and too few students. A second factor is the fact that many prospective students find themselves in situations that prevent them from completing their studies in three or four years of full-time study. They place a high value on convenience and efficiency, and they do not necessarily perceive as benefits longer and more traditional programs, faculty credentials, or on-campus residence. Traditional schools are competing with other educational providers who are selling a product rather than a process.[4]

4. See the Knight Higher Education Collaborative, "The Mission and the Medium," *Policy Perspectives,* July 2000, p. 4. The report notes that as colleges and universities (and seminaries) find themselves grouped together with a range of other educational providers, they are perceived more as vendors than as institutions. This is causing a shift from the traditional metaphor of "the gown" to "the badge." The gown "denotes a rite of passage, the culmination of a journey in which the student has met a succession of increasingly difficult challenges in more than one domain. Symbolically, as well as literally, the

These factors can create conflict for presidents as academic leaders. On the one hand, presidents are the first "quality control" officers and must ensure a high level of program quality. On the other, they must keep their institution financially healthy. This often means proposing new programs (or new packaging). Faculty have other priorities. Faced with the prospect of a new program initiative, they are likely to think first about their own immediate interests, especially schedules, time for writing and research, and workload. As one president notes, "Seminary faculty are generally clueless about the financial issues that drive seminary education. Their concern is — rightly — maximizing the educational experience. They tend to see attempts to increase enrollment as an assault on academic excellence."

Presidents need not initiate every new program, but they must develop an entrepreneurial sense that will enable them to identify emerging trends and determine how the seminary can best respond to these trends without drifting too far from the school's core mission. Presidents who fail to ask, "Should we be involved in this?" may end up producing the theological equivalent of buggy whips. It is important that presidents understand their role as leaders of strategic planning. They should suggest broad areas of program development (usually in conversation and consultation with other faculty and administrative leaders) while leaving precise implementation details to the dean and the faculty. This means avoiding the impression of micro-managing the program and undercutting the dean and the faculty, while still playing an important role in developing new initiatives or redirecting traditional programs. Presidents must also ensure that program development proposals are supported by solid data. This is a tedious (and sometimes expensive) process, but it is the only way to build new programs on a firm foundation. Presidents should expect the board to ask, "How do you know there is a market for this program?" and should be prepared with an answer that includes solid research.

---

gown extends over the student's entire body." The badge symbolizes "a contrasting approach that certifies a learner's mastery of a particular set of skills. Its purpose is to provide a credential, and [it is] about singular steps and achievements."

The President as Keeper of the Tradition

There is probably not a president out there who has not received a letter or a phone call asking, "Are you aware that your [faculty member/staff member] [did/said/promoted] this?" Such calls are bad enough when they come from concerned alumni; they are even worse when they come from bishops, pastors, or denominational officials.

Presidents are often in the paradoxical position of having to represent and preserve the church's tradition and at the same time promote dialogue and academic inquiry. While universities have both culture and policies that protect academic freedom, it is much more complicated within the seminary world. We want to promote inquiry and to pursue a fuller understanding of God's truth, but in many traditions there are clear boundaries of where God's truth is *not*.

New presidents must quickly identify the neuralgic issues in their denominations. They must develop a working relationship with faculty built on mutual trust. Faculty have to believe that, in the event of a truly conflicting situation, the president won't "hang them out to dry." They in turn must acknowledge the president's wider responsibilities. On the eve of a controversial publication, for example, a faculty member at one seminary requested the president's permission to send out a "fact sheet" to denominational officials. When the controversy broke, the church administration was prepared to speak in an informed and constructive manner to the public.

In many denominations, faculty speak for the church; to the extent that they do, they must speak prudently. Some presidents have found it helpful to urge the faculty to see themselves as an organic whole, with responsibilities to one another. The president might say, "If you write or lecture on a controversial topic, ask your colleagues about how it will affect them or how they think it will affect the seminary." This attitude can avoid division and contribute to a deeper sense of shared mission.

Shaping a Learning Community

Even though seminaries differ in many important ways from universities, university standards have affected us, and not always in a positive way. In some instances, such as the understanding of scholarship, we have picked up bad habits of arcane and excessively individualistic scholarship. We have also tended to focus too much on scholarly publication as the only acceptable form of scholarship outside of the classroom.

Even though few would dispute the importance of serious, sustained scholarship (and such an affirmation is important in North America, where there are strong strains of pragmatism and even anti-intellectualism), seminary presidents are still charged with the responsibility of preparing women and men who can preach the gospel, making a difference in real lives. Scholarship and teaching must always be directed "toward salvation," however we each define salvation. In this sense, seminary presidents must encourage theological scholarship *that matters* for the church and for the world.

This means two things. First of all, presidents should try to avoid the pointless dichotomy between "academic" and "pastoral." In seminary work, these two areas must necessarily go hand in hand and must inform one another. Second, presidents must sometimes be proactive in directing, or at least suggesting, scholarship that the church and the world truly need. This may involve research grants or released time to encourage faculty to explore such areas. Presidents should model the combination of academic and pastoral work in their own publications, speeches, sermons, and leadership. Presidents must also show an awareness of valuing the varied gifts within the faculty and the faculty members' desire to address differing audiences. Some seminaries have found faculty collaboration on a common project — for example, a volume of thematic essays — to be a very effective way of building a community of scholars.[5]

The President as Educator

The president's educational role should not be underestimated.[6] In the past, seminary presidents were usually chosen from the faculty. Today,

5. See *In the Company of Preachers,* ed. R. Siegfried and E. Ruane, by the Faculty of Aquinas Institute (Collegeville: Liturgical Press, 1993).

6. See Robert L. Payton, "Presidents as Public Teachers," in *The Advancement President and the Academy: Profiles in Institutional Leadership,* ed. Mary Kay Murphy (Phoenix: Oryx Press, 1997), pp. 3-10. Thanks to Carolyn Wright and Michael Havercamp for research assistance on this chapter.

they come from their own faculties occasionally, but far more often from other seminaries, from universities, from pastorates, or even from church management or administration. Some have rarely taught in a classroom. Presidents who arrive with an academic background have the advantage of familiarity with the rigor and culture of at least one academic discipline. On the other hand, the difficulty of moving from faculty peer to CEO should not be underestimated. Many presidents fail precisely because they are unable to negotiate this transition.

Presidents without academic experience have a different challenge. They must take special care to build rapport, acquire respect for academic culture, and gain familiarity with faculty scholarship and teaching. Academics or not, presidents will have to acquire a new discipline, namely, theological education. Careful attention to books and professional journals in theological education will not only enhance on-the-job learning but will also stimulate creative, strategic thinking.

It is also important to make the public relations or communications office aware of faculty scholarship and to actively cultivate connections between that scholarship — which is often not readily accessible to the general public — and the media. "Pitching stories" to the media on important faculty writing is an excellent way to do this. Some faculty resist this because they resent having to "dumb down" their work. Helping them to see this as "public preaching" and training them to field media questions and translate scholarship into more accessible language can help them feel more confident.

Classroom teaching is a valued task (and often a respite from the usual office routine) for nearly every president, but most find it difficult to maintain a regular teaching schedule. For those who can manage it, teaching provides a highly effective way of staying in touch with students, with one's academic discipline, and with the challenges that faculty face day to day in the classroom. Even though the president's vision has to be broader than any individual classroom, there is no substitute for firsthand experience of student abilities and problems.

Travel and other presidential responsibilities may make it impossible to teach a full-semester course. If so, team-teaching, lecturing in one's area of expertise in other classes, and teaching in Internet-based, summer, or cohort programs provide other opportunities.

The president must also "teach the trustees." People join the boards of educational institutions because they are interested in higher education. Seminary trustees often serve because they are looking for theological and spiritual enrichment. They should learn what the faculty members of their seminary teach and why that is important. The president sets the tone for this and should provide occasions to teach the board about the seminary's educational mission. Many seminaries provide "trustee enrichment" or "board education sessions" at each meeting. Whether led by a faculty member or an outside expert, they are an excellent way to enhance board participation.

There are two other kinds of presidential teaching. The first is what we would call "public teaching," which occurs when the president is asked, "What does the seminary [or the denomination] think about this particular issue?" Using the public relations office, the president will have to respond to important theological or social questions.[7] Many Catholic seminary rectors found themselves unexpectedly (and unpleasantly) thrust into this position during the clergy sexual abuse crisis. When the spotlight shifted from the abuse itself to the causative factors, rectors and presidents were asked, "What is your seminary doing to ensure that this will not happen again?" As in most other instances of media crisis, a "no comment" was not an option. Rectors and presidents had to try to explain what they had done or were doing to ensure high standards of professional conduct.

The second type of presidential teaching can be called "prophetic teaching." Presidents can be prophetic teachers when they initiate, rather than respond to, discussion of a certain topic. The manner in which this is done is determined largely by the extent to which the denomination enters into discussion of public policy issues. The Catholic tradition, for example, lobbies actively on certain issues, and bishops frequently issue statements or pastoral letters on them. If the seminary represents a "public" religious tradition, it is important to engage the crucial issues of the day. The president will usually be the official spokesperson; he or she might even issue a media release with thoughts on some important event. If this kind of participation in the public square is appropriate to the school's tradition, it can be a highly effec-

---

7. Rita Bornstein, "The Authentic and Effective College President," *The Chronicle of Higher Education,* July 30, 2004, p. B16, makes some helpful suggestions for public communication.

tive way of teaching and raising awareness about the contribution one's seminary makes to public discourse and to the common good.[8]

Four Essential Habits for the President as an Academic Leader

Presidents must cultivate at least four "habits" (in the sense of practices or disciplines) if they are to be successful academic leaders: they must ask the right questions; they must balance tradition and innovation; they must be persons of evident learning; and they must cultivate courage.

Asking the Right Questions

We have already noted irrelevance as one of the occupational hazards of academic life. It is simply a fact of life that the people we serve are sometimes not asking the questions that scholars want to answer. Asking the right questions also helps to maintain a sharp edge on the seminary's theological mission. Seminary presidents must be intentional about this at a time in history when psychological and therapeutic models of ministry threaten to overwhelm more traditional models that emphasize academics and critical thought. The president meets countless people and sees many perspectives on the church's role in the world. Successful presidents will learn to mine this experience and articulate for the seminary the questions that are important to the church and world in this time and place. This is crucial if the president is to lead what Ronald Heifetz describes as "adaptive" rather than merely "technical" change.[9]

---

8. Lack of public awareness about what seminaries do and why they are important is a serious problem. See the Auburn Seminary study by Elizabeth Lynn and Barbara Wheeler, *Missing Connections: Public Perceptions of Theological Education and Religious Leadership* (New York: Auburn Studies Series, 1999). The lack of public awareness of what seminaries do or why they do it is an important issue every president must attend to, not only to extend the seminary's educational mission beyond the campus, but also to assist fundraising.

9. See Ronald Heifetz's book with Martin Linsky, *Leadership on the Line: Staying Alive through the Dangers of Leading* (Boston: Harvard Business School Press, 2002). Meeting an

Balancing Tradition and Innovation

Some presidents fail because they grasp "the tradition" too tightly and miss important cultural shifts that affect the preaching of the gospel; others neglect the tradition because they never saw a cultural trend they did not like. The gospel is one and true, but it is affected by the time and place in which it is preached. It has been said that the Reformation was possible largely because Martin Luther knew how to use the printing press. As academic leaders, presidents must attend not only to what is taught and studied but also to the manner in which the teaching and studying are done.

Being Persons of Evident Learning

Whether they come from academic backgrounds or not, presidents must have intellectual curiosity; they must read widely and bring theology into dialogue with other important disciplines such as business, finance, social sciences, and medicine. Their own learning and intellectual inquiry will inspire the faculty in their teaching and their scholarship. It will keep faith vital in a secular world, and it will secure the seminary's place as an important social institution.

Cultivating Courage

It has been said that there are only two kinds of courage: the courage to die and the courage to get up in the morning. Most presidents would disagree. They have found that there are daily challenges that require sustained courage: hiring, firing, carrying on building projects, making changes in strategic direction, and admitting failure or bad judgment are just a few. One of the most important skills the president must acquire is the habit of well-tempered courage to take calculated risks — and to persuade others to accompany him. This courage is necessary to face the "little deaths" that a president must face in order to meet the demands of office: the death of anonymity, the death of certainty, and the

---

"adaptive challenge" requires that a leader "raise the heat" to a "productive level of stress" so that significant change occurs within the organization.

death of scholarship are just a few examples.[10] And yet, these deaths are not merely painful; rather, they are purifying and a necessary part of the process of professional growth.

Additional Resources

Bornstein, Rita. "The Authentic and Effective College President." *The Chronicle of Higher Education,* July 30, 2004, p. B16.

This article traces the significant changes that accompany the movement from presidential candidacy to the actual role as the primary institutional leader. This movement warrants a diminished individualism for the sake of institutional representation, creates "asymmetrical relationships" as one's social life becomes work, and can hinder a president's freedom to be vocal on public issues. To fulfill one's role as president without compromising one's personal identity, the author suggests an identification of a shared vision amid diversity, openness to divergent viewpoints, more subtle forms of political involvement, limiting external involvement, and honest accountability with trusted friends.

Coll, Edward G., Jr. "The Advancement President and the Faculty." In *The Advancement President and the Academy: Profiles in Institutional Leadership,* edited by Mary Kay Murphy, pp. 136-44. Phoenix: Oryx Press, 1997.

Increasing financial pressures demand a new kind of president — "advancement specialists" skilled in long-term strategic planning, effective management, and fundraising. Coll recommends an intentional distancing from the role of chief academic officer, responsibilities that should be delegated corporately to the deans, department chairs, and the provost. He advocates aggressive fundraising to prove oneself early in one's presidency and maintaining open communication to avoid an "insensitive administration" reputation.

Diamond, Robert M. "Curricula and Courses: Administrative Issues." In *Field Guide to Academic Leadership,* edited by Robert M. Diamond, pp. 135-56. San Francisco: Jossey-Bass, 2002.

---

10. See Charles Bouchard, "New Presidents Consider Death and the Presidency" (ATS newsletter, *Colloquy,* March/April 2005).

Good teaching, use of technology, and strong off-campus experiences are not enough to ensure that a school is providing an excellent education. Ongoing assessment and curriculum development must become an institutional practice. This article explores the design of curriculum and provides models for use. Administrative leaders assume a key role in appointing and supporting a curriculum task force. Strong curriculum proposals will incorporate outcomes assessment, provide a clear outline of competencies sought by a program or major, ensure that goals will be reached, and integrate new technologies, community experiences, and internships.

Guskin, Alan E., and Mary B. Marcy. "Pressures for Fundamental Reform: Creating a Viable Academic Future." In *Field Guide to Academic Leadership,* edited by Robert M. Diamond, pp. 3-14. San Francisco: Jossey-Bass, 2002.

This article predicts that, in the next ten years, financial and societal developments will warrant serious reform in the administrative and educational practices of colleges and universities. As costs of higher education outstrip institutional resources, society is demanding increased accountability via student learning outcomes. Increasing workloads and hiring non-tenure track faculty are not viable long-term solutions for financial shortfall. In order to safeguard faculty work life and continued student learning, institutions of higher learning are called to change academic structure (academic calendar, assessment of learning, faculty workload) and incorporate new technologies.

Higdon, Leo I., Jr. "Making the Team: One of the Best Legacies That a President Can Leave Is a Strong Management Team." *The Chronicle of Higher Education,* December 5, 2003, pp. C1 and C4.

Short presidential terms demand quality management teams to carry institutional vision. This article outlines three action steps to assemble and maintain a strong senior management team. New presidents must (1) set the tone from the beginning to calm anxieties, keep good people on staff and attract others, and employ a collaborative leadership style in corporate decision making; (2) assemble a management team to match institutional values; and (3) build dynamic teamwork through trust, communication, collaboration, and alignment (presenting a unified front).

Knight Higher Education Collaborative. "The Mission and the Medium." In *Policy Perspectives* 9, no. 3 (July 2000): 1-9.

One of a series of excellent essays on leadership, "The Mission and the Medium" describes two paradigms for education, namely, the more traditional "gown" approach, which covers the whole person and aims at character formation as well as knowledge, and the emerging "badge" approach, which focuses on discrete skills and achievements and tends to be proprietary and consumerist in nature. The emergence and rapid growth of the badge approach presents a serious challenge to seminaries and other traditional professional education programs.

Krebs, Paula. "Drifting Away: At Some Point Every Academic Who Moves into Administration Has to Set Aside Scholarship." *The Chronicle of Higher Education,* January 21, 2005, p. C1.

One of the "little deaths" that administrators face — the loss of time for scholarship — can be a major trauma to the new president. But it has its rewards, Krebs says, especially if it provides an opportunity for scholars to put their "money where their academic mouth was," by advancing the values they only wrote about before.

Lynn, Elizabeth, and Barbara Wheeler. *Missing Connections: Public Perceptions of Theological Education and Religious Leadership.* New York: Auburn Study Series, 1999.

An analysis of research by the Auburn Center for the Study of Theological Education, "Missing Connections," shows how little public awareness there is about the mission and value of seminaries to society at large.

McLean, Jeanne. *Leading from the Center: The Emerging Role of the Chief Academic Officer in Theological Schools.* Atlanta: Scholars Press, 1999.

McLean's seminal work outlines all aspects of the dean's job and shows how it is a vocation as well as a job. It includes "Advice to Prospective Deans" and statistical profiles. Chapter 3, "The Dean-President Relationship," provides an excellent basis for discussion of collaborative leadership.

Payton, Robert L. "Presidents as Public Teachers." In *The Advancement President and the Academy: Profiles in Institutional Leadership,* edited by Mary Kay Murphy, pp. 3-9. Phoenix: Oryx Press, 1997.

College presidents must maintain their societal role as steward of the norms and standards of truth and reason — the foundation of liberal education. Not authoritative tyrants or "public relations apologists," presidents must be public teachers and facilitators of continual dialogue. Payton stresses the need for presidents to return regularly to the question of the institution's purpose (teaching, research, and service to society).

Rile, Judith A. "The Changing Role of the President in Higher Education." 2001. Available at http://www.newfoundations.com/OrgTheory/Rile721 .html. Accessed July 26, 2004.

This article discusses the changing role of the office of president as institutions respond to societal developments. The Industrial Revolution, the financial crunch of the 1960s, and the demographic changes of the 1990s forced college presidents to adapt to the times or close. "Friend raising" and fundraising are the primary responsibilities of the modern institutional president. The college president today has power derived less from position and more from the collegially accepted norms and values of the institutional community. The dwindling population of traditional students, growing ethnic diversity, and increasing use of distance learning programs is changing the demands of the college president once again and charting the path for the future.

Shaw, Kenneth A. *The Successful President: "Buzzwords" on Leadership.* Phoenix: Oryx Press, 1999.

Former president of the University of Wisconsin System and current president of Syracuse, Kenneth "Buzz" Shaw offers practical advice on how to overcome inevitable obstacles in leading an academic institution. More "insights and guidelines" than a leadership "cookbook," Shaw discusses conflict resolution, use of power, motivation, working with groups, crisis leadership, and future selection and training of academic leaders.

The resources identified in this handbook are listed on the ATS Website where the list will continue to be updated as new resources become available: www.ats.edu > Leadership Education > Presidents.

CHAPTER 6

The President's Role in Financial Management

ANTHONY RUGER, Auburn Theological Seminary
JOHN CANARY, University of St. Mary of the Lake,
Mundelein Seminary
STEVEN LAND, Church of God Theological Seminary

Financial Reporting and Analysis

   Regular Reports

   Full Costs versus Incremental Cost Analysis

   Analysis of Campaigns

   Institutional Borrowing

Investments

   Cash Flow and Short-Term Investments

   Long-Term Investments

   Asset Allocation

   Spending Rates

   Social Responsibility in Investing

Regular Reminders for Presidents

Additional Resources

The Economic Purpose of a Theological School

Any discussion of financial management in theological schools can quickly turn into a specialized accounting and investment discussion full of arcane terminology and technicalities. Those conversations are important and have their place. But the crucial "big picture" questions are strategic: What is the economic condition of the whole school? Is it healthy? Are there areas of financial weakness? Are there "stable and predictable sources of revenue" that will sustain the school?[1] Where does the school seek growth in revenues? Are expenditures exceeding revenues? Are there "hidden" assets and liabilities?

    What should be the goal of financial management in a theological school? What is the economic purpose of a theological school? For-profit organizations, of course, point to the goal of profit, or maximizing the wealth of the shareholders, as a perpetual and predominant economic purpose. Not-for-profit organizations, like theological schools, do not have owners or shareholders expecting cash dividends or an increase in

---

1. The Association of Theological Schools in the United States and Canada, *Standards of Accreditation,* section 9.2.1.2.

their share price. A theological school has religious and educational purposes, to be sure, but what, then, is its *economic* purpose? Richard M. Cyert, former president of Carnegie Mellon University, answers that the economic goal of a nonprofit should be, minimally, "economic equilibrium." What is economic equilibrium? Cyert offers a three-part answer.[2]

First, to achieve economic equilibrium the not-for-profit organization must conduct its mission with adequate quality and quantity. Instead of dividends and increases in share value, the various stakeholders in the institution (both internal and external stakeholders) must be reasonably satisfied that the school is educating a sufficient number of students, contributing to the intellectual and spiritual life of the church, and serving the needs of its constituents consonant with the school's purpose. Failure to perform the mission implies that the economic activity of the institution — how the money is used — is misaligned or that the resources are sorely inadequate.

Second, Cyert specifies that the organization should maintain the purchasing power of its financial assets. In other words, the organization should be as financially strong (or stronger) than it was last year and the year before. The school's wealth has to keep up with inflation. If the organization is financially weaker each year, one can readily see that, unless things change, the mission will have to be curtailed or diminished in quality.

Third, the organization should maintain needed facilities in adequate condition. Deferring maintenance is not a sound practice. Neglected buildings take their revenge through higher costs for repair and a dispiriting appearance. Just as financial assets should be maintained on an ongoing basis, physical assets needed for the mission of the school should be maintained for the long term.

Cyert's definition of economic equilibrium is a minimum standard. It maintains the school in its current condition. Probably all presidents and trustees would like to build a healthier, stronger institution rather than just maintain the status quo. Indeed, achievement of new financial strength and health is a worthy goal. But if circumstances and external conditions are unfavorable to growth and seem to lead the

2. Richard M. Cyert and Chris Argyris, "Managing Universities in the 1980s," in *Leadership in the '80s: Essays on Higher Education* (Cambridge, MA: Institute for Educational Management, 1980).

school into decline, the president should strive to reverse the decline and at least achieve the stability of economic equilibrium.

Role and Responsibility of the President

Several presidential roles described in other sections of this *Handbook* include a significant financial dimension. Strategic planning, educational leadership, facilities management, and institutional advancement all have significant impact on the financial well-being of the school. As those topics are covered elsewhere, this section will focus more narrowly on the specific money-related topics of audit, budgeting, investing, and similar matters.

The president's responsibility in this area is a straightforward managerial and leadership role. Boards are particularly focused on the "bottom line" of financial health, as are major donors, so it behooves the president to give priority attention to the school's financial condition and performance. While there may be a chief financial officer charged with specialized duties in this area, the policies, practices, and results ultimately are the president's responsibility. The CEOs of for-profit companies immersed in financial scandals may try to deflect responsibility onto financial officers, but by and large they are held accountable for the activities on their watch. The same holds true for theological school presidents.

Finance Office and Staffing

Ensure that a competent staff is hired in the finance office. The chief financial officer should be able to oversee the staff responsible for all accounting, including the specialized tasks of accounts receivable, accounts payable, cashier, and payroll. In some schools the financial aid director also reports to the finance office. Depending on the size of the school and budget constraints, most schools will have to have one person perform several job duties. Staff should be adequate to ensure that reports are timely, inquiries are answered, and the service obligations of the office are routinely met. Staff inadequacies in this office, especially in the chief business officer and chief accountant, create costly and complex problems.

Staff should have a good relationship to students, faculty, and staff. The finance office should be relied upon as providing dependable information in a pleasant setting. While the finance office often takes the financial welfare of the school to heart, responsible financial behavior and concern for the financial integrity of the school are the obligation of all staff. The finance office should be cast in the role of Ebenezer Scrooge only for the skit at the Christmas party.

Audit

Every year independent auditors should examine the financial records of the school.[3] The audit assures various stakeholders — trustees, donors, grant-making organizations, sponsoring denominations, accrediting agencies, government bureaus — that the financial statements in the audit are not fictional or incompetent concoctions but have been examined by independent accountants who verify their reasonable accuracy.

Presidents do not need to spend much time on the annual audit, but the time spent should be quality time. The chief business officer and the accounting staff do most of the work. The audit, as a year-end report, should be accompanied by other year-end longitudinal summaries of key indicators of financial vitality.[4] These longitudinal summaries should show a number of years — at least three, but preferably five — so that long-term revenue and expenditure trends may be observed. The important task of the president is to understand the audit and other year-end financial statements, interpret the results to various constituencies, and address the problems revealed in the audit, audit process, and other year-end reports.

Audit Content

The report on the audit usually contains at least three financial statements. One is the balance sheet or statement of financial condition. This state-

3. An independent audit is required by the *Standards of Accreditation,* section 9.2.2.2.

4. Some examples of key financial and enrollment indicators may be found in *The Strategic Information Report* provided biennially by the Association of Theological Schools. See also KPMG LLP and Prager, McCarthy & Sealy LLC, *Ratio Analysis in Higher Education: Measuring Past Performance to Chart Future Direction, for Independent Institutions* (1999; 4th ed., KPMG LLP).

ment shows the condition of the school on the close of business on the last day of the fiscal year. It shows, as of that frozen moment, the things of value the school owns (assets), the definite financial obligations the school has to pay (liabilities), and the net equity or wealth (net assets) of the school.[5] The balance sheet shows whether or not a school is heavily in debt. Although most theological schools have little long-term debt, or have a manageable amount of long-term debt, it is possible that large and significant obligations can put considerable stress on the school's scope of activity. The balance sheet also shows the amount of financial assets, such as cash and investments, and physical assets, such as land, buildings, and equipment.

The statement of activities shows the revenues and expenditures of the school for the past year. This statement may not match exactly the school's internally generated statements comparing revenues and expenditures to the budget. This is because schools may use different accounting rules for their budgets than auditors must use in the audit. For instance, schools will use an endowment spending rule for the budget rather than actual income and gains, as auditors must. Similarly, some schools "exclude" unrestricted bequests from current income, directing those bequests, by policy, to long-term investments, but auditors must include them. A good practice is to ask the chief financial officer to prepare a schedule reconciling any differences between the audited financial statements and the statement of actual versus budget revenues and expenditures.

The audit also shows a statement of the sources and uses of cash and contains a number of explanatory notes.

Accounting Control

The audit is also an opportunity to make sure that sound accounting procedures and controls are in place. Auditors should test internal controls. They should make sure check signing limits are maintained, invoices are signed by department directors, deposits are prepared and deposited by separate personnel, bills are paid from original invoices, bank balances are reconciled in a timely way, purchasing is carefully

5. The term "balance sheet" comes from the "balance" or equality in the equation: assets = liabilities + net assets.

controlled, and other well-established control procedures are followed. A "management letter," a separate report of comments and recommendations prepared by the auditor regarding accounting procedures and controls, should accompany audits.

Small schools sometimes have difficulty in efficiently and economically meeting all the criticisms encountered in the management letter. The president and board audit committee should carefully review the management letter recommendations along with the business officer's response, and then determine if the auditor's recommendation should be followed. Problems described as material weaknesses and reportable conditions in the management letter should be addressed in the near term.

Audits may be delayed or late for many legitimate reasons, but a pattern of chronically late audits implies a weak accounting function and bears investigating.

Board Audit Committee

One sound practice is to establish an audit committee of the board. This could be a small committee for convenience. At a minimum the audit committee should meet with the chief business officer and the auditor to discuss the statements, the management letter, and the business officer's response to the letter. The audit committee should have an opportunity for a private discussion with the auditor. The audit committee would thereby be in a position to recommend changes in the school's accounting operation and, as appropriate, recommend retaining or changing auditors.

Budgeting

Purpose of Budgets

The budget is a powerful management tool. It shows in detail how the school plans to acquire resources and allocate or expend those resources. As such, it is probably the most concrete, thorough, short-term mission blueprint of the school. As a planning document it embodies

95

the next steps the school will take to fulfill its long-term plans and priorities. In addition to its unique status as a planning document, the budget is also a control tool. Part of the control involves the short-term monitoring of revenues and expenditures so that the school can measure progress toward financial goals, as well as provide a means for management to intervene when there are revenue shortfalls or excess expenditures.

The budget is the president's budget. The president will bear responsibility for all major decisions, plans, and priorities imbedded in the budget, and therefore he or she must participate fully in the review and development of the budget. The business officer should bear the responsibility for compiling the proposals and decisions, producing the budget drafts, and providing analyses, projections, suggestions, and assistance throughout the budgeting process. Some presidents will make some or all budget decisions, keeping their own counsel, with technical help from the business officer. Many presidents, however, rely on a small group of senior administrators (often including the chief business officer, chief academic officer, and chief advancement officer) to serve as advisers and problem solvers in the budget-building process. Group cohesiveness, maturity, and trust are essential, as budget building often involves difficult and painful choices.

Each school should have two budgets. The operating budget should list all the revenues and expenditures associated with the ongoing annual operation of the school. The capital budget should show the revenues and expenditures associated with strengthening the financial and physical capital assets of the school. For instance, the capital budget should show anticipated gifts to the endowment, and/or the gifts and expenditures anticipated for a special building project. Often capital projects stretch over several years; it therefore makes sense for capital budgets to show all the years of projected revenue and expenses until the projects' completion.

Both budgets should be in balance. That is, revenues should meet or exceed expenditures. The budgets should be built using policies designed to achieve economic equilibrium. For instance, part of the definition of economic equilibrium calls for the maintenance of needed facilities in adequate condition. This means that the operating budget should have sufficient allocations for ongoing maintenance, and the capital budget should have funds allocated for major repair and replacement of the buildings, building components, and equipment. Because the expense of major repairs and replacements varies considerably from year to year, an excellent practice is to include a line item in the operating budget for an allocation to a reserve fund for major repairs and replacements. The major repair and replacement reserve fund may then be used in the capital budget as the source of funds for major repair and replacement projects.

Budget-Building Process

A typical budget-building process starts with the senior administration determining guidelines for budget building. These guidelines may include assumptions about the number of students to be enrolled, how long-range plans and special efforts are to be reflected in the budget, and specifications on the amount by which expenditures are to be increased or decreased. Department directors, with help from the business office, can review the departments' past financial performance in preparation for proposing the new fiscal year's revenue and expenditure. Department directors' budget proposals are forwarded to the business office and, eventually, to the senior budget-making group.

Conventionally, proposals for upcoming budgets originate with the several department heads or cost center managers, using the guidelines mentioned above. The president and his or her budget-making group review these proposals. There are no objective standards as to the proper allocation of funds to different departments, but some benchmarking or comparative studies may be useful. The *Institutional Peer Profile Report* produced by the Association of Theological Schools shows each school's proportions of revenue compared to those of peer schools. Differences from peers may be interpreted in a number of ways, as the school may enjoy efficiencies in certain areas of operation that peers do not. Conversely, a school's expenses may be out of line with others. The comparisons may be useful and thought-provoking but certainly should not be determinative.

Revenues

The popular book *Good to Great* by Jim Collins advises leaders to "face the brutal facts."[6] Budget revenues should start there. The budget is no place for unrealistic expectations about enrollment or fundraising. Budgeting is an occasion to face squarely the question of whether revenues can increase, and if so, by how much. Presidents and advisers should ask tough questions. Can tuition rates be increased without diminishing enrollment or inducing excess borrowing by students? Can enrollment be increased in what has been a low-growth environment? Are we confident in our giving expectations? While it is helpful and motivating to have aggressive goals for fundraising, the budgetary expectations should be achievable, based on careful analysis of the giving history of known donors. If the school has an endowment or investments, the tough questions should continue. Does the budget use an equilibrium spending rate, or does it draw down extra amounts to cover expenditures? How is that problem to be dealt with? Endowed schools seriously jeopardize their future through the habit of overspending.

Expenditures

Theological schools are blessed with committed faculty and administrators who always want to do more to improve the school and the quality of its programs. Few of the proposals they submit to the budgeting process will be truly wasteful or utterly ill-conceived. Inevitably, good ideas for increased expenditures outrun the available funds. In broad terms, the budget-building challenge on the expenditure side is to allocate the available funds carefully amid many competing ideas. Strategic or long-range plans may be highly informative and useful, as they may identify the priorities that should be funded and, directly or indirectly, the areas of lower priority.

Operating expenditure budgets are generally organized into departments or cost centers. Authority to expend funds from the line items and responsibility for keeping expenditures within budget rest

6. James C. Collins, *Good to Great: Why Some Companies Make the Leap ... and Others Don't* (New York: HarperCollins, 2001).

with the administrator or manager assigned responsibility for the cost center. Having two or more administrators assigned to a cost center tends to cause confusion. Similarly, each capital project is usually budgeted so that responsibility can reside with a single manager.

Compensation

Compensation of employees typically represents 55 to 70 percent of the operating budget. Consequently, cost-of-living increases in compensation and benefits have a major impact on the expenditure budget, especially when inflation is high, as in the 1970s. Recent increases in medical insurance premiums have hit budgets hard. These realities imply that special care must be taken when expanding the roster of employees. One employee costing $50,000 per year ties up one million dollars of capital.[7] New permanent positions, as a matter of good stewardship, should be crucial to achieving the school's mission and should either help the school generate additional revenue or be fully funded for the foreseeable future. Retrenchment is sometimes necessary and always difficult; the likelihood of retrenchment is reduced if schools avoid unnecessary sprawl by careful and well-thought-out expansion of employee rosters.

The school should compensate employees at a fair wage for their area of expertise or skill level. Compare the school's compensation to that of local, regional, or national salary surveys and set guidelines or benchmarks for pay at the school. The Association of Theological Schools' Annual Data Tables (available on the ATS Website), the *Fact Book,* and the *Strategic Information Report* contain useful information concerning faculty and administrative officers' compensation.

The distribution of compensation increases is a complex topic. Many schools make across-the-board increases (often on a percentage of salary) to all employees who remain at the same rank and level of seniority. This approach has the virtue of treating all employees consistently. Some schools will additionally increase the compensation of a

7. It takes $1,000,000 in endowment to generate $50,000 per year using a spending rate of 5 percent. A faculty member costing $100,000 requires $2,000,000 in capital investment in order to generate that much annually.

limited number of employees on the basis of meritorious performance. Advocates for merit pay assert that good performance is thereby encouraged, and the retention of excellent employees is strengthened. Advocates of equal raises note the difficulty of establishing and administering a consistent and fair set of criteria for merit raises, and they argue further that an equitable ethos is fostered.

Retrenchment

Schools with persistent, serious deficits will have to consider retrenching faculty as well as administration and staff. This should not be done lightly or casually, but only when serious financial problems confront the school. Faculty, including tenured faculty, may be terminated if there is a situation of financial exigency. In some instances, school policies define financial exigency and the procedures the administration and board are obligated to follow as they consider the termination of faculty. In the absence of written definitions and procedures, the president should take care to make sure that decisions are reached carefully and evenhandedly and that the actions taken may be successfully defended from accusations of bias, favoritism, or a lack of consultation and due process. The financial exigency of the school must be substantial and real, to the point where the future viability of the school's mission is at risk. That said, the school should not wait to act until its existence is threatened.

The advice and commentary in this book is not intended to be used as legal advice; that is especially true when dealing with the complexities of faculty contracts and terminations. The advice and guidance of the school's legal counsel should be sought early in the consideration of faculty terminations.

Financial Reporting and Analysis

Regular Reports

Ongoing financial reporting and analysis should be part of the business officer's regular duties. The president should typically receive a statement of monthly revenues and expenditures, comparing the actual revenues and expenditures to the budget. The business officer should also interpret the statement for the president and board, explaining whether or not the performance shown in the statement is likely to improve or deteriorate by year-end. Department directors should receive regular reports on their expenditures versus budget. Monitoring of financial performance follows from an effective reporting system.

Full Costs versus Incremental Cost Analysis

Presidents need to understand the financial implications of programmatic decisions. Financial analysis of proposals is a key step. The chief business officer is best equipped to conduct such analyses, as he or she has access to and familiarity with all the available financial information and is likely to have knowledge and experience in cost accounting. The president, however, should always investigate, with the business officer's help, the financial implications of budget proposals, program initiatives, and other plans. The paragraphs that follow discuss some of the types of financial analysis and problems often encountered.

In budgeting and planning it is important to distinguish between what might be called a "full" cost analysis and an incremental cost analysis. For instance, a full cost analysis of a Doctor of Ministry (DMin) degree program would list costs of the DMin office, the cost of adjunct faculty, allocated costs of regular faculty teaching in the program, and allocated overhead costs for space and general administration. In many schools the full cost of the DMin program, so accounted, exceeds the tuition receipts. On a full cost basis, the degree often loses money. Should the degree be dropped? Would that save money?

In most cases dropping the degree would hurt the school financially. How is that possible if costs exceed revenues? Dropping the degree certainly ends the tuition associated with the degree. What costs would be saved? Only the incremental costs, that is, the costs *directly incurred* by the program. Unless the school terminates regular faculty when it ends the DMin program, no regular faculty compensation is saved. Those costs and all the administrative overhead costs continue. Although the degree loses money on a full cost basis, the tuition receipts — the incremental revenue from the program — often cover the incremental direct cost of the program — that is, the costs of the DMin office and the adjunct faculty. Put another way, the program may lose money on a full cost basis, but it may cover its incremental costs and make a positive contribution to overhead. The analysis of incremental revenues and costs thus determines a break-even financial standard for a program — that is, that the program covers its direct incremental costs. Of course, the school may apply a higher financial standard and decide that the program should cover its full costs or a certain portion of its overhead.

A similar methodology may be applied to proposals for program expansion. For instance, a proposal to offer classes at an extension site should examine carefully all the incremental costs directly associated with the new site. Thus rent, staff at the site, adjunct faculty, travel, local expenses for recruitment, identifiable added costs on the home campus, and other direct costs should be tallied as part of the ongoing costs. If regular faculty teach at the remote site as part of their regular responsibilities, the cost of their time should not be considered a direct incremental cost of the site. On the other hand, the cost of travel and lodging at the site would be an incremental cost of the site. The cost of the dean on the home campus, the president's office, the business office, and all the rest of the shared overhead costs of the whole school should not be included in the incremental analysis. Once the incremental costs are fully compiled, one may compute the number of class registrations needed to break even. As in the previous example, the school may decide that it must have better financial performance than break-even viability and that the site should provide a substantial contribution to overhead.

If new programs or centers do not cover their incremental costs from program receipts, the president, along with his or her advisers and the board, must decide whether or not the new program or center should be launched or continued, and whether it should be subsidized by the general revenues of the school. If the new program or center is considered a key expression of the school's mission, it may be justifiably subsidized, so long as all parties recognize and affirm that the subsidy for this high priority program implies fewer resources and possible cutbacks for other projects, programs, and needs.

Analysis of Campaigns

Special fundraising campaigns should be subject to incremental cost analysis. Sometimes a campaign "goal" combines all expected receipts, adding annual fund receipts and bequests to the amounts that the special or capital campaign solicitations are expected to yield. This is done to have an impressive fundraising figure for public relations purposes. There is nothing particularly wrong with conflating all of these sources of funds, provided that the administration, board, faculty, and other key constituents understand that the conflated total does not represent "new" money for the school, and that in fact a considerable portion of the campaign total would be received in the normal course of business — even if there were no special campaign. Indeed, it is not unusual to find out that the incremental gain from the campaign — the actual "new" money raised through the special efforts of the campaign — is less than half of the conflated total. Any special campaign for funds should be carefully analyzed to determine if the campaign has the objective of strengthening the school's financial structure and to what extent.

Some capital gifts and special grants cost money, or at least obligate the school to spend more money. This is most often the case when foundation grants are restricted to new programs or activities. The new grant monies fund new grant activities — that is, new expenses that were not part of the normal course of operations before the grant was received. The new money flows out to new expenses. The net financial gains from some restricted grants are very small, limited to a modest allocation of the grant for overhead expenses. Additionally, the expiration of the grant may result in the school funding the expenses previously covered by the grant. This happens often enough that foundations routinely require grant applicants to explain how funding will be secured after the grant expires.

Another occasion for gifts that cost money, or at most break even, is when new funds are raised for new programs. One example is a new endowed chair. If a school receives new money to endow a chair and expands the faculty roster by hiring a new faculty member to fill the chair, the bottom line of the budget is not necessarily improved. The new expenses for salary, benefits, and other items associated with the new faculty member can consume all the new endowment revenue generated by the gift of a chair. On the other hand, if a current faculty member could be appointed to fill the chair, the bottom line for the school is strengthened considerably, as expenses remain the same while endowment revenue increases.

Of course, new chairs with new occupants and foundation grants that spur the school in new directions make the school better because they increase the teaching and learning of the school and advance the school's mission. Financial analysis is needed to ascertain whether or not they also help the bottom line, making the whole school more financially secure.

Institutional Borrowing

Colleges and universities commonly borrow large amounts to finance new buildings, laboratories, athletic facilities, and the like, principally with the aim of attracting more students.[8] Such borrowing is less common in theological schools. Why are theological schools hesitant to borrow and more likely to seek capital funding from donors? The habit may be an expression of church and ecclesial traditions and values, but it could also be attributed to hardheaded realism about potential revenue increases. Investment in new facilities and program capacities may improve the environment and potential of the school, but they don't necessarily produce the large increases in tuition revenue that colleges and universities are betting on. If new revenues are not forthcoming, principal and interest payments on the debt could burden rather than benefit future programs.

Investments

Presidents need not be experts in investing, but as with any area of oversight the president should have a thorough understanding of what the school is doing and should have enough knowledge of the field to be constructively critical. Relying solely on trustees produces mixed re-

8. Martin Van Der Werf, "Colleges Turn to Debt to Finance Their Ambitions" and "Poor Bond Ratings Don't Deter Some Colleges from Seeking More Debt," *The Chronicle of Higher Education,* March 19, 1999, pp. A38ff.

sults. Surprisingly, many trustees who are accomplished business leaders do not have the experience or perspective needed to guide the school to excellent long-term investment performance. Thus the president's responsibility is to make sure the investment committee is well equipped and continually educated on sound principles and perspectives on institutional investing. Some trustees, unsure of their knowledge, defer to the sometimes erroneous instincts and impulses of other, high-status trustees, and thereby inadvertently hurt the school. The best defense is to have well-educated trustees with a thorough understanding of the school's well-thought-out, written strategy, which should include the following.

Cash Flow and Short-Term Investments

The business officer is usually charged with handling the issues involving cash flow. These duties include managing the bills that are due and investing excess operating cash in interest-bearing accounts, such as money-market accounts. Cash flow management, in some situations, requires the school to have a line of credit to meet payroll and other expenses when the school is short of cash. Extensive use of credit is a signal of financial trouble and should be monitored and investigated. The school's auditors should look closely at cash management in order to help the school maximize its return and assure careful control.

Long-Term Investments

Schools with nonexpendable endowments and other monies that are not needed for operations may invest those funds for the long term and use a portion of the investment return to support the operations of the school. The term "endowment" is usually used loosely to describe all the monies invested for the long term. More precisely, the long-term investments may include (1) nonexpendable funds that donors have given to the school with the restriction that the principal not be expended (such funds are often called "true" endowment and are also known as "permanently restricted" net assets); and (2) expendable funds that the board has directed to be retained and reinvested for the long term. These are often referred to as "board-designated" funds, as distinct from "donor-restricted" funds. The term "quasi-endowment" refers to such board-designated funds.

As mentioned, donors may permanently restrict the use of the principal. They may also restrict the use of the return. They may indicate, for instance, that the return is to be used for scholarships. If the donor restricts the return to a specific purpose, the return must be accounted for with "temporarily restricted" funds — that is, the funds must be specially earmarked until expenditures are made that fulfill the donor's restriction. When expenditures fulfilling the restriction are made, the temporarily restricted funds are released from their restriction. Donors may also restrict the purpose of expendable gifts and grants; those gifts and grants must also be classified as temporarily restricted.

Schools may also be the beneficiaries of trusts or gifts held and managed by trustees or by a denominational foundation external to the school. These funds function as endowment in that they are invested for the long term and provide a return to the school. The school does not, however, actively manage them. Insofar as these amounts are substantial, a theological school should consider adjusting its internal investment and spending policy so that the combination of assets held internally and externally are appropriately allocated and the combined spending or draw rate from internal and external sources meet the equilibrium standard. A well-managed endowment connotes good management on the part of the school and its trustees, and it engenders confidence in potential donors that their gifts to the school will be wisely invested and prudently used.

In many independent schools a board committee takes responsibility for oversight of investments. In schools that are part of a larger university, diocese, or religious order, or whose investments are managed by a denominational entity, the theological school may not have or exercise direct control over investment policy. In most cases where a school has direct responsibility for investing, the board committee develops investment policies, hires the investment managers, evaluates performance, and changes investment management when appropriate. Schools with large endowments or schools that are heavily dependent upon investment returns often find it wise to employ independent investment counsel as a resource for the investment committee in an effort to be sure that this crucial resource is excellently managed. The role of the independent counsel is to assist in creating investment strategies, developing appropriate policies, selecting investment managers, evaluating performance, and investigating issues of interest to the committee. Such independent counsel does not invest money directly but assists the investment committee in managing the managers. Schools whose endowment plays a smaller strategic role may not find it cost-effective to hire independent counsel; in those cases the schools will tend to rely on the expertise of the committee members or the resources of their money managers.[9]

Asset Allocation

Asset allocation is a key decision in investing. Many academic studies have confirmed that asset allocation is a key determinant of the total return from an investment portfolio; some say that asset allocation determines 90 percent of the return. What is asset allocation? It is the decision to invest in various "asset classes" or types of investments. There are many asset classes. Stocks, bonds, real estate, and money market funds may each be considered an asset class. In addition, there are asset classes within asset classes. There are various kinds of equities or stocks, such as stocks of large companies, small companies, and international companies. Asset classes may include different styles of investing, such as investing in "growth" stocks or in "value" stocks. The idea of "passive" investing, in index funds, has gained some popularity in recent decades. Bonds or fixed-income instruments also have varieties in terms of their yield, quality, term, and issuer. "Alternative investment" asset classes have also gained attention in recent years. This category includes anything that is not a traditional stock or bond investment and includes hedge funds of many kinds, private equity, and real assets.

What should the asset allocation strategy be for a theological school? Proper fiduciary oversight may be achieved through a range of strategies. The investment committee should select a strategy that prop-

9. The Commonfund provides education and investment services for educational institutions and other nonprofits, and it is considered by many to be of service for smaller endowments. See its Website: www.commonfund.org.

erly weighs and balances both risk and return. Percentage allocations for asset classes should be adopted for the long term. Without such long-range targets, the investment committee may be tempted to "time" the market — that is, to guess whether or not stocks will outperform bonds, or vice versa, over the next three months. Professor J. Peter Williamson of Dartmouth notes, "If short-term shifts in asset allocation are to be based on hunches, or a 'feel' for the market, whether on the part of trustees or professional managers, then skepticism is appropriate."[10] Most experts recommend establishing long-term asset allocations and rebalancing investments in them to their long-term proportion each quarter.

Spending Rates

Long-term investments generally produce two kinds of return: (1) they generate income in the form of dividends on stocks and interest payment on bonds; and (2) the price of a stock or bond may also change. An increase in the value of stocks or bonds is called appreciation. A decrease in the value of investments is called depreciation. Thus the total return to an investor is the income plus the appreciation or minus the depreciation.

From year to year portfolio returns vary widely. Because a school needs a stable source of revenue, a school will typically employ a spending formula to determine the amount of investment return that should be budgeted. The formula is designed to smooth out major fluctuations in investment returns. The most common spending formulae tie the amount to be spent to an average market value of the portfolio. The most common formula in use in higher education is to spend a percent of a three-year (twelve-quarter) average of the endowment market value. The percent should be a long-term equilibrium rate such as 5 percent. There are variations that take inflation into account as well.

The once-popular policy of spending just the *income* (interest and dividends) from endowment and reinvesting all the appreciation has severe drawbacks. The most significant is that the decisions about invest-

---

10. See J. Peter Williamson, *Funds for the Future: College Endowment Management for the 1990's* (Westport, CT: The Common Fund Press, 1993), pp. 7-156.

ments are distorted by the need for income. For instance, most of the total return from bonds comes in the form of income, that is, interest payments. By contrast, most of the return from stocks comes from appreciation. If a school spends only income, it could be tempted to emphasize bonds rather than stocks to increase the flow of interest payments. Many excellent investment opportunities for appreciation and growth might thereby be missed. The total return approach of spending a specified percentage of the endowment market value permits the investment managers to invest for the best long-term health of the school without an unnecessary constraint of income generation.

Return is either spent or reinvested. The endowment spending rate plus the endowment reinvestment rate equals the endowment's total return. One approach to the spending/reinvestment rate decision is to try to balance the needs of the present (for spending) with the needs of the future (for reinvestment). There should be enough reinvestment in the endowment that it will keep pace with inflation, so that in the future the institution will have at least the same level of endowment support it has enjoyed in the present. Such a rate would be an equilibrium spending rate, designed to maintain the purchasing power of the investments. Experts in the 1960s and 1970s concluded that a spending percentage between 4.5 percent and 5.5 percent for an endowment invested 60 percent in stocks "probably" would keep pace with inflation.[11] This finding became, for all practical purposes, the norm for U.S. colleges and universities, as many adopted a spending rule of 5 percent of the average market value of the endowment over the past three years.[12]

A president is strengthened if the equilibrium spending policy is firmly enforced by the governing board. A widespread perception that the spending policy may be violated — through special appropriations, or special circumstances, or chronic deficits that, in effect, increase the spending rate — puts enormous pressure on the president and adminis-

11. *Managing Educational Endowments: Report to the Ford Foundation by the Advisory Committee on Endowment Management* (The Ford Foundation, 1969); and *Funds for the Future: Report of the Twentieth Century Fund Task Force on College and University Endowment Policy,* by the Twentieth Century Fund, Inc. (McGraw Hill, 1975). Investment returns in the 1980s, 1990s, and 2000s confirm the earlier finding that 4.5 to 5.5 percent spending would keep pace with inflation over the long term.

12. Williamson, *Funds for the Future,* p. 111.

tration to permit the overspending to continue. In those instances the president must make heroic efforts to educate the board *and* the administration, faculty, and students that equilibrium must be achieved and that fiscal discipline is required.

Social Responsibility in Investing

Some denominations and schools choose to reflect their ethical and social commitments in their investments.[13] Three popular ways of achieving this aim are (1) screening the portfolio to avoid owning stocks of corporations whose products or business activities are disapproved of and to seek investments in corporations whose behavior is praiseworthy; (2) engaging in shareholder advocacy with particular corporations on particular issues, including initiating and voting on proxy resolutions and lobbying directors; and (3) practicing community investing, that is, finding ways to assist disadvantaged communities by providing capital for local investment. Issues of social responsibility in investing are complex, and considerable study and discussion are likely to be required to reach a consensus in the governing board.

Regular Reminders for Presidents

Managing finances is a complex but critical task for any institution. A president should delegate most of this responsibility to a competent finance office, but a president needs to remind himself or herself regularly of critical issues and principles and should monitor these regularly. The following are some of these critical issues:

- Responsible financial management of a theological school should help the school perform its mission with adequate quantity and quality while preserving or enhancing the purchasing power of the

13. According to the June 2002 National Association of College and University Business Officers survey of participating colleges and universities, 27 percent of schools employ some social criteria in investing.

school's financial assets and maintaining needed facilities and equipment in adequate condition.

- It is important to pay attention to the annual audit of financial statements. The audit provides an external professional review of the accuracy of the school's accounting records and the adequacy of control procedures.
- The annual operating and capital budgets of the school are a uniquely detailed and powerful expression of the school's plan for its mission. Budgets should be balanced and realistic. Faculty and staff compensation typically dominate the expenditure budget and make cost reduction and retrenchment difficult.
- Proposals and plans for new programs, projects, or campaigns should be analyzed to determine their true financial impact on the school. Incremental cost and revenue analyses are especially useful in decisions to launch new programs or fundraising campaigns.
- Investments should be well managed by trustees, who may use consultants to assist them as appropriate. Asset allocation is crucial in determining total return. The spending rate should be low enough to permit reinvestment of returns so that the principal will keep pace with inflation. Some schools apply social responsibility criteria to their investment selection.

Additional Resources

Anthony, Robert N. *Essentials of Accounting*. 6th ed. Reading, MA: Addison-Wesley Longman, 1997.

This book by Robert Anthony is a basic introduction to financial accounting, designed for those who have little or no prior knowledge or experience. Although it is not crucial for the chief executive to have this knowledge, it is helpful when one attempts to understand the financial statements in the audit.

Association of Theological Schools. *Fact Book*.

The ATS *Fact Book* and Annual Data Tables (www.ats.edu) show industry-wide financial trends, including revenues, expenditures, library data, compensation, and numerous other tables.

Association of Theological Schools. *Institutional Peer Profile Report.*

ATS's *Institutional Peer Profile Report* compares the recipient school to selected peers along a wide range of enrollment and financial data.

Association of Theological Schools. *Strategic Information Report.*

ATS's *Strategic Information Report* shows the recipient school's financial data on assets, liabilities, revenues, and expenditures in a graphic format. Some comparisons are also included. Enrollment data and trends are also included.

Auburn Studies (Auburn Theological Seminary) (www.auburnsem.org).

Auburn Studies reports on research conducted by Auburn's Center for the Study of Theological Education. Publications include studies of theological school revenues, student educational debt, faculty, board members, and various other topics. Supplemental background reports and resources are available also.

The Commonfund (www.commonfund.org).

The Commonfund (formerly The Common Fund) provides education and investment services for educational institutions and other non-profits and is considered by many to be of effective service for smaller endowments. It has numerous publications in addition to the Williamson book cited below.

In Trust.

In Trust magazine specializes in governance in theological schools, especially at the board level, and consequently frequently publishes articles regarding financial policies and the fiduciary duties of trustees.

KPMG LLP and Prager, McCarthy & Sealy LLC. *Ratio Analysis in Higher Education: Measuring Past Performance to Chart Future Direction, for Independent Institutions.* 1999.

This book explains financial ratios, based on audited financial statements, which measure the viability and financial performance of the school. Some of the ratios are in the *Strategic Information Report* provided by ATS.

Schneider, William, Robert DiMeo, and D. Robinson Cluck. *Asset Management for Endowments and Foundations.* New York: McGraw Hill, 1997.

This is an excellent overview of the issues involved in investing.

Williamson, J. Peter. *Funds for the Future: College Endowment Management for the 1990's.* Westport, CT: The Common Fund Press, 1993.

This book is an excellent and thorough overview of college and university investing.

The resources identified in this handbook are listed on the ATS Website where the list will continue to be updated as new resources become available: www.ats.edu > Leadership Education > Presidents.

CHAPTER 7

The President's Role in Managing Facilities

WARD EWING, General Theological Seminary
THOMAS GRAVES, Baptist Theological Seminary at Richmond
ROBERT LANDREBE, Gordon-Conwell Theological Seminary

OVERVIEW
Introduction: Two Cases
The Role of the President
Working with the Board
Strategic Planning
Important Questions to Ask
Potential Problem Areas
Financing Capital Projects
Life-Cycle Budgeting for Annual Refurbishment and Renewal
Additional Resources

Introduction: Two Cases

People become presidents of seminaries for many different reasons, but
rarely is it because of their expertise in maintaining buildings and facilities. Two stories illustrate this point.

The new president was attending her first meeting of the facilities
committee of the board of trustees. She was aware that deferred main-

tenance was a major problem for the seminary. The purpose of this meeting was to hear the report from the engineering firm that had been hired to assess the extent of the problem and to estimate costs for repairs. As the engineer began his report, talking about flashing, re-pointing of buildings, wood-frame versus steel-frame construction, conductors, and windowsill deterioration, she looked around at the members of the committee and realized that many were confused. She had served as the senior pastor in an old Victorian downtown church; she had dealt with old buildings in that position and had learned a great deal. The engineer moved on to describe some of the wiring and fire protection problems. When one of the more knowledgeable members of the committee asked what "M/E/P/FP" stood for (mechanical, electrical, plumbing, fire protection), she suddenly had the sinking feeling that she knew more about buildings and maintenance than any trustee on the committee. What was she to do? As a woman, her voice might be largely ignored with regard to buildings and maintenance. As president, she could not spend a great deal of time with the facilities committee, yet given the severity of the problems and the lack of competency in this committee on these issues, how could she prevent these tasks from demanding far too much of her time?

In another similar story, the new president was also meeting with the facilities committee as it was receiving the report regarding the plans for remodeling three of the buildings on campus. He listened politely to the architect, to the mechanical engineer who was a member of the committee, to the developer who was helping to arrange the financing, and to the city rector who seemed to know a lot about old buildings. They talked about heating systems that included fan-coil units and cooling towers on top of the building. They talked about ADA standards in the halls and the bathrooms. They talked about multiple water services with one-inch and one-and-a-half-inch services needing upgrading. They talked about constant pressure booster systems with duplex pumps, cushion tank, and controls, about heating and cooling load calculations, steam condensate receiver, and feed pumps. They talked about electrical service, amperage, HVAC equipment, total electrical loads, and deficiencies in code compliance issues. As his eyes glazed over, the president got the sinking feeling that he was in way over his head when it came to being involved in the decision-making processes for the seminary's facilities. He realized that this was a technical field in which he had almost no knowledge; yet, the long-term implications of the decisions that would be made about such items would be very important in the life and mission of the seminary. The seminary had a record of poorly made decisions that did not solve problems but produced more of them. Inadequate and non-functioning facilities had added dramatically to a sense of dissatisfaction and low morale among faculty and students. How could he provide leadership when he was so inadequately prepared to deal with this critical issue for the quality of life at the seminary?

Most presidents can relate in some way to these two examples because most theological schools have facility issues, inadequate staff, and often inadequate expertise to deal with the issues. The president's primary duty cannot be focused on facilities, as there are other issues of leadership, program, personnel, and development that demand greater attention. The way a place looks, feels, and functions, however, greatly influences what people will feel and what they will perceive is possible for them and for the school. Inadequate or poorly functioning facilities have a major negative impact on the quality of life in the seminary. The president must provide strategic leadership to ensure appropriate maintenance and improvements to facilities. This chapter will look at the nature of that leadership and how the president can prevent these issues from taking too much of his or her attention and time.

The Role of the President

While it is easy to say that the president's attention cannot be focused primarily on buildings, it is much more difficult to understand the appropriate role for the president in this area. Many factors influence what is appropriate: the physical condition of the facilities, the age of the facilities, the costs involved in physical plant refurbishment and maintenance, the quality of the plant and maintenance staff, and the expertise available for planning and implementing projects. An additional factor is the existence (or lack thereof) of plans for funding renewal and replacement, responding to deferred maintenance, systematically refurbishing buildings, maintaining current facilities, evaluating and modernizing heating and electrical utilities, and responding to special needs like those found in the library or related to information technology instructional needs.

Whether facing severe facility problems or planning for major renovations or new construction, the president will have to take a leadership role in planning and setting priorities. Fortunately, taking such a role does not mean that the president must directly manage studies, contracts, or personnel, nor is it necessary for the president to have great knowledge about infrastructure, construction, or building codes (though some knowledge wouldn't hurt). As in other areas of the seminary, leadership involves keeping the focus on the mission and vision of the school; developing and guiding an appropriate process; recruiting, hiring, and appointing qualified and talented people; asking probing questions; keeping the issue in front of the board; maintaining cooperative relations with the town; and seeking to balance long-term budget planning with immediate problems.

Working with the Board

The president must ensure that the board is given appropriate information to deal with long-term facilities issues. In the absence of presidential leadership, boards may focus on immediate pressing problems rather than on long-term solutions, on fighting off alligators rather than on draining the swamp. When this occurs, decisions often respond to particular crises but neglect long-term planning with appropriate budgeting. Combine this short-range focus with the reality of overall restricted financial resources and we have the primary causes of accumulated deferred maintenance in many of our schools. The president and senior administration must continually encourage the board to focus on the long-term issues and to deal with the financial implications.

The president's leadership begins with personnel. Whether there is a single chief operations officer (COO) or whether those functions are included in the job description of another senior administrative officer, such as a vice president for administration, the president and this officer must work together in focusing on the long range by developing an appropriate planning process. The facilities committee of the board (again, there are many different structures in different schools) must take the lead in directing and implementing this planning process. This means that a facilities committee chair must be interested in buildings and infrastructure and must have or develop an ability for guiding the planning process. The chair does not need to have expertise in the field; in fact, such expertise can interfere with an appropriate process when the chair believes that he or she knows the proper solution. Clergy who serve in older, downtown congregations often can serve well in this capacity. A president knowledgeable about facilities will take an active role in recruiting appropriate leadership; a less knowledgeable president must find trustworthy experts (e.g., architects, engineers, or contractors) to assist in putting together a good team.

Too often the talents of board members do not include skills in engineering, architecture, and construction. When this is the case, the chair of the facilities committee, in cooperation with the president, must recruit additional volunteers who have these needed skills to serve on the committee (either as committee members or as resource persons, depending on the bylaws of the board). This situation provides an opportunity to involve volunteers who have needed technical skills. These volunteers become more engaged and committed to the seminary, gaining satisfaction by sharing their professional experiences and training.

Finally, the head of maintenance must have the ability to gather the data needed for the studies involved in long-range planning. Having a board committee chair, a COO, or the head of maintenance, none of whom understand the necessity of focusing on planning, will add to the president's difficulty in developing long-term solutions.

Strategic Planning

The planning process is not overly complex, but it does involve much detail work. While the president is not usually deeply involved in planning for facility maintenance and improvement, knowledge of the process and constant pushing toward completion (including annual updates) will be the primary factors that determine if a responsible plan is developed and implemented. Once knowledgeable and skilled personnel are in place, the main task for the president is to keep the group focused on the mission and vision documents for the school and to insist that accurate and timely information regarding the program is available. The planning group must have clear descriptions of the educational program and demographics of the school — the number and nature of the student body, the sizes of needed classrooms, the size and needs of the faculty, expected changes for the future — that will determine the facility needs.

While there are many different planning processes, all basically follow the same steps: identify the problems (or opportunities); analyze the seriousness of the problems (or the importance of the opportunities) by weighing costs and benefits; set priorities for dealing with the improvements; and develop a plan for funding. The first step is for the staff (or an outside consultant) to prepare a "facilities audit" for each building on campus. Projects that are small in scope or cost are designated as part of the annual budget for operations and maintenance. The remaining identified projects will become part of the long-range plan for facilities renewal and replacement. A well-functioning facilities committee, working with staff, will analyze the extent of these problems for each facility and set priorities for the projects. Finally, the president is ultimately responsible through the COO to see that the facilities audit is updated on a regular basis, possibly annually.

Important Questions to Ask

Important questions must be asked as part of setting priorities. The president's role (possibly through the COO) is to be certain that these probing questions are addressed. A president's knowledge of facilities can be a great help in developing the questions. A list of questions might include the following (these are in priority order, but are not exhaustive of all possible questions):

- Are current conditions hazardous? Are they life threatening in any way?
- Is the seminary in legal compliance?
- Do the problems affect accreditation requirements (e.g., library, classrooms)?
- What requirements of the Americans with Disabilities Act (ADA) apply to this project? Even if not required, can we make the building more accessible?
- What will the future cost be if we do not do the needed repairs now? Will doing the work now save money in the future? How much? Can the work reasonably be deferred?

- How critical is this project for the mission of the school?
- Will the proposed work reduce utility costs? How much? How long will those savings take to cover the expense?
- Should we seek to preserve this historic building? Is the building beyond saving? Will preservation attract more support than replacement with a new building? Will the results of renewal of the historic building be functionally and aesthetically successful? Can we make the building ADA compliant?
- How long will the project take to complete? How will it affect operations while it is under way?
- How will we pay for it?

In setting these priorities, it will be important for the director of admissions to submit trends and projections, for faculty to discuss pedagogical implications for classroom remodeling, for the director of the library to be involved regarding plans for the library, and for the vice president for institutional advancement to comment regarding fundraising potential. The president is responsible for seeing that all parties are included and provide appropriate data.

If the president, the COO, and the chair of the facilities committee of the board do not ask such questions and expect as complete answers as possible, then the director of maintenance (staff) and the board will tend to make their recommendations and decisions based largely on cost and available financial resources. The result may be cheaply done work, continued accumulation of deferred maintenance, and an approaching financial crisis.

If the input from the broader seminary constituency is not included, there is increased risk that the project will not be appropriate in scope, programming needs will be inadequately included, and the users of the facility will be dissatisfied with the completed work.

Potential Problem Areas

There are particular areas that may be overlooked until they become a major problem. Few board members truly understand the needs of the library. Information technology (IT) is of growing importance in the classroom, in the library, and as a communication tool for all constituencies on and off campus. Making older buildings accessible to persons with disabilities is desirable and may be legally required when other work is done. Food service and student housing may continue for years before there is any remodeling and upgrading of the standards. These areas all relate in one way or another to the mission of the school. As is implied in the series of questions above, next to life-safety issues and legal compliance, fulfilling the mission of the seminary is the highest priority. The president does not need to be an expert regarding the library, food service, IT, or accessibility, but he or she must be certain that appropriate input and expertise regarding these areas are part of the planning process.

Major facility renewal or construction, while forward looking, usually raises anxiety for at least some community members, resulting at times in anger. People tend to be protective of space, and everyone has an opinion regarding how space should function, be arranged, be decorated, and be used. The president must deal with the community's anxiety and anger in a way that does not allow it to disrupt or misguide the process. It is easy for the president to be blind-sided, thinking that he or she is doing a good thing for the community. Regular communication and a process that encourages "buy-in" of key stakeholders will help avoid much conflict and anger.

Financing Capital Projects

Once the project priorities are set, the plan is completed by addressing the question of funding. Funding of large capital projects typically comes from four sources: (1) a plant reserve fund created from special gifts, unrestricted bequests, unrestricted endowment, and annual income; (2) a capital campaign; (3) debt; and (4) realization of the value of certain campus assets, such as collectors' items (art work or library books), land, or asset value of buildings (rental possibilities).

While the first source, a plant reserve fund, is an important tool for financing capital projects, few seminaries have the capability of developing such a fund.

The second possible source of funding is a capital campaign. The president's role in developing such a campaign is covered in Chapter 8 of this handbook.

The third possible source is debt. The use of borrowing must be carefully planned so that the debt can be repaid in a manner that does not negatively impact other budget priorities. Great care must be taken if debt service is to be included in the operating budget. Identification of a particular revenue stream outside the regular operating budget is one way to repay debt with minimum repercussion. Tax-exempt bond financing may be a possible method of reducing the cost of debt incurred in any development. Crucial in any of these arrangements is getting expert legal and financial advice.

The fourth source of funding — the realization of the value of certain campus assets — involves creativity and discipline. Schools may own valuable paintings, important artifacts that could be in a museum, or books that are important collectors' items but less important for academic purposes. Such assets may be sold, and sometimes they realize large sums for the school. The basic criteria guiding the process of divesting of assets, after appropriate safeguards for gift restrictions, is whether or not an item is essential to the mission of the school. Again, the president must be active in ensuring that these criteria are appropriately applied. When assets such as valuable books from the library collection are sold, if the publicity around these sales is not clear and focused on the mission, the public will see the sale as "selling the seed corn," as seeking survival of the institution while diminishing its functions. One seminary sold a copy of the Gutenberg Bible, a valuable collector's book with little academic importance; thirty years later this sale is still seen as a sign of the school's financial fragility. In the sale of assets, the president must make certain that mission criteria are applied and *appropriately publicized* so the public understands and can support the action.

The proceeds from realizing the value of capital assets should be invested in capital projects or board restricted endowments. If the funds are simply used for the annual operations, then, in fact, the asset value of the school is diminished. The obvious impression (probably true) that the school is financially insecure will diminish financial development potential.

Many campuses have large unused asset value in land purchased for future expansion or in under-utilized buildings, both old and new. Through the use of innovative techniques, these can create an income source for capital renewal and replacement. The simplest way to realize this unused asset value is by renting space. For larger projects (and therefore greater financial return), the seminary may choose to work with a private developer to remodel space or build new facilities. Options include a development that the seminary owns and controls, some sort of land-lease arrangement, or an outright sale such as developing condominiums.

The president's role, again, is to ask probing questions. In one case, a seminary was a year or two along in working with a developer when the president learned (by talking with another seminary president) that, even though the seminary was a tax-exempt institution, there were methods by which it could sell the federal and state tax credits it was accumulating by refurbishing a historic building — a sale worth several million dollars. Development is a complex area; the president (with the COO) must keep asking questions and seeking information. (See Matthew 7:7.) The COO implements the plan.

Finally, the president must play a significant role in raising support for whatever plans and projects for renewal and replacement emerge. At this point, the president who feels ill-informed technically will discover how much he or she needs to know about facilities. One needs to know at least enough to tell the story so others can get on board. This role is obvious in a capital campaign. It is also important to build constituencies among faculty and staff, on the board, and among alumni/ae and other supporters. Raising support begins with communicating that there is a problem, involving key people in developing plans to respond to the problem, and then supporting those key people as together the president and leadership recruit advocates for raising the necessary funds and implementing the plans.

Life-Cycle Budgeting for
Annual Refurbishment and Renewal

How did so many seminaries end up with large backlogs of deferred maintenance? Answer: one year at a time. In a school where income is restricted, denominational support limited, students unable to bear the burden of high tuition, and program expenses constantly rising, the most difficult task is to develop a plant reserve fund that will allow annual maintenance of facilities before the entire building needs major work. This is the key to avoiding excessive accumulation of plant problems: the president along with the chair of the board, the COO, and the chair of the facilities committee must develop guidelines for regular plant renewal and become disciplined in following them. If the president and the COO do not support and encourage such action, it will be ignored by others.

"Life-cycle cost analysis" is a method commonly used to calculate the funds needed for regular plant renewal. Based on the replacement cost of each building on campus and the life expectancy of the buildings, maintenance staff can develop a reasonable budget target, using this method. Manuals and software are available to assist staff. The colleges and universities that have used this method discovered that, as a rule, the annual target for the budget for regular plant renewal equals 1.5 to 3 percent of the replacement value of the campus facilities. Given this number, one can quickly see how excess space or space that is not maintained is costly to the school and why it will hasten the move toward financial crisis as deferred maintenance accrues.

Presidential leadership in the area of facility maintenance does not require special expertise or an inordinate amount of time, but unless the president and top administrators insist on appropriate planning and budgeting for facility renewal and replacement, most institutions will follow the easy way of deferring large expenditures until a crisis has developed.

Additional Resources

Note: Most of the materials available regarding maintenance and capital renewal are written for large colleges and universities. Most seminaries are considerably smaller. This will require the COO to discern which material is applicable.

Publications

Kaiser, Harvey H. *Crumbling Academe: Solving the Capital Renewal and Replacement Dilemma.* A publication of the Association of Governing Boards of Universities and Colleges, 1984.

Though not very recent and out of print, this short monograph was the most complete resource we were able to find. It discussed all aspects of deferred maintenance and capital renewal. While written for larger institutions, the information is easily translated for smaller schools.

Two magazines frequently have articles that are pertinent to this topic and that give references to additional information: *NACUBO Business Officer* and *University Business*. Two recent articles that were helpful with this chapter are:

Biedenweg, Rick. "Why You Need Life Cycle Planning." *University Business,* March 2003.

Medlin, E. Lander. "The Deferred Maintenance Dilemma." *NACUBO Business Officer,* March 2003.

Websites

Several Websites provide useful resources. As with the other resources, they are primarily aimed at larger institutions.

College Planning and Management Magazine (www.peterli.com/cpm/index.shtm)

Diversified Intelligence (www.telligence.net)

Pacific Partners Consulting Group (www.ppcg.com)

VFA (www.vfa.com)

Regarding issues of accessibility, there are Websites focused on Americans with Disabilities Act compliance. The National Organization on Disability is a not-for-profit organization that focuses on accessibility issues and provides advocacy and helpful information to ensure full involvement of people with disabilities.

National Organization on Disability (www.nod.org)

U.S. Department of Justice, Civil Rights Division, Disability Rights Section (www.usdoj.gov/crt/ada)

The resources identified in this handbook are listed on the ATS Website where the list will continue to be updated as new resources become available: www.ats.edu > Leadership Education > Presidents.

CHAPTER 8

The President's Role in Institutional Advancement

REBEKAH BURCH BASINGER, In Trust , Inc.
C. SAMUEL CALIAN, Pittsburgh Theological Seminary
ROBERT F. LEAVITT, St. Mary's Seminary and University

OVERVIEW

Introduction

Whenever two or three seminary presidents are gathered together, it is not long before the conversation turns to money. Survey after survey identifies fundraising and resource development as being at the top of the list when it comes to institutional concerns of leaders in theological education. Almost no president these days is exempt from fundraising, and success in financial development has become synonymous with effective leadership.

To be sure, most institutional stakeholders understand the importance of the school's connections with alumni/ae, church leaders, and prospective students, but when it comes to allocating the president's precious time, consensus points in the direction of fundraising. It is simply assumed that presidents will be involved in securing the friends, funds, and connections necessary to undergird the mission of the institution.

Not surprisingly, new presidents can feel as though they've been tossed into the deep end of the institutional advancement pool — and without a lifeguard in sight. Fortunately, most learn to enjoy the advancement waters, and many become quite expert swimmers.

What Is Institutional Advancement?

The phrase "institutional advancement" applies to the wide range of activities that contribute to the realization of the mission and purposes of a theological school. The functions most often bundled under the advancement rubric include fundraising, alumni/ae relations, public relations, church relations, and student recruitment. Strengthening ties with church and civic leaders, keeping track of alumni/ae, publicizing the school, and engaging in fundraising are interrelated functions, with each building upon and complementing the others. All are necessary to the forward movement of the institution, and all are worthy of the president's attention.

Yet when board members, faculty, and other constituents speak of the president's role in institutional advancement (used almost interchangeably with financial development), what they usually have in mind are fundraising and donor relations. There may have been a time when seminary presidents did not have to concern themselves with such matters, but if so, those days are long past. For more years than any of us care to remember, theological schools in the United States and Canada have lived with chronic financial shortfalls, and the situation grows ever more urgent by the year. Writing in the early 1990s, Leon Pacala, who had just retired as executive director of the Association of Theological Schools (ATS), observed:

> The nature of theological school leadership is influenced by the requisites of financial development to a greater extent than any other single factor. . . . As a result, there is a growing distinction between presidents who come to office with a clear recognition and acceptance of these requisites for their leadership roles and those who do not.[1]

Expectations of the president's leadership in fundraising have only continued to increase.

Defining the President's Advancement Role and Responsibilities

Although this chapter focuses on the role of the president in institutional advancement, this does not mean that he or she should (or must) go it alone. Indeed, the strongest advancement programs are the result of a team effort, with the president, development staff, board members, and other key volunteers all doing their part on behalf of the institution. Yet the president's commitment to and involvement with advancement

---

1. Leon Pacala, "The Presidential Experience in Theological Education: A Study of Executive Leadership," *Theological Education* 29, no. 1 (Autumn 1992): 25.

activities are critical to the success of those activities, beginning with the following essential tasks.

Articulate the Mission of the Institution and Translate It into Fundraising Objectives

It is a truism of fundraising that money follows mission, and the president is the public embodiment of what the institution is said to be about. Seminary presidents who can translate mission and vision plans into a winsome, compelling case for support are the most effective in garnering that support. Mission clarity not only propels the institution forward with confidence but also encourages would-be friends to invest in the purposes and future aspirations of the school.

Presidents are the chief and most frequent spokespersons for their institutions, and by their words they build confidence among key constituents in the gift-worthiness of their schools. They have the joyful role and responsibility of communicating to constituents, "We are all engaged in the task of divine development (spiritual formation) that unifies heart, mind, and soul as well as resources of time, talent, and money into a totality of stewardship before God."

Participate in Shaping the Advancement Work Plan

There is nothing like putting plans in writing to hold the feet of staff and volunteers to the fires of accountability, and all the more so when it comes to fundraising. Effectiveness in advancing the institution begins with both a well-thought-out operational plan for the short term and a longer range strategic plan for advancement goals and activities.

For presidents who are new to the development function, participation in shaping a fundraising work plan is an excellent entry point into the development process. The plan lays out the entire program for the CEO and makes evident the linkages between the various activities. In short, planning documents provide a checklist against which the president, staff, and volunteers (including board members) can assess the progress of the advancement effort at various points along the timeline. A solid plan also helps to focus the president's priorities and workload in fundraising.

Lead in Cultivating Major Donors, Including Planned Giving Prospects

It is the president's responsibility to seek out and establish relationships with potential generous supporters who will become lifelong friends of the school and whose gifts can assure the institution's future economic vitality. High-end donors and prospects expect to have the president's attention. In turn, the president needs to understand his or her work with donors as an extension of his or her leadership ministry.

Seminary presidents who are fortunate enough to work with an effective development staff can look to these individuals for help in designing strategies for reaching out to different segments of the school's constituent base. For example, non-alumni friends of the school may not have the same issues or interests as alumni. The former are more future oriented, while the latter may have longer memories and attachments that impede certain types of development. Different methods are needed to reach these groups with messages that increase their confidence, engage their imaginations, and engender energy for development.

Hire Professionally Expert and Theologically Mature Fundraising Staff

The president must hire fundraising staff whose skills and sense of call prepare them for the challenges of raising funds in support of theological education. When institutional funds are tight, adding staff in the development office can be viewed as an unnecessary or impossible luxury, especially by faculty and other campus personnel. However, without adequate staffing, the president too often is pulled into levels of fundraising that are time consuming and that may actually work against the long-term financial goals of the school.

A primary consideration in hiring a chief development officer (CDO) is to find someone who is authentic and passionate in his or her commitment to the school's mission and vision. It also helps greatly if this person is able to envision creative connections among donors that are not immediately obvious. A solid relationship between the president and his or her CDO rests on the duo's ability to work together on projects, a realistic understanding of each other's strengths and weaknesses, a commitment to setting and meeting program targets, and, above all, a willingness to speak the truth to one another with candor and care. As an experienced president advised, "Get the best person you can find for the leadership position and be willing to try special arrangements to have the most competent person you can afford. Never hire anyone who is untrained in systems or organizational development. Managing data and keeping it under control is essential to a well-run development operation."

Remember the Importance of Theological Fit

The difficulty in finding good development staff encourages some presidents to overlook the importance of matching the personal faith commitments of a prospective fundraiser with the theological underpinnings of the organization, and this is a grave mistake. For a fundraiser to accurately and personally convey the uniqueness of a seminary's mission and program to the donors, he or she must understand and embody the theological tradition of the school. To paraphrase Henri Nouwen, seminaries must seek out fundraisers for whom every word spoken, every advice given, and every strategy developed is tested by a heart that knows God intimately.[2]

Encourage Board Participation in the Advancement Program

At those theological schools where the board is active and effective in helping to advance the institution, the president spends considerable time educating and encouraging trustees for their assignments. In fact, some longtime presidents devote as much as 50 percent of their time to nurturing board members for development success. This is no small commitment for a president, but board members who benefit from this kind of interaction with the president report high levels of satisfaction with their own service to the institution.

2. See Henri J. M. Nouwen, *In the Name of Jesus: Reflections on Christian Leadership* (New York: Crossroad, 1989).

In addition to board members, there are usually key volunteers, such as former board members, advisory board members, women's guilds, alumni/ae, or persons who have special interest in the seminary and its mission, who can provide significant time, contacts, and personal resources. They too require special presidential time and attention in order to involve them effectively in advancement activities for the seminary.

Getting Started: Strategies for the Early Years of a Presidency

Escalate the Learning Curve

The financial fragility of most seminaries demands that presidents embark on a crash course in the basics of institutional advancement even as they are adjusting to the many other challenges of the job. Newcomers to the presidency should seek to acquaint themselves with the language, conventions, ethical practices, and performance standards of the fundraising profession. And they must be prepared to put their new knowledge to work almost immediately in assessing the strengths and weaknesses of the school's development program and in suggesting innovative strategies and tactics.

Fortunately, learning the rules of the development game is not much of a problem these days, thanks to the rich array of helpful books, newsletters, Websites, seminars, and workshops from which new presidents can choose. In addition, presidents speak with appreciation of the valuable learning that comes from interaction with peers who have enjoyed success with fundraising. Five or more years into the job, many seminary heads look back with appreciation on the wise counsel provided by fundraiser mentors from institutions of similar size and theological tradition — experienced leaders who were willing to share what they had learned over the years through trial and error. Other newly appointed presidents are fortunate to discover fundraising mentors within the school itself — an expert, seasoned chief development officer, for example, or a board member with a personal history of fundraising success.

Cultivate Planned Giving

While it is impossible (and unwise) for presidents to double as planned giving officers, it is essential that presidents have at least a rudimentary grasp of the instruments of the trade. A massive intergenerational transfer of wealth is under way in Canada and the United States, estimated at $40 trillion and climbing, and it is crucial that seminary leaders talk with longtime friends about their estate plans. The good news is that many denominations and religious bodies employ planned giving staff and are more than willing to make these experts available to their seminaries. The wise president seeks out this kind of assistance early on and takes full advantage of the help. Development staff members should all have some basic knowledge of planned giving principles and methods. Where possible, it is very helpful to a development program to have one person who can focus fully on planned giving.

Check Institutional Performance against Industry Standards

In addition to acquainting themselves with the characteristics of an effective institutional advancement program, new presidents must acquaint themselves with the track record of their school's advancement activities. Assuming the school has a good development database, it should not be much of a problem for staff to pull together a quantitative analysis of the fundraising program. And even at schools where recordkeeping by the development office has been less than ideal, the president should press for good management data. The data needed includes the following:

- the number of donors who give for general operations; for capital purposes only;
- annual fund giving at various gift levels (e.g., major gifts of $5,000 or $10,000 and above; $1,000 to $5,000; $500 to $999; $250 to $499; $100 to $249);
- the top ten annual fund donors to the institution during the past five years and the top ten capital donors during the past five years;
- the percentage of alumni/ae giving for each of the past five years;

- the number of congregations supporting the seminary, in what amounts, for what purposes, and the frequency of gifts;
- the pattern of giving by board members, and by faculty and staff;
- the churn rate — that is, how many people who gave the previous year failed to give in the current year;
- the number of new names that were added to the database each year and what portion ended up giving (the quest for new names that are productive is an important measure of whether communications programs and publicity are working).

While it is challenge enough in many institutions to consolidate key quantitative data, assessing the qualitative aspects of the development program can be even tougher. As a solution, many presidents turn to a development audit conducted by an outside expert for help in judging the effectiveness of the current program. An audit provides the opportunity for a thorough and impartial review of all components of the current fundraising effort, including the following:

- the fundraising work plan and the school's planning documents;
- support constituency, their past performance and future possibilities;
- fundraising case statements, appeal letters, and brochures;
- general purpose print pieces and marketing activities;
- board leadership and participation in fundraising, including board minutes for the past year;
- technology, budget, and staff (including position descriptions) in support of fundraising.

Board members and others expect the president to be involved in suggesting the best methods for meeting the school's funding goals, to introduce techniques or strategies that maximize the efforts of limited staff, and to hone in on the best funding sources for the school. With a head full of new fundraising knowledge and an audit report in hand, the new president is better prepared to meet those expectations.

Meet and Spend Time with Donors

Over the past forty years or so, the funding future of graduate theological education in North America has shifted away from religious bodies and church-wide support and onto the pocketbooks of individuals. As Daniel Aleshire, executive director of ATS, warns at every opportunity, general church subsidies for seminary education are rapidly declining, the trend will not be reversed, and leaders in theological education should look elsewhere for support. So while it is important for seminary presidents to be visible in local congregations and at regional and national denominational meetings, it is essential that they increase the time they spend with major donors in one-on-one situations.

During the crucial first year on the job, new presidents should seek to meet personally with as many of their schools' most generous benefactors as is possible. At a minimum, the president's development portfolio should include the ten or more donors who have contributed the most dollars during the past three years. It is also a good idea for the new leader to seek appointments with program staff at foundations from which the school has received or hopes to receive a grant. Add in civic and church leaders, alumni/ae, and prospective students, and the president's advancement plate fills quickly. As one longtime seminary head responded when asked how much time a new president should expect to spend on development work: "At least 50 percent in a 'normal' year, and during a campaign as much as 80 percent."

Undertake Capital Campaigns

At some point most seminaries will find it necessary to undertake a concentrated effort to secure capital gifts for new buildings, the refurbishment of old buildings, new programs, scholarships, endowments, etc. A successful capital campaign requires a good base of annual donors and lists of significant prospects for large gifts. Thus, a successful annual fund is an essential first step in a capital effort. Such campaigns may require additional development staff, outside consultants, a feasibility study, and a commitment of more time and leadership from the president. The primary prerequisite, however, is a clear and persuasively articulated case of mission and goals for the seminary and the need for additional funds to achieve those goals and fulfill that mission. The full understanding, commitment, and involvement of the board are also essential.

Consider Foundation Funding

Foundations are great places to turn when seeking funds for building projects, student scholarship endowments, or start-up support for new programs or technology. However, very few foundations provide grants for current operations or for continuation of existing programs. Nor are foundations likely sources of quick money. Most operate on a strict timeline, with two or three proposal review meetings a year. That means it can take as long as six to nine months from the point of proposal submission until a grant check is received at the school. That said, however, foundation grants can be a tremendous boost to seminary communities, and presidents should be on the lookout for foundation funding opportunities that fit with their seminaries' priorities.

Maintain an Excellent Development Staff

Unless the situation within the development office is completely out of hand, it is a good idea to give continuing staff the opportunity to rise to new challenges. We've all seen how personality differences can influence performance, and a change in leadership style may bring fresh creativity and energy to a seemingly tired and uninspired fundraising team. The simple step of introducing measurable goals for the development program very quickly separates out staff persons who don't or won't fit with the new president's expectations. Performance indicators worth tracking include:

- the number of contacts, based on an agreed-upon configuration of types (e.g., twenty-four face-to-face contacts per month, thirty phone calls per month, thirty letters per month);
- the number of new donors worked with;
- the number of lapsed donors returned to the giving fold;
- the number of increased gifts over the previous year.

If, after a reasonable period of time (six months or so), or based on recommendations from a development audit, it is apparent that a change needs to be made in the development staff, do not drag out the decision and action. It is up to the president to encourage trusting relationships among the staff and with potential donors so that all parties can become a blessing to one another. Conflict in the development office almost always sets a fundraising program back, discourages donor confidence in the school, and saps a president of precious time and energy. Decisive action, as painful as it may be, is the only solution to a problematic personnel issue.

Conclusion

The days are past when seminary presidents did not need to concern themselves with institutional advancement (if indeed there was ever such a time). The pursuit of money is a constant and pressing aspect of seminary leadership. It is also a joyful responsibility if viewed through the lens of ministry. When seminary presidents ask for support in ways that invite donors to give as agents of God's grace, and when donors respond with faithful, generous hearts, seminaries will have all that is needed to support their mission, vision, and programs.

Additional Resources

Books

Dove, Kent E. *Conducting a Successful Capital Campaign*. Revised and expanded edition. San Francisco: Jossey-Bass, 2000.

> This revision of an already good resource provides newcomers to fundraising with everything they need to know about planning for and carrying out a capital campaign. The information is presented in handbook format and includes helpful checklists, suggestions for campaign reports, and sample publications.

Dove, Kent E., Jeffry A. Lindauer, and Carolyn P. Madvig. *Conducting a Successful Annual Giving Program*. San Francisco: Jossey-Bass, 2001.

This book provides a complete guide to planning and managing the school's annual giving program. The authors address such important topics as the case for annual support, best approaches to direct mail, making the most of special events, strategies for personal solicitation, and tips on foundation relations.

Jeavons, Thomas H., and Rebekah Burch Basinger. *Growing Givers' Hearts: Treating Fundraising as Ministry.* San Francisco: Jossey-Bass, 2000.

Based on a three-year, nationwide study of fundraising programs of faith-based organizations, this book explores the dynamic interplay between encouraging spiritual development of donors and raising essential resources for ministry.

Rosso, Henry A., et al. *Achieving Excellence in Fund Raising.* San Francisco: Jossey-Bass Publishers, 1991.

This volume provides a detailed introduction to all aspects of a comprehensive fundraising program, explaining the profession's major principles, concepts, and techniques. Now considered a classic in fundraising circles, the book is a must read for every seminary president.

Schumacher, Edward C. *Building Your Endowment.* San Francisco: Jossey-Bass, 2003.

This book provides step-by-step guidance on understanding and implementing an endowment program. Included is help in making the case for endowment, selecting fundraising vehicles most likely to attract gifts for endowment, and strategies for soliciting and renewing gifts.

Willmer, Wesley K., editor. *Advancing Small Colleges.* Washington: CASE Books, 2001.

The strategies for success in alumni/ae relations, communications, fundraising, marketing, and enrollment management outlined in this book are as applicable for seminary development staff as for fundraisers working in small college settings.

Zimmerman, Robert M., and Ann W. Lehman. *Boards That Love Fundraising: A How-to Guide for Your Board.* San Francisco: Jossey-Bass, 2004.

This easy-to-use workbook is an ideal resource for boards and presidents who are finding their way together into the world of fundraising. The authors provide information on board structure and its impact on raising money, outline the concepts that will empower board members to ask boldly and thank sincerely, describe the wide variety of methods nonprofits use to raise money, and show how to recruit board members who can help with fundraising.

Newsletters

Seminary Development News

Seminary Development News is published twice a year by the Development and Institutional Advancement Program (DIAP) of the Association of Theological Schools and features articles by experienced development officers and presidents. It is available online at www.ats.edu.

Successful Fund Raising and The Major Gifts Report

Successful Fund Raising and *The Major Gifts Report,* both from Stevenson, Inc., Sioux City, Iowa (www.stevensoninc.com), provide easy to read and practical advice on structuring an effective, well-run development program.

The resources identified in this handbook are listed on the ATS Website where the list will continue to be updated as new resources become available: www.ats.edu > Leadership Education > Presidents.

CHAPTER 9

The President's Role in
Enrollment Management and Student Issues

DAVID MCALLISTER-WILSON, Wesley Theological
Seminary
CRAIG WILLIFORD, Denver Seminary
DAVID NEELANDS, Trinity College Faculty of Divinity

What Is Enrollment Management?

Presidents often see fundraising as their most important role, and they have a special relationship with the Development Office. Since the 1970s, many new presidents have been referred to as "development presidents." But if a president's primary concern is funding, he or she will also need to be an "enrollment president" and will want to establish a similar relationship with that side of the seminary's advancement program. This requires more than simply getting more involved in student recruitment. Beyond the work required to bring a student to the first day of class is all the work it takes to keep a student in seminary and moving effectively toward graduation and placement. Furthermore, an enrollment president must ensure that enrollment objectives are balanced with other objectives, including the budget. This whole process has become known as "enrollment management." This chapter will explore the key issues in enrollment management.

What's at stake? In a large percentage of ATS seminaries, tuition is the biggest revenue source and falls in that precious accounting category of "unrestricted income." Each new full-time student is like a three-year grant of $30,000, not including the additional income generated through denominational funding per student, room and board, and other auxiliary services. As seminary enrollments have become more volatile in the rate of retention and more dynamic in the hours per student, and as competition for seminary students has increased, new presidents are discovering that tuition revenue is no longer a relatively reliable and stable source of income. By the same token, they are finding that a surge in enrollment can float the school across dangerous financial shoals. Moreover, as the demographic nature of student bodies has changed, particularly with the infusion of second-career students, many seminarians also become significant donor prospects.

Enrollment requires the attention of the president for other equally important reasons. First, the bad news: students can be the source of the president's greatest involvement in legal issues. Several areas of federal law and many state and local ordinances are implicated in the recruiting, funding, housing, feeding, and teaching of seminary students.

Now, for the good news: the work of an "enrollment president" can profoundly affect the mission and the ethos of the seminary. Students are the school's mission, or at least are the primary means by which a seminary accomplishes its mission. Students are the organic link between the president and the faculty and between the seminary and the church. Their needs and their concerns challenge the operative assumptions about the curriculum, community life, and theological commitments of the resident academy. A president may not have enough time to transform the quality and character of a faculty, but he or she must have time to affect the nature of the student body.

Most importantly, God has entrusted these students to the seminary's care. Their call to ministry is the spiritual source of the seminary's energy, and a seminary's interaction with them can be a source of its own renewal. The seminary can be a great blessing to them, and, if treated faithfully, they will rise up and call their alma mater "blessed" in ways that profoundly strengthen the institution.

Recruitment and Admissions

At one time, the Admissions Office simply processed applications. The church sent students to seminary, and few seminary applicants applied to more than one institution. Moreover, the demographics were simple: young males straight out of college who were clear about their vocational direction and were ready to be full-time seminary students. Whatever "recruitment" was done occurred on college campuses where this "traditional" student could easily be found.

Now, recruiting seminary students is much more competitive. In most cases, the cost of educating clergy has shifted from the church to the student. That means younger prospective seminary students are behaving more like prospective college students: they are shopping. At the same time, the diversity of the seminary enrollment and the increased complexity of degree and non-degree offerings have meant that there are many more market niches to probe.

This new reality has caused most seminaries to become familiar with the mind-set and methods of recruitment marketing. This fact has brought an expansion in the staffing and an increase in the budgets of Admissions Offices, with the bulk of the work focusing on recruitment rather than admissions. There has also been an increased professionalization of both the recruitment and admissions processes. And financial aid has become an important factor in determining the nature of each entering class.

This means that presidents of seminaries now have to attend to this vital operational division of the institution. They need to compete for the best staff. They need to be a part of the shaping of the schools' recruitment messages, in addition to maintaining high standards for admission. And they have to respond to an increasing demand for marketing and financial aid budgets to ensure a certain level and quality of enrollment.

Strategic Marketing Plan

The elements of an effective recruitment program should include:

1. a Website providing contact information or, better yet, on-line inquiry and application functionality;
2. advertising placed in denominational publications and regional media outlets;
3. visits by seminary representatives to colleges, key churches, and other venues where prospective students gather;
4. a set of printed informational material;
5. a schedule of regular mailings to those who have inquired and applied;
6. opportunities to host prospective students individually and in groups on campus;
7. a staff that is market oriented, high energy, and goal driven.

Effective seminary recruitment in today's competitive environment requires that these strategies be deployed according to a strategic marketing plan. This plan should include:

1. market analysis that takes into account the seminary's missional objectives, programs, reputation, competitive position, and demographic profile;
2. institutional "branding" that carries consistently across the entire seminary's communications and that considers the prospective student to be the primary audience;

3. high quality "look and feel" for all print and electronic material packaged to match the findings of the market analysis;
4. targeted placement of advertising and recruitment visits determined by the market analysis;
5. identification and cultivation of "influencers," who help candidates make decisions about seminary;
6. a set of discrete and accountable recruitment goals.

This marketing plan should be an integral part of the overall institutional strategic planning process. Strategic planning should consider what level of enrollment is *achievable.* It is an occasion for the board and the faculty to take a clear-eyed look at the institution's current reputation and competitive position and to understand the limitations imposed by internal factors like scarce financial aid and external factors like geography and denominational weaknesses, even as it considers the opportunities for more aggressive recruitment. The stakeholders of the institution must also consider what enrollment is *desirable.* Almost certainly, the possibilities for expansion involve adding elements of demographic, cultural, and theological diversity that would change the seminary's existing ethos and practice. Some schools may have to consider scheduling and curricular changes in order to adapt to the "nontraditional" students. And strategic planning should consider what level of enrollment is *sustainable.* Increases in enrollment impact all areas of the budget, and, because seminary enrollments are more volatile today, it is prudent to plan to be pleasantly surprised by enrollment increases, instead of scrambling to make up a shortfall.

The President's Role

The role of the president in recruitment is fivefold:

1. to insist that student recruitment be guided by a careful marketing plan;
2. to approve the overall marketing message;
3. to hold staff accountable for recruitment goals;
4. to provide budget and technological resources commensurate with the importance of tuition revenue;

5. to align the development of academic programs with student marketing strategies by upholding both mission and budget as the frame in which everyone is held accountable.

In order to accomplish the final point, the president must give time and leadership internally to interpret and help faculty, staff, administration, and board to understand the enrollment management process and the critical role it plays in the seminary's aims of fulfilling its mission and remaining economically vital.

Financial Assistance

All seminaries provide some form of financial assistance to help students bear the increasing cost of seminary education. The best approach is to bundle financial assistance as a package that includes aid coming from the seminary's budget and from outside sources. The elements of the financial assistance package can include:

- merit-based scholarship aid
- need-based financial assistance
- denominational grants and loans
- government-guaranteed student loans
- government work-study positions on campus
- campus employment for the student and/or spouse
- paid internships in ministry settings.

Sometimes the availability of post-seminary placement opportunities are part of the services a seminary offers to make seminary education financially feasible.

The critical nature of financial assistance to enrollment management requires a new level of professional staff who is able not only to comprehend the many new federal, state, and church regulations and procedures in this area, but to understand it as a part of the overall enrollment management program of the seminary.

Effective Tuition Rate

A critical policy decision is the way the effective tuition rate is set. Seminaries can control the effective tuition rate by holding the growth of the nominal, published rate. Alternatively, tuition can be "discounted" by charging less for a full load or by granting merit or need-based assistance for some or all students. Discounting gives the seminary greater budgetary control and can be a powerful factor in the student marketing strategy. Like undergraduate colleges, seminaries are divided over the use of "merit" scholarships as a tool in shaping enrollment. On the one hand, seminaries can get caught in the trap of a bidding war with competitor schools and endanger the seminary's internal egalitarian culture. On the other hand, merit aid helps a seminary target candidates deemed to be of high quality.

The awarding of seminary financial aid should be guided by a carefully wrought internal policy and may be awarded either by staff or by committee. The Financial Aid Office/officer plays a pivotal role, attending to the financial aid policy, the budget, and the laws and regulations governing the awarding and reporting of government student loans. This office is also the place where information about outside grants and loans, internships, and campus employment are researched and promulgated.

The president's role is to ensure that the financial aid process, including the management of government student loans, conforms to the law and is aligned with the student marketing plan.

Deconstructing the Silos:
Structuring for Enrollment Management

One method of increasing the quality and number of students is to develop a transparent and seamless coordination between all of the functions of enrollment management. This goal may turn out to be harder to accomplish than it first appears to a new president. Decades of conscious and subconscious departmentalization among recruiting, admissions, financial aid, registrar, student services, placement, and alumni offices create silos that can seem impenetrable. The unique forms, languages, processes, foundational approaches, and differing styles and skills of personnel in these areas can all be used to justify a multitude of reasons to prohibit coordination among them.

Presidents also often face the challenge of changing the style of the enrollment-related departments from protection and enforcement of rules and regulations to service to students. For example, at some seminaries the Registrar's Office personnel perceive their main purpose to be guarding the academic integrity of the seminary. However, they could better serve the seminary by appropriately expanding their pri mary focus to assisting and advising students in course selection. Examples can be listed for any of the departments within the enrollment management process.

Where should enrollment management be lodged organizationally? In some institutions the functions are distributed, with some under the dean on the academic side of the house and others under the administrative side. Many presidents tackle these challenges by combining all of the enrollment functions and offices into one department under the leadership of a vice president of enrollment management (VPEM). Usually the VPEM reports directly to the president and serves on the senior leadership team. Some seminaries have also created a new enrollment management committee of the board to provide counsel for the president and VPEM. These two steps (direct reporting to the president and the creation of a board committee) reinforce the importance of this new approach and can communicate a powerful message to the seminary community. Relocating all of the physical offices in close proximity to one another sends a visual message that all of these staff members are now focusing on student service as a team, not on individual priorities.

The Metrics of Enrollment Management

Numbers, statistics, charts, acronyms, and abbreviations abound in the art and science of enrollment management. Understanding basic information contained in these figures allows the president to identify the most important variables in successful enrollment management and to focus on determining the health of the enrollment efforts of the seminary.

While the Association of Theological Schools (ATS) provides precise definitions and methods for measuring most of the areas listed below, some are more art than science. ATS allows individual seminaries to determine how they wish to measure these imprecise areas. Please consult the ATS Website (www.ats.edu) and manuals for this information. Also, ATS provides the annual Institutional Peer Profile Report, which includes pages of helpful comparison of these data between your seminary and up to fifteen "peer" schools that you select. Most presidents keep a copy of this report easily accessible for their use.

A conceptual tool for monitoring the effectiveness of the recruitment/admissions program is a concept called the "admissions funnel," moving from inquiries to applicants to students.

- **Number of inquiries:** the total number of people making inquiries to a seminary through any means.
- **Percentage of applicants from inquiries:** a measure of the number of people who move from inquiring to completing an application.
- **Percentage of applicants to acceptances:** a measure of the number of applicants who receive acceptance compared to the number who apply.
- **Percentage of acceptances to enrollment:** a measure of how many applicants actually enroll. This number demonstrates the effectiveness of a school's overall enrollment management process. From 66 to 70 percent may be an appropriate target.
- **Average cost to recruit:** a number that results from dividing the entire operational costs needed to recruit and matriculate a student by the actual number of students enrolled in a given year at an institution.
- **Total institutional head count:** the total number of students (full-time and part-time) enrolled at the school, excluding audits.
- **Full-time equivalency (FTE):** A measurement equal to one student enrolled full-time for one academic year. Total FTE enrollment includes full-time plus the calculated equivalent of the part-time enrollment. The full-time equivalent of the part-time students can be determined first by deciding how many hours per academic semester is regarded as full-time and then dividing that number into the total enrollment hours of all part-time students. ATS has guidelines for determining hours needed to be counted as full-time, which can be found in the ATS Annual Report Form instructions for the ATS-EF-1 form. Usually a school's registrar

who has filled out the ATS Annual Report Forms can educate a new president on this calculation. In any case, this figure is one of the most important in enrollment management.

- **Billable hours:** the total number of credit hours taken by all students in a given term or academic year, multiplied by the cost of tuition.
- **Average class load per student:** the total billable hours divided by the total number of students enrolled during a school term.
- **Faculty to student ratio:** the measurement of the ratio of faculty to students at an institution. It is determined by dividing the FTE for students (explained above) by the FTE for faculty as determined by the ATS formula and an institution's decision as to what constitutes a full-time load for its faculty members. Too large a faculty to student ratio is considered by many to indicate a lower quality education setting; too small a ratio means too high an instructional cost per student, which can present budget problems for the school.
- **Retention rates:** a measure that is looked at in two ways. First, what percentage of the students who originally enroll eventually graduate? With current enrollment of more part-time students, it is increasingly difficult to accurately measure the percentage that graduate. A second, and perhaps more important, retention number is what percentage of students who were enrolled one semester actually enroll for the following semester? The number is determined first by subtracting the number who graduate and the newly enrolled students in the new semester. The remaining number of students is divided into the number who have enrolled for the new semester. This percentage is the current retention rate. Schools are learning that they must track and encourage each student to enroll the following semester. Otherwise, particularly with part-time students, they can easily fail to register for a variety of reasons. Many students are lost along the way due to the inattention and lack of active pursuit of them by the seminary staff. Finally, this retention number can help the seminary better plan the level of enrollment it can count on for the future. A president should be alert to how his or her seminary compares in retention of students to other seminaries. A low retention rate may indicate a major systemic problem at an institution.

An "enrollment president" understands these metrics and uses them to guide both management and strategic planning. For example, the recruitment metrics and attention to retention rates helps ensure that the cost of recruiting and matriculating students is used efficiently. When projecting billable hours for a new budget, many schools review how their billable hours have increased, decreased, or stabilized over a three- to five-year history. They then determine a conservative budget number based on tuition rate increases for the upcoming year and the average of the billable hours over the time period they reviewed, plus any impact new initiatives might have on FTE. If a school's projections are overly aggressive and not attainable, they find themselves in a budget reduction mode within a budget year, which mostly discourages faculty, staff, and students and takes the institutional focus away from the strategic initiatives for growing and fulfilling the mission.

The President's Role in Spiritual Formation

The word "formation" is being used frequently by theological educators, like a group of contractors wondering why the concrete isn't setting up properly. One problem is an old one: the lack of academic preparedness as shown in the inability to write and think at the graduate level. In addition, two new issues have to do with the lack of formation in what Joseph Hough calls "the Christian identity." First, more students now enter seminary with little knowledge of the Bible, liturgy, or the basic doctrines of the church. Second, many students lack vocational formation and are now categorized as "searchers" or "seekers" because they are not sure what they intend to do with their theological education. In previous generations, there might have been concern about the lack of preparedness or sophistication among entering seminarians, but there was little concern about their earnestness or lack of Christian identity. These are the new "formation issues."

The formation issue comes to the president from two directions: the faculty and the church. Often, our desire is to push the blame back upstream to lack of formation in the church. In the past, the seminary community itself provided a simple, sturdy framework for formation. Now, the diversity among the student body and its part-time nature present additional challenges. Differences in gender, theological background, ethnicity, age, and life experience further complicate the process of formation. Part-time students who come on campus and take only one or two courses are difficult to engage in other more formational activities such as chapel, discussion groups, common meals, prayer groups, and so on.

Traditionally, faculty advising and counseling with students was understood to play the central role in student formation, but this role is also made more complex by the diversity of enrollments and the increased presence of part-time and commuter students. Typically, seminaries looked first to curricular reform, trying to find ways to integrate the disparate disciplines and contextual education through its field education requirements. Most now recognize that formation is not just about courses. It also has to do with other aspects of community life: worship, counseling, small group experiences, dormitory, library, and food service. These issues cut across the divisions of the seminary, though they may be lodged administratively with an office/ dean/director of "student affairs" or "community life." A critical issue for a seminary is whether it can understand "community life" as part of the enrollment management process, whose goal is not only to bring students into the seminary but to sustain them through their educational and formational program into the ministry to which they have been called.

What is the role of the president in formation? Perhaps the most important thing is to acknowledge the issue and identify the intentional and unintentional formation forces at work in the institution. The president's role is then to signify the importance of formation as the transcending issue in seminary education. The president must ensure that the community practices hospitality and justice for all segments of the student body. And the president also plays an important symbolic role. In today's seminary the president is often perceived as the CEO, concerned only with money and management. It is vital that the president be one of the spiritual leaders of the community. This involves both formal acts, such as preaching and leading in worship, and the many informal ways a president comes to know and share in the spiritual struggles of seminarians.

Conclusion

Presidents look for ways to get their institutions moving and steer them when it sometimes seems like they are just spinning their wheels on a slippery slope. There is a good rule for cars that are in that predicament: put the traction under the wheels that turn. Your time spent as an enrollment president will give you traction and new energy, because it relates the administrative and governance functions with the greatest source of institutional vitality.

Additional Resources

Websites

The Association of Theological Schools (www.ats.edu)

> The Association of Theological Schools is the primary resource. Mention has already been made of the comparative reports that are available from ATS. Other information and resources are available through its Website.

The Council for Advancement and Support of Education (www.case.org)

> The Council for Advancement and Support of Education (CASE) is the professional organization for advancement professionals at all levels who work in alumni relations, communications, and development. CASE offers a wide range of publications and services.

STAMATS (www.stamats.com)

> STAMATS is a for-profit consulting firm specializing in providing integrated marketing solutions to higher education. Their Website offers a rich variety of seminars, publications, and consulting services.

Graduate and Professional School Enrollment Management (www.gapsemc .com)

> Graduate and Professional School Enrollment Management (GAPSEMC) is an organization that has worked many years with seminaries and other graduate schools on issues of recruitment and admissions.

The following publications may also be useful, though they are written primarily for an undergraduate market:

Dennis, Marguerite. *A Practical Guide to Enrollment and Retention Management in Higher Education.* Westport, CT: Greenwood Publishing Co., 1998.

Penn, Garlene. *Enrollment Management for the 21st Century: Institutional Goals, Accountability and Fiscal Responsibility.* ASHE-ERIC Higher Education Report, Volume 26, Number 7. Washington: George Washington University Graduate School of Education and Human Development, 1999.

Seidman, Alan. *College Student Retention: Formula for Student Success.* ACE/Praeger Series on Higher Education. Westport, CT: Praeger Publishers, 2005.

The resources identified in this handbook are listed on the ATS Website where the list will continue to be updated as new resources become available: www.ats.edu > Leadership Education > Presidents.

CHAPTER 10

The President's Role with External Authorities

VINCENT CUSHING, Washington Theological Union
DONN MORGAN, Church Divinity School of the Pacific
ALBERT AYMER, Hood Theological Seminary

OVERVIEW

Introduction

Relating to External Agencies

    Initiate Relationships

    Communicate, Communicate, Communicate

    Make a Strategic Plan

    Step Carefully When Necessary

    Keep the Board Informed

Church and Accrediting Agencies

    Reporting to Agencies and Academic Freedom

    Working with Accrediting Agencies: Best Practices

Other Concerns: Legal Counsel and Auditors

Conclusion

Additional Resources

Introduction

The presidency of a school involves numerous institutional tasks. It is important that the president focus on those key institutional tasks that only the president can address. One task that requires presidential attention is the maintenance, and indeed the development and enrichment, of key relationships with external authorities. Note that the emphasis is on relationship and institutional well-being, and not the mere meeting of a prescriptive list of regulations. This larger view of developing meaningful institutional relationships will necessarily entail being institutionally accountable. The task is more than filling out forms, more than rendering a perfunctory accounting, and more than merely acknowledging an external agency. It entails presenting the institution in its best light as a graduate school of theology and ministry.

In developing relationships with external authorities, the president needs to be sure that the institution's work and response are characterized by due diligence. Particular agencies have specific requirements, and these requirements govern the shape of an institution's response. Responding to these requirements necessitates oversight of details to be sure that an institutional response is on target. In all cases, a president needs to make an informed judgment on the degree of accountability accorded an external agency and to respond to what is legitimately asked — no more, no less. If an agency wants more detailed information it will usually make that request in terms that are clear and helpful.

Relating to External Agencies

Who or what are these external authorities? Every theological seminary is broadly accountable to at least three external authorities, from each of which come legitimate calls for accountability with an eye to reviewing the integrity of the educational endeavor as carried out by a particular institution:

- the church, in regard to educating a range of ministers, both lay and ordained;

- the state, in terms of licensing, charter, observance of non-discrimination guidelines, safety, and building laws;
- accrediting agencies, which are concerned both with institutional functioning and with the development of curricula and the maintenance of professional and academic standards.

Even when a school of theology or seminary is not specifically accountable to a particular church (e.g., in the case of interdenominational seminaries), or not accountable to the state by virtue of separation of church and state, it nevertheless has enduring relationships with both entities that affect its educational program and institutional licensing. Finally, in seminaries that participate in the Student Federal Loan program or Work Study program, there will be a relationship with the U.S. Department of Education.

Initiate Relationships

In most cases, the best approach to dealing with external authorities is one initiated by the president, characterized by personal relationships, and done in a timely fashion. Delay, obfuscation, and careless or summary treatment inevitably spell disaster and serve neither party well. In all cases, the president will need to draw upon institutional resources as well as an array of personal skills. The task, as always, is to read the climate as accurately as possible and to design the best strategy to address the particular regulatory agency.

A new president should send a letter of notification to all agencies with which the institution has a relationship to inform them that he or she is now president. If someone on the president's staff knows the appropriate contact person, then the president should write to that person. In this letter, ask for confirmation of the date of the next accrediting visit and ask to be placed on the mailing list for workshops and forthcoming information.

It is essential that accurate information be filed in a timely fashion to meet deadlines. The president must oversee this and make sure that staff will prepare the material and submit it to him or her for review.

When possible, the president should confer with knowledgeable people — other presidents and key institutional personnel — to get a reading of the regulatory landscape of church, state, and accrediting agencies. This should involve a candid, in-depth discussion of possibilities and pitfalls, potentially sensitive areas, and issues or practices that might adversely affect an institution. Part of this conversation should be the listing of key people who can be potentially helpful or harmful to a school.

Communicate, Communicate, Communicate

David Hubbard, the late, esteemed president of Fuller Seminary, offered sound advice for dealing with interested public constituencies: communicate, communicate, communicate. This is true when things are going well, but even more so if things are not going well. Nothing substitutes for a reasonably open line, a friendly spirit, and a cooperative approach. A president's job is, of its nature, a public position, and the president should be ready to look to the institution's welfare and well-being. Institutional well-being is supported by sound, accurate, and timely communication. There is just no room for personal pique or institutional grudges. The president will do well to show that he or she will walk the extra mile, even when that entails travel or long discussions with accrediting agencies or church officials. Effective communication will include the following three tasks.

> *Assemble a packet of information for the agency*
> *in accordance with the agency's requirements.*

This information packet should include, first, a personal cover letter from the president, highlighting the mission of the school and its wish to be in a productive relationship with the agency. In this letter, the president addresses directly the queries or concerns of the regulatory agency.

Second, the information packet should provide other supplemental information that might be helpful, including the following:

- the most recent institutional catalog describing degree programs, faculty, institutional governance, and accreditation, both special and regional;

- when appropriate, enrollment data and key financial issues, especially endowment;
- student financial aid;
- a summary statement of goals and future directions;
- assurance of policies of non-discrimination and equal opportunity employment;
- any specific additional items in which the agency expressed an interest.

Familiarize yourself with the agency and with significant agency personnel who have a legitimate role with respect to your institution.

Obtain pertinent information from the agency on current regulations, working policies, or confessional statements that have a bearing on your institution and have significant import for your institution's educational mission.

Be clear on the nature of the current inquiry to your institution. Is it in regard to a normal review, to a new issue that has arisen, or a past issue that was or was not addressed?

Review files for past reports, official letters, and agency actions in regard to your school. Go back at least as far as the last state, church, or accrediting agency visit and review the actions that were recommended, how they were or were not implemented, and what your institution's reporting history has been to that particular external agency.

Initiate conversations with other schools that have had interaction with the external agency with which your school is interacting.

Find out their "take" on that agency and discuss what you are preparing to address. Be especially alert to the particular agency's working policies that challenge an institution in substantial ways. Listen carefully for peculiar idiosyncratic actions characteristic of the external agency and their import for your institution.

Make a Strategic Plan

Presidents should recognize the key role of strategic planning and assessment in responding to external authorities. A school will fare well in addressing church, state, or accrediting concerns if it has implemented those internal institutional processes that sound evaluation entails. This is best achieved when an institution undertakes, on its own and prior to any external prompting, the strategic planning needed and remedial actions called for that enable it to fulfill its mission more effectively.

Particular key areas for review are:

- fiscal soundness according to recognized criteria;
- quality of faculty as professionally assessed;
- curriculum goals and processes for review;
- orientation, composition, and operation of the board;
- student admission criteria (e.g., program, numbers, geographical distribution);
- faculty development;
- building of endowment;
- physical facilities;
- student welfare, and especially financial aid;
- short- and long-term goals for the institution.

This list, by no means exhaustive, highlights the vital link between reporting to external authorities and maintaining internal institutional health. The maintenance of quality is best achieved through strategic planning that is active, implemented, and reviewed annually by the administration and board. If an institution does not monitor its ongoing health, it risks having problematic issues arise without warning.

Step Carefully When Necessary

The president needs to understand clearly that he or she is the chief spokesperson and protector of an institution and must be prepared to do all that is necessary to ensure the inherent autonomy and culture of a graduate academic institution. With most church agencies and accrediting agencies (but not all), the president serves the institution best by establishing a friendly, candid institutional relationship with the authorities of the agencies. The president should cultivate such relationships even when there is no "official business" to conduct.

In some instances, however, the president may need to step carefully, to respond courteously but in a circumspect way to inquiries. This can be a particularly sensitive issue in regard to accrediting or church agencies. In regard to accrediting agencies, it can happen that a visit takes on the appearance of a review of an institution by the inspectors general, thereby creating an atmosphere of defensiveness and occasional mistrust.

When a denomination treats its seminary or school of theology as an "owned" subsidiary corporation, claiming that it is not for the school to decide how it shall respond to inquiries or assessment, similar mistrust can emerge. Additionally, confusion can arise when divinity school trustees have *officially* divided loyalties: as an official of the institution *and* as a representative of the church. In this case, the president needs to educate the board to understand that the school has certain inherent rights and that full commitment to the institution is needed for the institution's well-being.

At root, the conflict is between legitimate concerns of the church and the need for a school to exercise the institutional integrity and autonomy proper to a graduate school. The president's task is to maintain a balanced tension and educate all parties about the role of a graduate school in both contexts of society and church.

Keep the Board Informed

Finally, the president should keep the chairperson and the executive committee of the board of trustees fully informed about how the relationship with external agencies is faring. The board of trustees is not in any sense an external agency. Indeed, it is the very foundation of an institution. No board reacts well to being surprised by a difficulty with a church, state licensing agency, or accrediting agency. Indeed, some board members may have contacts with officials in such agencies, in which case their assistance can be of inestimable help. In any case, the board members must be kept informed and their guidance sought in addressing a specific concern.

Church and Accrediting Agencies

Accountability to church agencies, judicatories, general conferences, and dioceses will vary from denomination to denomination. Some denominations have a separate authorization agency. In this case, a denominational seminary will relate to this agency on a regular and consistent basis, because it is a "way of life" for that denomination and its seminaries. The president will do well to stay informed on a range of denominational requirements and to respond promptly and carefully to periodic reviews or serious inquiries. It is especially important in relating to church agencies that trust and confidence be fostered. The president should spend significant time each year with the professional staffs of local, regional, and national denominational offices. In some denominations, annual gatherings of the seminary presidents are held. These become important opportunities for developing networks among colleagues and also for becoming aware of emerging trends and requirements.

When a seminary trains persons for another denomination, it needs to relate to that denomination's authorization agency. At a minimum, a president needs to be familiar with that denomination's guidelines and timelines. Clearly, churches and denominations have choices regarding the schools they will approve or encourage their ministerial candidates to attend. Moreover, the informal network of communication between and among denominations operates quite effectively. In every case of denominational review or inquiry, the response must be custom-tailored to the particular culture of that denomination and to the concerns of denominational officials.

The president needs to make sure that he or she, or a trusted and acceptable alternative member of the staff, represents the institution at key church conventions or assemblies where the school's name, program, or actions are likely to be discussed. Seek introductions to key officials to tell them of the institution's interest in having an open, cooperative relationship with the denomination. If warranted, invite denomination officials to visit the institution.

Reporting to Agencies and Academic Freedom

It can happen that a church or denomination is not sensitive to issues of academic freedom. Each school should have in writing its understanding of what academic freedom entails at that institution. When issues about curriculum or instruction arise, as they do now in more than a few denominations, the task for the president is both sensitive and diplomatic. The president has to attend both to the possibly bruised sensibilities of faculty and to the occasionally aggressive queries of a church or denomination. In all cases, the task is to bring light rather than heat. No faculty member should have to answer directly to a church agency, even though this practice exists. A faculty member is part of an academic collegium that ought to be characterized by processes for professional internal review, debate, and the exercise of due process to ensure faculty welfare. The task of the president is to remain in open communication with all parties and to insist that the school can best handle the issue within professional canons and institutional due process. Issues cannot be hurried, processes need to be observed, and equity must be served. Difficult as it may be, the president needs to be both guide and active mediator in this type of issue, and he or she must aid both faculty and church in coming to a reasonable and just adjudication of issues.

Working with Accrediting Agencies: Best Practices

Working with accrediting agencies is certainly one of the president's key roles. Tasks include decennial accreditation reviews, interim periodic review reports and visits, annual reports, and scheduled follow-up reports and/or visits stemming from specific agency requirements. Each is important and merits careful attention. A president needs to work on two levels: both fostering amicable relations and implementing written guidelines and regulations. In the case of seminaries and schools of theology, this also entails participating in annual or biennial meetings of the Association of Theological Schools and regional accrediting agencies, serving on committees and visiting teams as time and schedule permit, and observing within the institution the best practices recommended by the accrediting agencies.

The president should have a comprehensive understanding of the standards and regulations of the accrediting agencies of his or her institution. There are six regional accrediting agencies in the United States. Most accrediting agencies have published a number of helpful documents that need to be read and implemented. Observance of these published guidelines will usually assure smooth passage through accreditation visits and periodic reviews. The guidelines also provide excellent starting points for strategic planning and internal evaluation. They also cover the areas that most visiting teams will be reviewing when they engage in institutional assessment. The president's comprehension of the standards of the accrediting agencies will enable him or her to guide the institution in its satisfaction of those requirements.

Other Concerns: Legal Counsel and Auditors

Are there other agencies to which a school is individually accountable? A distinction must be made between official accountability, such as accountability to accrediting agencies, churches, and state licensing agencies, and the normal accountability that a school owes to interested constituencies such as alumni/ae, public supporters, and the general public. Two areas, however, do merit consideration: relations with legal counsel and accounting regulations. Both are increasingly important in institutional life and both merit special attention. The guidelines are simple: first, be sure that everything you say to counsel is true and presents a rounded, accurate picture, and second, be sure that the certified overview of financial records and transactions accurately reports actual operations. A host of negative experiences will be avoided when the president makes a professional commitment to candor in legal counseling and to accuracy in reporting finances. Understandably, the president may rightly require that confidential conversations remain private, but that is distinctly different from not being candid with legal counsel or certified auditors.

New presidents upon assuming office should schedule a meeting with legal counsel for the seminary. Legal counsel should *not* be a member of the seminary's board. Ask counsel to summarize legal issues or concerns that have been raised by the seminary in the past two years. In addition, ask counsel when best to consult with him or her and how such consultation can become part of the president's routine. A presi-

dent needs to talk to counsel about any matter that concerns employment, property, fiduciary responsibilities, rights of students, due process for faculty, trustee liability, and any issue that might result in
litigation.

Accuracy in reporting is necessary in regard to statements of financial position. Recently in North America there have been painful experiences of certified audits not accurately portraying the financial situation of a few large corporations. The same can and sometimes does
happen with institutions of higher education. This is a mistake. Negotiations can take place regarding what, in good practice, may be included
and released in financial information, but care must be taken that what
is released is a fair representation of the financial situation of the institution.

A new president should schedule a meeting with the firm that produces the seminary's audit and financial statements. Ask the auditor to
review the audited fiscal reports and management letter (with responses
from the seminary) for two prior fiscal years, and note any concerns the
auditor highlights. If an institution participates in federal loans, have
the auditor review the last two audits of the federal loan program. Next,
review the terms of the contract that the auditing firm has with the seminary and when the contract is subject to renewal. Finally, seek the auditor's opinion about the best practices for your business staff.

Conclusion

The presidential burden is, indeed, taxing. Experience teaches us that
observance of regulations is time consuming, demanding, and never
ending. Experience also teaches that it is to the distinct advantage of a
school and to the credit of the president when he or she pays careful attention to working cooperatively with external agencies. To fail to do so,
or to be careless in meeting deadlines, filing reports, and attending to issues, inevitably leads to tension and occasionally leads to an official
warning or institutional rebuke. No president wants to undergo such
professional disappointment, nor will a functioning board ignore it.

Additional Resources

The Association of Theological Schools of the United States and Canada (ATS)

ATS is very helpful in assisting schools to meet the Standards of Accreditation. Presidents will find both the staff and the available printed materials very helpful.

Guidelines for ministerial education

Churches or judicatories sometimes publish official guidelines for ministerial education, both ordained and non-ordained, such as the Roman Catholic *Program of Priestly Formation.*

Reference works for specific church bodies

Reference works such as *The Episcopal Church Annual* or the *Catholic Directory* can be very helpful. These volumes contain valuable information on the number of congregations, demographic distribution, as well as various institutional and congregational locations regionally and nationally.

Regional accrediting agencies

Most regional accrediting agencies have published helpful material on such issues as outcomes assessment or how to prepare a response to agency queries. They are frequently willing to provide professional staff assistance when requested.

The resources identified in this handbook are listed on the ATS Website where the list will continue to be updated as new resources become available: www.ats.edu > Leadership Education > Presidents.

CHAPTER 11

Personal and Professional Well-being
of a President

DONALD SENIOR, Chicago Theological Union
MAXINE BEACH, Drew Theological Seminary
BYRON KLAUS, Assemblies of God Theological Seminary

OVERVIEW

Introduction

The role of a seminary president can be demanding, and it takes its toll on the physical and spiritual well-being of the one who holds this public office. From the outset, for his or her own good as well as for the sake of the institution, the new president should be attentive to avoiding undue stress and to taking the necessary measures to ensure a healthy way of life. This is not just common sense but also a form of leadership by example. Faculty, staff, and students should be able to look to the president as an example of Christian leadership that can be dedicated and effective without being self-destructive.

Provide for Leisure Time

The role of the Sabbath in our Judeo Christian tradition reminds us that making a place for rest is integral to a physically and spiritually healthy life. Exodus 31:15 reminds us, "Six days shall work be done, but the seventh day is a Sabbath of solemn rest, holy to the Lord." The diffuse demands of the president's role can easily lead to long days and nights on the job. There are so many events, so many people to be met, so much paper work to be done, perhaps a lot of travel. No one is invincible, and a frenetic schedule will take its toll on a president's well-being and ultimately impact job performance and family life. Too many presidents of seminaries burn out prematurely and have to leave office because of the physical and emotional stresses of the job. It is important, both for the president and for the institution, that from the outset the president strives to lead a well-balanced life that makes room for rest and relaxation.

Everyone has his or her own way of relaxing, but common wisdom has reminded us of some constants. Work in some amount of physical exercise each day, whether this is a brief walk in a quiet spot or a regular visit to a gym or a quick swim. Often these moments apart also serve to calm one's nerves and to put difficult issues in perspective. For more extended times of leisure it is good to get away from the concerns of the president's office all together and to do something different. One president who grew up in a rural community found great satisfaction and refreshment in tending to his garden and growing his own vegetables at home. A game of golf or tennis — as long as it is not simply another venue for business — can also be restorative. So, too, are other pursuits: the opera, hobbies, etc. The key is to be determined not to let the job be all consuming and to find time for physically and spiritually refreshing diversions built into your schedule.

Regular vacations during which the president is able to get physically and mentally away from the job are also crucial. These should be built into the contract and taken seriously. The pressure of work to be done should not be used as an excuse to forgo vacation time. Remember that the president's job is not done in a day, and one has to pace one's energies for the long haul for the sake of the institution.

Nourish the Pastoral and Spiritual Dimensions of the President's Role

While the leader of a school of theology should make use of the best practices of good management developed in business and other professions, the spiritual dimension of the president's role should not be forgotten. First of all, the president should be attentive to his or her own spiritual life. Financial concerns, the stresses and strains of personnel issues, the fast pace of one's daily schedule — all of these administrative concerns can drown out or flatten the spiritual dimension of our lives. We should resolve to intensify our spiritual life in this role, giving time to prayer and devotions, recalling God's presence in our lives and in our decisions. While traditions differ in how one's Christian life is nourished, many presidents find it useful to schedule a few days each year for a spiritual retreat — time set aside for reflection, rest, and quiet prayer in a place of beauty conducive to the spiritual life. It is also helpful to have a trusted friend or mentor who can serve as a kind of "spiritual director" to whom one can entrust anxieties and cares and speak honestly about one's spiritual life.

The president or rector of a school of theology is also a spiritual and pastoral leader for the institution. While this role is conceived differently in various schools and traditions, all schools of theology look to the president as an exemplary Christian and a thoughtful leader whose values are consistent with the gospel. Many presidents who are ordained find it helpful to occasionally preach and lead worship in a parish or local congregation. Others who have a particular theological or professional background find it useful to lead workshops for pastors or programs in continuing education. These occasions help presidents of theological schools to keep in touch with the life of the church and remind them of their own calling as Christian leaders. International travel, especially to developing countries, is also very useful and salutary

— giving one an understanding of the global church, sharpening one's sense of economic justice, and providing a perspective on one's work of theological education for the sake of the whole church.

There are often occasions in the life of an institution when the president will be required to assume a particular pastoral role: a special anniversary, the death of a student or faculty member, a crisis in the collective life of the institution, a shattering world event such as the outbreak of the Iraq war. At moments like these it is often the president who guides the institution to respond in an appropriately Christian way. Being attentive on a daily basis to personal and professional spiritual responsibilities can better equip the president to be of pastoral service to the school community.

Find the Necessary Supports

Successful presidents understand the importance of finding support in others as the pressures of the job mount. Obviously the president should ensure that his or her key administrative colleagues and office support staff are competent and trustworthy. A style of administration that includes proper delegation is also crucial. The president cannot do it alone. Over time the new president will see opportunities to delegate some tasks and responsibilities to others within the institution. It is important to know when to "let go" of some tasks, rather than trying to keep control of everything. Presidents should also be self-conscious about their use of time. Time management is a personal matter that requires discovery of an individual style. If a new president is coming from a faculty role or from a more solo type of work, he or she may be initially overwhelmed by the multiple meetings, phone calls, e-mails, and complex issues that come tumbling into his or her daily schedule. The president has to give thought to how best to manage his or her time and how best to use the skills of the staff in organizing the day and sorting out the traffic that can come through the office. In other words, presidents should work smart — finding ways to delegate properly, looking out for more effective ways of managing time, and pacing the work of their office. These practices go a long way toward reducing stress and fostering well-being.

Finding some trustees or other sponsoring officials who can be discreet and trusted sounding boards when difficult issues arise is also an important source of support. In most cases this should be the chair of the board, but sometimes a president might have more personal rapport with another trustee to whom he or she can occasionally turn as a trusted friend and counselor. There can be no substitute for a friend outside of the institution from whom the president can count on receiving guidance and support, one who knows him or her well enough to be able to listen and, when necessary, to challenge him or her, and one who has nothing to gain from the friendship with a president. Such friends, who may be neither educators nor clergy, can tell the truth and give a realistic perspective about the president's concerns.

Another helpful source of support is the experience of peers from other institutions. Many presidents testify that talking with a fellow president from another school can be a great source of comfort and wisdom. A president who may feel beleaguered by financial pressures or discouraged by an antagonistic faculty or staff member can find real relief in learning that many other presidents face the same problems and, in some instances, have found ways to alleviate them. This, in fact, is one of the advantages of taking time to attend programs sponsored by the Association of Theological Schools (ATS) or by other professional societies. Besides the benefits of getting away from the campus for a few days and having the stimulant of hearing new ideas, attending these meetings also brings one into contact with peers who can be a genuine source of wisdom and support. And one need not feel obligated to participate in every session or event. Here, too, is potential time for rest and reflection mingled with opportunities to learn and interact.

Personal Ethics and Boundaries

Presidents are not guaranteed sainthood in assuming their office. They are just as human and frail as they were before becoming president of a school of theology. Yet the public nature of the president's role and its impact on the tone and spirit of the seminary require that the president more than ever before lead a life of integrity and virtue. This renewed commitment to Christian discipleship should also be evident in the virtues of truthfulness, compassion, a sense of justice and fairness, and a spirit of hope that the president brings to his or her leadership of the seminary. The legitimate expectations of the seminary community that their president will be a person of faith and lead a life of virtue can be a stimulus to renewing one's spiritual life and to asking God for the grace to live up to these new responsibilities.

While seeking the support of colleagues and friends is essential, as mentioned above, the president must also be aware of possible pitfalls and maintain proper professional boundaries in dealing with others. The position of president holds power within an institution, however small the school may be. There may be individuals who give great attention to the president because of this power and position, and that can be flattering to one's ego and sense of worth. It is possible to maintain a productive working relationship with such individuals, but in some instances this situation could also be full of danger. Other factors can also bear risks: the isolation of the president's role can lead to feelings of loneliness and being cut off from others in the organization; fatigue or stress can weaken one's good judgment. Many people will not want to say no to the president; maintaining proper personal and professional boundaries helps reassure a president's colleagues that he or she is trustworthy. The president, as a responsible leader and as a Christian, will want to be alert to situations where professional and spiritual intimacy could stray into an inappropriate relationship. The relationship of an employee with the president of the institution is never equal, and it is the responsibility of the president to maintain the proper spiritual discipline in such situations and to prevent them from becoming a personal and professional disaster.

While maintaining professional boundaries with staff and conducting oneself in a mature and honorable manner have always been an expectation of the president of a school of theology, the present climate, in which so many instances of harassment and abuse have commanded the headlines, should make a Christian leader all the more alert to this issue. Here reducing stress, maintaining good health, and pursuing a vigorous spiritual life combine to help the president avoid the pitfalls of ignoring professional boundaries and exploiting relationships with others.

Family and Spouse

A president with a family obviously does not come alone to this responsibility. The role of the president is too difficult to take up without the support of his or her spouse and family. The decision to uproot from familiar surroundings and move to a new location is a cause of stress on any family, particularly on adolescent children. One's spouse and family have to be part of the decision to accept this role.

It is important to understand the expectations of the board and the seminary community about the role of the president's spouse and family in seminary life. Also important are the living arrangements for the president and his or her family. While these expectations may be unwritten, they are still very real. If those expectations are incompatible with the convictions of the president's family, then there should be clear negotiations about the possibility of changing expectations. No doubt the spouse of a president should find some "niche" in the life of the seminary where he or she can make some contribution and have appropriate connection to the life of the school. Regardless of the spouse's own professional career, the realities of the seminary presidency usually involve some visibility for the president's spouse and, to some extent, the family as well. The key is finding the right level of involvement that is compatible with the commitments and desires of one's spouse and with the reasonable expectations of the president's public role in the community. To ignore these issues in the beginning is to invite tensions and difficulties over time.

In many respects the life of the president can be a solitary one. The president and spouse will have few peers on campus who will understand exactly what the pressures of the presidency may be. The president often has information about the institution or personnel that cannot be shared with others. Or the president may have opinions about individuals or situations that it would be inappropriate to express in front of others in the institution. Relationships with staff and faculty cannot become too familiar. To help offset such isolation, various denominational caucuses within ATS provide a place for peer support for both president and spouse (e.g., the Fellowship of Evangelical Seminary Presidents). ATS also provides programs for new presidents and other opportunities for professional development. These programs can be a source of information, inspiration, and personal support for a president and his or her spouse.

Contract

Obviously many elements go into a proper contract between the new president and the institution: fair compensation, adequate benefits, housing, length of service, lines of accountability, and so on. Each institution has its own way of drawing up contracts. Presidents should not be passive or hesitant about asserting their value to the organization at the times of contract renewal, or else they risk having a bad contract, which in turn can lead to feelings of hostility and victimization. ATS has data that can help a board and president calculate fair compensation. The attention to one's personal and professional well-being discussed above underscores some elements that can be overlooked in forming the contract or work agreement between a president and the seminary. The contract should include a satisfactory amount of vacation time, and perhaps also, as some have done, a designated amount of time for spiritual renewal such as some days for retreat. Some contracts have included membership in a local health club as part of the compensation. The contract might also include opportunities for attending professional meetings and participating in professional development programs for presidents. While the expected role of one's spouse and family may not be spelled out in the contract, the contract negotiations are an opportune time to discuss this issue.

The time of renewing the contract can also be an opportunity for the president to invite feedback from trustees and others in the institution about the quality of his or her work and relationships within the seminary community. Some have established a special committee on the board that periodically confers with the president about his or her well-being. The renewal of the contract can be a good occasion for this committee to swing into action. The contract renewal is also an appropriate time to set new goals for the president in conjunction with the board or church body.

Leaving the Presidency

For new presidents just entering their role, it may seem premature (or ominous) to discuss leaving the presidency! But even if the completion of one's service as president may be years away, there is merit in thinking about it from time to time at the outset of one's presidency. Awareness that one "holds" an office rather than "owning" it can be salutary. Some seminaries have set terms of office for the president; others may have the president serve indefinitely at the will of the board; but in every case the term of the president is finite. At some point, God willing, the president will leave office and turn to another task or ministry: teaching, pastoring, consulting, or just enjoying a leisurely retirement.

The sure prospect of eventually leaving the office can give the president what the ancient spiritual writers called a sense of "detachment" — that is, the healthy realization that one is not irreplaceable or invincible. Presidents are called to serve for a time and should give their full commitment to doing so. But, at the same time, they do not have an exaggerated sense of their own importance that could lead to arrogance or an exaggerated anxiety from a fear of failing. One long-term president refrained from putting too many personal mementoes in his official office to remind himself that the office belonged to the seminary and not to him. Such an attitude can help prevent one from being "wedded" to the job — leaving time and space for one's spiritual life and for taking care of one's health. It can also help the president be aware that many others in the institution are also important to its ongoing success. Paradoxically, having a sense of the transitory nature of the job can help a president be more committed to it and more effective in carrying out its responsibilities.

Additional Resources

Bakken, Kenneth L. *The Call to Wholeness: Health as a Spiritual Journey.* New York: Crossroad, 1985.

All persons are in need of healing in every aspect of life. The author, a physician specializing in preventive medicine, integrates learning from both science and religion to present a holistic approach to well-being that is rooted in an understanding of Christian principles.

Bass, Dorothy C. *Receiving the Day: Christian Practices for Opening the Gift of Time.* San Francisco: Jossey-Bass, 2000.

Time management is more than scheduling. In this book on the spirituality of time, the author invites readers into a way of living that is both alert to contemporary pressures and rooted in ancient wisdom. She identifies specific practices for ordering the day, the week, the year, and the lifetime — practices that enable us to live more richly and rightly in time.

Cicero, Marcus Tullius. "Laelius: On Friendship." In *The Good Life*. Translated by Michael Grant. Penguin Classics Series. Harmondsworth: Penguin, 1971.

Cicero's treatise on friendship is worth returning to from time to time.

Daugherty, Rose Mary. *Group Spiritual Direction as Support for Ministry*. New York: Paulist Press, 1995.

A helpful guide to spiritual direction in a group setting, Daugherty's book can be applied to many situations in which people wish to deepen their sense of God's presence in their workplace.

Jones, Kirk Byron. *Rest in the Storm: Self-Care for Clergy and Other Caregivers*. Valley Forge, PA: Judson Press, 2001.

Jones's book contains practical advice on ministry and spiritual questions for more effective leadership.

Kisly, Lorraine, ed. *Ordinary Graces: Christian Teachings on the Interior Life*. New York: Bell Tower, 2000.

This is a good desktop volume for dipping into from time to time. One Jesuit commentator put it: "this book is 'spiritual reading' in the old fashioned sense of the term."

Larsen, Bruce. *There Is More to Health than Not Being Sick*. Waco: Word Books, 1981.

The intent of the book is to give hope about oneself and one's physical well-being. It explores spiritual healing that is both biblically based and clinically sound.

Moore, Thomas. *Care of the Soul: A Guide for Cultivating Depth and Sacredness in Everyday Life*. New York: Harper Perennial, 1994.

Moore is a psychotherapist whose Christian faith informs his wide notion of spiritual attitudes.

Muller, Wayne. *Sabbath: Finding Rest, Renewal, and Delight in Our Busy Lives*. New York: Bantam Books, 2000.

Muller's book is a useful resource for theological practice and reflection. This highly engaging book is a best-seller on the more popular reading charts.

Muto, Susan, and Adrian Van Kaam. *Growing through the Stress of Ministry*. Totowa, NJ: Resurrection Press, 2005.

Co-founders of the Epiphany Association, which assists clergy, religious, and lay persons in deepening the life of the spirit, Muto and Van Kaam offer helpful strategies for moving *through* stress rather than trying to go *around* it.

Oswald, Roy. *Clergy Self-Care.* Washington: Alban Institute, 1991.

A practical volume written by a seasoned church consultant that contains nuggets of wisdom for leaders at every stage and in every setting of ministry.

Rolheiser, Ronald, O.M.I. *The Holy Longing: The Search for a Christian Spirituality.* New York: Doubleday, 1999.

The book is accessible but not squishy, learned but not supercilious.

The resources identified in this handbook are listed on the ATS Website where the list will continue to be updated as new resources become available: www.ats.edu > Leadership Education > Presidents.

CHAPTER 12

The President's Role as Symbolic, Culture-forming Leader

RICHARD J. MOUW, Fuller Theological Seminary
WILLIAM McKINNEY, Pacific School of Religion
BRIAN STILLER, Tyndale University College and Seminary

Donors

Church Leaders

Nurturing "Inner" Resources

Additional Resources

The Core Task

When Derek Bok announced that he was stepping down as Harvard's president in 1990, he remarked that he would have some strong advice for his successor. University presidencies have gotten very complicated in the last few decades, Bok observed, and the danger is that presidents will become exclusively managers and disconnected from the center of the institution, which is, of course, intellectual education and research. Bok said he would highlight this danger by advising his successor that he would not be able to keep this from happening unless he was aware of the problem from the very beginning. "You are going to have to be much more creative in keeping it from occurring than I was," he said. A university president, Bok insisted, must observe very carefully what is happening in the minds of other people and what is happening intellectually in order to see how the university can pick and choose among new opportunities thrown up by changes in each of these areas.

While presidents of theological schools obviously face some different challenges than the presidents of large universities, leaders in theological education do well to heed Bok's general advice. If anything, the danger he points to is increased when the management of the practical dimensions of congregational and denominational relations are added to the mix. In all of this, a seminary president must be intentional about maintaining a focus on the overall mission of theological education. "Intellectual education and research" — which Bok rightly notes are at the center of what any institution of higher education is about — will surely take on a different tone in a theological school than in other academic contexts. But however we may spell out the aims and purposes of theological education in our diverse seminary settings, scholarly reflection that nurtures vital teaching and learning is essential to the theological school's mission.

In a talk he has often given to new Association of Theological Schools (ATS) presidents, Robert Cooley identifies several "burdens" of presidential leadership, including "the burden of accumulated griev-ances." In stepping into the presidential role, Cooley observes, a leader immediately becomes the symbolic bearer of various institutional sins — even some sins about which he or she may be completely unaware. This is a poignant example of the symbolic dimension of presidential leadership, but that dimension also includes many positive things, not the least being the way in which the president is the symbolic bearer of the school's mission. The presidency brings with it an unavoidable obligation to represent in a special way in words and deeds, not only the basic aims and purposes of the seminary, but — even more — its highest aspirations.

Naming and Shaping "the Main Thing"

Not all presidents will fulfill this obligation in the same way. Seminary communities — more so than many other kinds of academic institutions — draw upon various spheres of expertise in choosing their leaders. Some come from the faculty ranks and others from pastoral and denom-inational leadership contexts. Still others are recruited from parachurch ministries or from various segments of public life. There is no one-size-fits-all formula for exercising missional leadership in theological educa-tion, but this much is clear: that kind of leadership must be exercised. Some presidents will do so out of a long history of academic involve-ment. Others will bring gifts that come from experience in other fields of leadership. Whatever the background, a seminary president must at the very least *see to it* that all who have a vested interest in the success of the theological school are regularly reminded of — and inspired to maintain their commitment to — "the main thing" in theological education.

Indeed, it often falls to a person stepping into the presidential role to sharpen the school's focus, articulating in fresh ways matters that may have been taken for granted by a previous leader — and thus may have been obscured in the minds of many others. Nor is this sharpen-ing/articulating role merely a matter of helping the seminary commu-nity better *understand* what it is doing. The president is not merely a symbol and a clarifier of the institutional mission; he or she is also re-sponsible for actively shaping an organizational culture that is appro-priate for the carrying out of the school's mission. A seminary can have a clear understanding of its mission but be poorly served by its communal culture — that is, by the way it organizes in the light of an explicit understanding of its core tasks and its life together — as it faces those internal and external obstacles and opportunities that have a direct impact on the effective pursuit of its mission. It is the centrality of this culture-shaping role that Edgar Schein highlights when he observes that "the only thing of real importance that leaders do is to create and manage culture."[1]

The Presidency as Teaching Ministry

As Neely McCarter has stressed in his important book on the seminary presidency, the office brings with it an important and unique *teaching* ministry.[2] It is as a teacher that the president not only functions as a symbol of the school's mission but also takes responsibility for the shaping and proper pursuit *of* that mission. Furthermore, to use an old distinction, the president teaches both *ad intra* and *ad extra:* the president teaches both to the inside and to the outside of the seminary community. The "internal" audience is rather easy to define; it includes all of those who are directly involved in the life of the seminary community. The "external" audience is the more difficult to delineate. We will look at the *extra* audience first, then the *intra*. Lastly, we will conclude with a brief word of encouragement to make room for the necessary "inner" preparation for these roles.

Teaching Outside the Seminary

Presidential leadership should not only focus on the cultural formation of the internal life of the seminary community but must also be directed toward the ways in which other communities understand and shape the patterns of their lives together. Obviously, seminaries must care deeply about the cultural patterns of the churches they serve. Because churches

1. Edgar Schein, *Organizational Culture and Leadership,* 3d ed. (San Francisco: Jossey-Bass, 2004), p. 2.

2. Neely McCarter, *The President as Educator: A Study of the Seminary Presidency* (Atlanta: Scholars Press, 1996).

themselves have a mission to the larger human community, the cultural-formation concerns of a seminary leader must have a broad scope.

Presence in the Community

The record of theological schools in fulfilling their external teaching role has not been an outstanding one. In 1998, researchers at the Auburn Center for the Study of Theological Education visited four U.S. cities and interviewed leaders in various sectors of public life about their views of religious leaders and their education.[3] Their conclusion was stark: "Seminaries are virtually invisible to leaders of secular organizations and institutions, even those in the seminary's own region." Seminaries are known to religious leaders of their own traditions and to some large and nearby congregations, but they are rarely seen as civic or educational assets. And seminary leaders are as invisible as the schools they serve.

There were exceptions, of course: African American seminary presidents tended to be known in the black community, and liberal rabbis were said to be visible on social issues. But generally speaking, seminaries and clergy were seen as not being present at the tables that count.

That presence is missed by many secular leaders. Some of those interviewed wished that religious leaders would speak out on controversial issues or sponsor social programs once run by governments. Even more expressed the desire that religious leaders would at least "raise the moral tone, not by advocating for a specific kind of morality, but by remind[ing] us of the 'tough questions.'"[4]

Barriers to and Avenues for the Public Role

Why is the public teaching role of seminaries and their presidents — the larger task of cultural formation, namely shaping the patterns by which human beings organize their collective existence — not more evident

---

3. Elizabeth Lynn and Barbara G. Wheeler, *Missing Connections: Public Perceptions of Theological Education and Religious Leadership* (New York: Auburn Theological Seminary, 1999).

4. Lynn and Wheeler, *Missing Connections*, p. 9.

than it is? The answers are complex. Most seminaries are small, even tiny, institutions and their presidents are pulled in many directions. The central activity of many schools is the preparation of persons for ministry in particular denominational traditions — churches whose members and leaders are not all of one mind on public issues. A visible public role on social issues can risk alienating large portions of the president's key constituencies.

Other schools, by contrast, have a long history of engagement with social issues. Some seminaries have played highly visible roles in the Social Gospel movement of the early twentieth century, providing both support for and opposition to World War II and the Vietnam conflict, and promoting racial justice, gender equality, and the gay rights movements. It is important to attend to the theological basis for these activisms.

Often, the most significant role of the seminary president is to provide encouragement and support for faculty and students as they express their social convictions. Occasionally, however, presidents themselves are in a position to take direct action in support of a particular cause, either as educators or as advocates. Some care must be taken, however. New presidents sometimes struggle to recognize that their voice often carries more weight than they were accustomed to in previous roles. Casual observations are sometimes read as proclamations from on high: "Well, I heard the president of the seminary say. . . ."

How can a theological school president exercise the teaching office beyond the walls of the seminary campus? It is important, first, to root such a public role in the mission of the school itself. This can take time in a seminary that has not expected such activity from its presidents. As Christians and as citizens, presidents have the right to speak out on social issues as individuals; doing so *as president* requires trust that comes only from years of building relationships with the board, faculty, staff, and others.

For schools that claim a role in public life, the role of the communications officer is very important. For example, at one seminary the communications director schedules a luncheon on campus with every new religion reporter in its metropolitan area. The school wants to connect people in the media with the president and faculty who are willing to respond quickly to reporters' requests. The communications director is also responsible for helping school representatives prepare for interviews.

Seminaries can sometimes take the initiative when an issue is coming to public attention. Pacific School of Religion, a seminary that is open in its commitment to the full inclusion of gay and lesbian persons in the life of the church, has been very proactive as issues facing the LGBT (Lesbian, Gay, Bisexual, Transgender) community have arisen, using op-ed articles in the local and national press, a Website on gay marriage, and press releases on ministry issues. Some evangelical seminaries, on the other hand, have taken the lead in supporting the traditional idea of marriage and the rights of the unborn.

Presidents and seminary leaders are often in a position to play a convening and educational role on controversial public issues. In the days after September 11, 2001, many seminaries sponsored special events for area clergy and civic leaders to assist in helping communities deal with the trauma of the 9/11 events. Audio versions of the seminary events available on the World Wide Web were useful to hundreds of clergy across the country. Schools often have teaching resources that are welcome and needed at times when the public is wrestling with difficult issues. One of the roles of a president is to find ways to make these resources more broadly available without placing undue burdens on the faculty.

Presidents sometimes underestimate the readiness of public audiences for serious theological engagement. Our media culture may tempt us to think that the public is unwilling or unable to handle more than sound bites, but folks in churches expect seminary presidents to have something significant to say on the issues of the day and to connect those issues to Scripture and tradition (and vice versa).

Teaching Inside the Seminary

In recognizing the need to address the theological school's larger public constituencies, we are acknowledging that the presidency serves as a platform from which to engage in a teaching mission about some of the key issues of the day — and again, that is a crucial mission. Presidents often are tempted to shy away from taking on controversial social topics — and they worry about faculty members who are inclined to do so. That nervousness is understandable, but it must not stand in the way of seriously engaging the agenda of the larger culture. As the Lilly Endowment's Craig Dykstra has often observed, theological schools will be clear about their mission if they can stay focused on these three questions: What is God doing in the world? How can the Christian community be aligned effectively with what God is doing in the world? And how can theological schools best equip the Christian community to be aligned with what God is doing in the world?

Addressing the Larger Issues

Thinking about the purposes of God in the larger creation and the issues that must be addressed there from our specific faith perspectives is no mere side issue in theological education. It is at the heart of our mission. Keeping the questions before the school is a primary obligation of the presidency. This means that the president must demonstrate an interest in, and a commitment to, that larger agenda by addressing the "big" cultural issues as well as by encouraging others in the seminary community to do so.

There is, of course, a necessary link between "external" and "internal" leadership. A president who energetically takes on the larger issues of church, academy, and society cannot be effective if he or she fails to establish a strong leadership role within the seminary community itself. The presidential teaching role must also be directed toward all who participate significantly in the carrying out of that mission: students, faculty, staff, the administrative team, trustees, and close friends and supporters of the school.

This teaching ministry can be carried out in many ways, but the ceremonial events are one fundamental opportunity for exercising presidential leadership. In their book-length study of academic leadership, Michael D. Cohen and James G. March make a rather cynical comment about the ceremonial addresses delivered by presidents. "Almost any educated person," they observe, "can deliver a lecture entitled 'The Goals of the University,'" but there are very few people who will voluntarily sit through that kind of lecture. This is so, they judge, because, "for the most part, such lectures and their companion essays are well-intentioned exercises in social rhetoric, with little operational content."[5]

We can hope that in the case of seminary leaders the "for the most

---

5. Michael D. Cohen and James G. March, *Leadership and Ambiguity: The American College President* (New York: McGraw-Hill Company, 1974), p. 195.

part" clause is an understatement. The kind of people who study, teach, administer, and support theological schools bring religious commitments to their institutional involvement that are often absent in other academic settings. This is true to the degree that such people actually look at the ceremonial events, where an account is provided of "the State of the Mission," as occasions to be inspired and reinforced in their dedication to the school's mission.

Internal Audiences

The seminary president has a unique opportunity to use many different occasions to articulate a vision for the school's mission, as well as to point to dimensions of that mission that need special emphasis. A piece of advice from Max De Pree serves as an important axiom for such occasions: keep articulating the vision; if you think you are being too repetitious, this means that you probably have it about right.

Students

Students may never take a course from the president, but they rely on the presidential vision to shape the nature of their studies and to provide them assurance that the education they receive both is valuable to them in their career and will carry with it a reputation that will act as valuable currency in their careers and personal life.

Faculty Members

Even if they have a love/hate relationship with their president, faculty members are the essential carriers of the vision, as it transplants its life into the hearts and minds of its students. They — especially younger faculty — need to hear the president's vision, including strong words of support for their central role in the seminary's mission.

Staff and Administrators

The staff and administrators provide the operational infrastructure of the school. They, too, need to be assured of their crucial role in the mission; if there is no strategic planning, or if the phones are not answered, or if the heating/air conditioning does not work, the mission will fail. These people need to know of the president's gratitude for their work, and they need to see the president as someone worthy of their trust.

Potential Students

Potential students are looking for a place in which they will be well trained. Even when the school has already been described by faculty, alumni, current students, and friends, it is often the president who becomes the symbol of the seminary. Students looking to invest time and money in their education will want the president's goals to match their own.

Alumni/ae

Graduates of the school will want the primary symbol of their alma mater to represent what they hope others will see as being of substance. They will draw on the strengths of their seminary's reputation. They need to be aware of, and instructed by, the president's vision.

Trustees

Trustees directly supervise the work of the president, but they are also — in an important sense — "students" of the president. Trustees typically come to their work with a desire to be educated and inspired. They, too, must draw strength in their commitment from the articulation of the seminary's mission.

Donors

Donors need more than the development staff for nurture. Some in particular need very personal attention from the president, but all donors need to be educated and inspired by the presidential vision.

Church Leaders

Church leaders will relate to different seminaries in different ways. However that relationship is structured, the relevant church leaders must be kept current about the seminary's mission. The benefits here are bi-directional: while church leaders need to be reminded of the importance of seminary education, they also need to provide necessary feedback to the seminary regarding the ways in which the mission of theological education can better serve the church's mission.

Nurturing "Inner" Resources

It should go without saying that practicing the spiritual disciplines is a non-negotiable activity for seminary leaders. A healthy spiritual life is essential to effective leadership. In the light of what we have said here, however, we must emphasize the fact that cultivating and nurturing the inner resources for leadership also requires time set aside for *thinking* — for reading important materials about issues in church, academy, and the larger culture and reflecting on these matters in depth.

In addition, these times "apart" — for practicing the spiritual disciplines and for feeding the mind — must be *scheduled*. They will not happen unless they are made a part of the normal rhythms of the presidency. Nor are they to be thought of as "off-duty" activities — as if they are to be taken out of the time devoted to recreation, family relations, and friendships. They are to be considered as a part of the regular "work" of the presidency — an expectation that must be clarified in explicit terms with trustees and office staff. The duties described in this chapter deal with issues that are crucial, not only for the success of an individual presidency, but for the health of the larger mission of theological education.

Additional Resources

Cohen, Michael D., and James G. March. *Leadership and Ambiguity: The American College President.* New York: McGraw-Hill Book Company, 1974.
This book is a classic study of the life of a college or university president. Presidents of seminaries will understand and appreciate the insights in this work.

De Pree, Max. *Leadership Is an Art.* New York: Dell, 1989; and *Leadership Jazz.* New York: Dell, 1993.

These short and readable books by Christian businessman and long-time seminary trustee Max De Pree give a refreshing perspective on leadership for seminary presidents who need to lead decisively but without heavy control.

Lynn, Elizabeth, and Barbara G. Wheeler. *Missing Connections: Public Perceptions of Theological Education and Religious Leadership.* New York: Auburn Theological Seminary, 1999.

This study sought to learn what the public knows and thinks about theological education. The authors report on the near invisibility of seminaries in the civic and public arenas.

McCarter, Neely. *The President as Educator: A Study of the Seminary Presidency.* Atlanta: Scholars Press, 1996.

Based on a three-year study, this book traces the background of the office of president and looks at the chief dimensions of a president's work today.

Schein, Edgar. *Organizational Culture and Leadership.* 3rd edition. San Francisco: Jossey-Bass, 2004.

In this third edition of his classic book, Schein shows how to transform the abstract concept of culture into a practical tool that leaders can use to understand the dynamics of organizations and change.

The resources identified in this handbook are listed on the ATS Website where the list will continue to be updated as new resources become available: www.ats.edu > Leadership Education > Presidents.

CHAPTER 13

The Unique Issues for Racial/Ethnic Presidents

EDWARD WHEELER, Christian Theological Seminary
MICHAEL BATTLE, Interdenominational Theological Center
DAVID MALDONADO, Iliff School of Theology

Where Can One Find Resources to Support Racial/Ethnic Institutions?

How Does One Assess a School's Commitment to Racial/Ethnic Inclusiveness?

How Can One Avoid Making Race the Issue When It Is Not *the* Issue?

Supports and Resources for Racial/Ethnic Presidents

Additional Resources

The Purpose of This Chapter

This chapter is intended to identify and discuss some of the issues that are unique to a person who becomes the president of a theological seminary and who identifies himself or herself as a racial/ethnic person. This chapter seeks to complement the other content of this handbook. Most of what a racial/ethnic president will encounter will mirror what any other president will face or has faced. Therefore, it is important that a racial/ethnic president also be familiar with the other essays in this handbook.

This chapter is important for the racial/ethnic person who assumes the presidency because in the United States (and to a lesser degree in Canada) race has been and still is important. While it is our sincere hope and belief that racism is not as pronounced or as acceptable as it has been in the past, racism is still alive and well and all of us in this culture have been affected by it. Thinking along racial lines is a fundamental aspect of American culture, and few have successfully moved beyond that, even if they have come to value diversity and racial inclusiveness. Therefore, a president who is racial/ethnic must come to grips with what it means to be a racial/ethnic president in the context in which he or she serves.

There are two very different but equally important contexts in which these presidents operate: institutions that have been and are predominantly racial/ethnic, and institutions that are and have been predominantly European American (white). This chapter attempts to identify distinctions in the way a racial/ethnic person might operate in these two contexts even as the chapter provides some more general observations that are applicable to both contexts.

The Role and Responsibility
of a Racial/Ethnic President

Expectations Related to Racial/Ethnic Communities

The role and responsibility of a racial/ethnic president is complicated by the culturally influenced expectations that exist, whether or not they are articulated. Some of these expectations result from lack of awareness of the nature of racial/ethnic communities; others are rooted in the history of racial/ethnic communities. A theological seminary, for example, may select a Spanish-speaking (Latina/Hispanic) president who identifies herself as Puerto Rican with the expectation that she will help recruit Latino/Latina students from a largely Mexican population base. What the search committee may not appreciate is the fact that there is tremendous diversity within the Hispanic Latino/a community and that one cultural perspective does not always relate well to another.

In the African American community, the church has historically been the center of the community's life. Therefore, the community has often seen the role of the pastor as the highest call/vocation available to human beings. Though tempted by call and tradition, an African American president must be careful not to see himself or herself as the "pastor" of the seminary. While there are some aspects of the presidency that correspond to the role of the pastor, the two roles are not the same, and an African American president must realize that fact early in his or her tenure or that tenure may not last long. One important difference between the roles of pastor and of seminary president is that African American pastors have far more autonomy and independent authority than most seminary presidents. Shared authority is the norm in most seminaries. The president who ignores this reality will find his or her presidency to be an uncomfortable experience.

Preaching and Community Involvement

Another expectation relates to preaching. While the expectation that the president of a theological seminary should be a good preacher is not exclusive to racial/ethnic communities, it is almost a requirement in the African American community. Preaching is the primary way a racial/

ethnic president relates to and connects with the African American community. A good preacher can earn the respect of the African American community and thereby open up other opportunities for building strong cooperative relationships between the church and the seminary. This can also be problematic, however. A good preacher must work at balancing the expectation of the community that he or she will be available to preach on a regular basis with the institution's expectation that the president's schedule will be more flexible to accommodate its needs. One thing is clear: any racial/ethnic president who tries to fill both expectations and is guilty of working seven days a week on a regular basis to accomplish them will end up not doing either task well.

In addition to preaching, the racial/ethnic president is likely to face requests to serve on several external boards, committees, commissions, and other community organizations in the local ethnic community, in the denomination, or within the broader theological network. The racial/ethnic president must be careful to find the balance between these external activities (which may be beneficial to the seminary in many ways) and the internal responsibilities that come with leading a theological school.

Maintaining the Tradition while Embracing a Future of Change

In a predominantly or historically racial/ethnic theological seminary, the racial/ethnic president may feel a natural kinship to the community (especially if the president and the institution share a common racial/ethnic identity). Nevertheless, the president has the role and responsibility, which may go unspoken, of remaining loyal to and protective of the institutional history and heritage while at the same time moving the institution into a more open and inclusive future.

Major Issues Facing Racial/Ethnic Presidents

Beyond the role and responsibilities of any seminary president, the racial/ethnic president must be aware of a multitude of issues that are in some ways unique. Understanding these issues and finding ways to address them will strengthen his or her presidency. Some of these issues are more prominent when a European American or white institution selects a racial/ethnic person as president, especially if the person selected is the first racial/ethnic president in the history of the institution.

Recognizing the "Cloud of Suspicion"

Because racism and white privilege are often institutionalized, the racial/ethnic president must often overcome the unspoken perception among faculty and staff (if not trustees) that he or she was selected for reasons other than his or her skills and competencies. While all presidents must earn the trust of the communities they are to serve, the racial/ethnic president of a predominantly white school often enters the office under a "cloud of suspicion." This "cloud" may include questions about the selection process, about the person's ability to lead a "white" institution without making it a "racial/ethnic" institution, about the person's commitment to maintaining "excellence," and even about the appropriateness of the theological fit. The inherent presumption that the standard for excellence is white and male means that the racial/ethnic president must constantly prove to the Euro-American/white community that he or she belongs in this role.

Church historian Justo Gonzalez observes that a far more subtle but no less deadly and hidden racism surreptitiously suggests that the new racial/ethnic president should be grateful for his or her appointment to a white institution and should therefore be more malleable than a Euro-American president. The racial/ethnic president of a predominantly white institution may even find resistance from whites who have been leaders in the fight against racism but who may unconsciously resent giving up that leadership to a racial/ethnic president.

Carrying the Community's Hopes and Aspirations

Another closely related issue is the fact that the racial/ethnic president carries the hopes and aspirations of the racial/ethnic community. When a racial/ethnic person is selected to lead a predominantly and historically white institution, the racial/ethnic community often sees this as a triumph for that community and a tangible sign of progress. Because of the community's vested interest in the racial/ethnic president, however, that community can have unrealistic expectations as to what the president can do. Furthermore, because the racial/ethnic community places so many of its hopes and dreams on the success of the racial/ethnic president, the president often lives with the added burden of "carrying the race on his or her shoulders."

Furthermore, the racial/ethnic president must be aware of the history of relations between the institution he or she leads and the racial/ethnic community. This is important because both the institution and the community may think that the racial/ethnic person should bridge whatever gaps exist between the two and reconcile any continuing tensions. While this is an unrealistic expectation, the racial/ethnic president must be aware of past history and tensions.

Handling Personnel Matters

Personnel matters are a major concern for every president. The racial/ethnic president at a largely white institution is likely to find personnel matters complicated by the fact that racial/ethnic personnel may assume that a president who looks like them and has an appreciation for the cultural dynamics of the racial/ethnic community will automatically be more understanding and perhaps more lenient in handling their particular situations.

While the president may indeed bring a different perspective and, it is hoped, would respect the dignity of every person serving the seminary, it is crucial that the racial/ethnic president avoid handling personnel matters in a personal way. The president must be sure that an adequate process for handling personnel matters is in place and that the process is followed whenever personnel matters arise. Such processes may make the president the final arbiter of personnel matters but only after a rather extensive process of checks and balances has been completed. Following the process closely will lessen the likelihood that there will be legal grounds to challenge personnel decisions and will keep the president from becoming the focus of matters related to personnel that should be determined at other levels of the institution.

The racial/ethnic president needs to be prepared for the possibility that racial/ethnic employees and/or students will not appreciate what may appear to them as the president's "hands off" approach — or, at worst, the president's unwillingness to "stand up" for racial/ethnic personnel. Nevertheless, the personal and institutional toll for the racial/ethnic president (or any president) acting outside the rules and regulations of the institution are far greater than the personal snubs or misrepresentations that might arise.

Overcoming the Stereotype of Being "Second Class"

While the racial/ethnic president of a racial/ethnic institution may not have to deal with such issues as the presumption of inferiority or the "cloud of suspicion" based on race, he or she may have to contend with a history of isolation and the presumption that the institution itself is "second class" because it is racial/ethnic. The historical beginnings of most racial/ethnic theological seminaries are tied to a history of racism and segregation that did not allow people of color (especially African Americans) the opportunity to enroll in predominantly white schools. Even those institutions that prior to the 1960s accepted African Americans into their graduate programs in religion had quotas that limited acceptance of racial/ethnic students to two or three per year. The historically African American theological schools emerged in this context, and they still feel the need to prepare their graduates for leadership of historically marginalized communities. In some ways, the desire of some Asian communities to develop their own theological institutions parallels the development of African American seminaries.

Despite the historical reasons for the development of racial/ethnic institutions, racial/ethnic presidents of these institutions must now overcome the isolation of the past. These presidents must also overcome the racial stigma that these institutions are inherently inferior, even among the partners that make up theological consortia in some areas of the country. In the words of one African American leader, "Why is it that a white school close to our institution would not allow its students to take a course at our school offered by an outstanding professor while he was at our institution? However, when they were able to lure him away from us with a much more lucrative contract, all of a sudden he was good enough to teach their students the same courses for credit."

Racial/ethnic presidents are forced to deal with these realities even as they must do all the other things needed to maintain an institution.

Creating a Culture of Inclusion and Diversity

One last issue for the racial/ethnic president is that of cultural/racial diversity. This issue is facing all seminary presidents, especially in light of the clear message carried in the Association of Theological Schools (ATS) accrediting standards that racial diversity/inclusiveness is a worthy goal. However, there seems to be a special twist to this matter both for the racial/ethnic president of a predominantly white school and for the president of a racial/ethnic institution.

In a predominantly white school, the racial/ethnic president needs to assess the institution's commitment to racial/ethnic inclusivity and help the institution understand racial/ethnic diversity and inclusiveness as God's gift to the whole church. This understanding should be cultivated at every level of the institution, beginning with the trustees and including faculty, staff, and students. The racial/ethnic president cannot be afraid to make this concern an institutional issue. The development of clear guidelines requiring the identification of qualified persons of color that represent racial/ethnic diversity in every institutional search can help remove the personal aspects of the process. Furthermore, the racial/ethnic president would do well to embrace the idea that his or her election was a mandate for the institution to change, even though that change must be managed carefully. Unless the election of a racial/ethnic president was mere "window dressing," the president needs to build on the mandate. As one African American president said, "If I simply do what all my white predecessors did, what is my contribution to making the institution better?" What this president meant was that prior presidents had not pushed for a racially/ethnically diverse faculty, staff, or student body. While the institution had clearly articulated this as a value, it had not made racial/ethnic diversity a reality. The African American president in question felt it was essential to the institution's future for it to become what others had only envisioned.

For the racial/ethnic president of a racial/ethnic institution, the challenge of cultural/racial diversity is tied in with racial stereotypes that we have already discussed. However, at a time when many second-

and third-career students are choosing seminary based on location rather than denominational or even theological considerations, the racial/ethnic president who is intentional in attracting non-racial/ethnic students, staff, faculty, and trustees has a good chance for some success if the institution can reach out and build a broad-based and diverse constituency.

Key Questions for Racial/Ethnic Presidents

As with any presidency, the racial/ethnic president needs to identify some key questions that have the potential to seriously impact his or her work. The racial/ethnic president must identify and seek to answer questions that relate to the racial/ethnic reality he or she brings to the presidency and to the racial/ethnic reality of the institution he or she seeks to serve. Some of these questions relate to the role and responsibility of the president while others relate to the issues we have discussed. Once again, it is important to recognize that some questions are different for a president in a racial/ethnic institution than for a president in a predominantly white context.

How Can One Celebrate Heritage while Welcoming and Creating a More Diverse Community?

For the president of a racial/ethnic seminary, a key question is this: How does the president celebrate and promote the value and uniqueness of a historically racial/ethnic institution while also attracting Euro-American students and financial support?

Associated with this question are two related questions: What is unique about the educational experience at a historically racial/ethnic institution that makes such an educational experience valuable for persons outside that racial/ethnic experience? And how does a historic racial/ethnic institution adjust or how much adjustment should it make in order to accommodate increased numbers of non-racial/ethnic students?

Presidents will need to give thoughtful and creative attention to these questions.

What Pedagogical Method Is Best for Preparing Leaders of Racial/Ethnic Communities?

Several racial/ethnic schools are now examining their pedagogy in light of their commitment to prepare leadership for the African American church. In Puerto Rico, the seminary prepares persons for ministry for both Puerto Rican and U.S. contexts. Some Asian American schools offer classes in the native language of their constituency in the hope of providing a quality theological education for persons who do not have English as their primary language and whose ministry is to communities where the native tongue is not English. Other racial/ethnic schools have sought to attract a diverse population by adjusting some courses to reflect the concerns of non-racial/ethnic students.

Where Can One Find Resources to Support Racial/Ethnic Institutions?

The struggle to find adequate financial resources for theological education is certainly not restricted to presidents of racial/ethnic seminaries. It does appear, however, that the problem of limited resources is magnified at historically racial/ethnic schools, especially among African American institutions. The limited amount of denominational support available for theological education from historic African American denominations, added to the large amount of financial aid needed by students and the limited resources available in the African American community, often means that these schools have to be extremely prudent in the use of their funds. In such an environment, how do racial/ethnic presidents of racial/ethnic institutions compete with wealthy institutions for the best racial/ethnic students and the most promising racial/ethnic faculty? Furthermore, how might the president enter into partnerships with other theological schools that are predominantly white — partnerships that would be mutually beneficial and respectful rather than dominating and paternalistic?

These questions are not easily answered, but racial/ethnic institutions need not give up too early in the search for top quality students or faculty members. Select, intensive recruiting at historically African American colleges and universities as well as connecting with campus ministers and African American pastors in towns where predominantly white colleges are located may uncover strong candidates. Working with the Fund for Theological Education may also prove invaluable for identifying young scholars and potential students. Partnerships that are mutually beneficial often emerge out of personal relationships that are based on commonly held values and ideals. It may not always be easy to find partners, but it helps to know what one wants from a partnership and what one brings to such an enterprise that will help both institutions achieve their goals. At a time when many strong white theological schools want to find ways to be diverse and cross-cultural, historically racial/ethnic schools may be surprised by the potential for partnerships that are mutually beneficial.

How Does One Assess a School's Commitment to Racial/Ethnic Inclusiveness?

The racial/ethnic president of a predominantly white institution needs to ask the seminary, How committed is the institution to racial/ethnic diversity and inclusivity? How important is racial/ethnic diversity to the institution's strategic plan and overall mission? This conversation must begin with the board of trustees, but it needs to be extended to the entire community. Unless the broad community is clearly committed to diversity as part of the mission and strategic plan of the institution, attempts to create a more racially/ethnically diverse community will most likely fail regardless of the individual efforts of the president. A racial/ethnic president should not be surprised if there is institutional resistance to this institutional culture shift. After all, there is always some resistance to change.

The president can know the level of resistance based on such indicators as how much effort the faculty puts into locating solid racial/ethnic candidates for faculty vacancies, whether the board seeks out racial/ethnic persons for board membership, and tracking the efforts made to recruit racial/ethnic students. If these efforts are inconsistent with the statements on paper and the verbal articulations made by the institution, the president needs to identify these inconsistencies and begin to rectify them with the support of the board. If the board is not supportive, the racial/ethnic president may need to reconsider whether he or she is a good match for the school.

How Can One Avoid Making Race the Issue
When It Is Not the Issue?

Another important question that the racial/ethnic president of a non-racial/ethnic institution must raise for himself or herself has important consequences for the well-being of the president and for the success of the president's tenure. The question is this: How does a racial/ethnic president avoid prematurely concluding that an issue or a concern is racially motivated?

Racial/ethnic persons who have experienced the demeaning and debilitating effects of racism and racial discrimination must be careful not to think that every instance of opposition, disagreement, or even disrespect is racially motivated. Some of the tensions and opposition, misunderstandings and conflicts that a president will encounter are simply the baggage that comes with the presidency. A racial/ethnic president who wants to avoid unnecessary stress and who wants to prevent polarizing the community on issues of race needs to be very careful that he or she does not prematurely conclude that normal conflicts are always racially motivated. At the same time, when it is clear that issues are racially motivated or have their genesis in disrespect for racial/ethnic leadership, the president must find ways to address that openly and with integrity.

It is important that a racial/ethnic president in a predominantly white institution identify persons (preferably board members or outside persons) who can help him or her determine when an issue is racially charged. Identifying persons to talk to about this sensitive matter is not always easy, but it is not impossible. While the presidency is most often lonely, it is rare for racial/ethnic presidents not to have someone in their institutions they might trust. A good rule to follow is never to react when you are angry. Wait until you have had time to reflect on the situation before talking to anyone. Once the emotions have calmed, the racial/ethnic president might then have the conversation about the incident. Usually a board member who has been supportive is a good person to talk to, as is the chair of the search committee that selected the president. Another person who might prove helpful is a senior pastor whom the racial/ethnic president knows and trusts. Such conversations can provide solid insights into what occurred and how it might best be addressed.

Erring on the side of caution is always wise for any president, but it is especially important for a racial/ethnic president dealing with potential issues of racial prejudice and racism.

Supports and Resources for Racial/Ethnic Presidents

Unfortunately, there is not a large body of written resources a racial/ethnic president can turn to for help in learning this wonderful but difficult vocation. There are, however, some books that can provide helpful insights into how some other racial/ethnic persons handled difficult leadership opportunities. A few of these resources are identified below.

Nevertheless, there are other learning opportunities that are very useful. Among the most helpful are the ATS-sponsored seminars for new presidents and the weeklong "President's Leadership Intensive." While these gatherings are not specifically designed for racial/ethnic presidents, there is much to be learned about the work of a president in these meetings. One key insight gained in these meetings is just how involved and complex the job is and how much presidents across the theological spectrum share common concerns and challenges in their work.

Another important meeting is a gathering of African American presidents and CEOs that is facilitated by ATS. At the time of this writing, the group is relatively new, and its agenda is still quite flexible. The meetings are important for fellowship, conversations about particular problems facing these presidents, and exploring ways in which theological education as a whole can benefit from the experiences, challenges, and insights that emerge from the racial/ethnic perspective.

Insights into the challenges of theological education and into creative solutions also emerge from participating in accreditation site visits. These visits are rarely convenient, are sometimes difficult, and always require commitment, dedication, and hard work, but persons who are involved in this process of peer evaluation come away from the encounter with a better understanding of the nature of presidential leadership. The insights acquired are adaptable to racial/ethnic presidencies whether they are in predominantly white or racial/ethnic institutions.

Racial/ethnic presidents can also benefit from having a mentor. Where does a racial/ethnic president turn for mentoring? Although finding a good mentor may not be easy for any president, it is particularly difficult for racial/ethnic presidents because there are not many racial/ethnic persons who have been presidents of theological schools and have retired and remained active. Therefore, a racial/ethnic president who wants to establish a meaningful relationship with an experienced mentor may have to turn to a white colleague for mentoring.

While there is no "one size fits all" solution to this issue, there are some things that need to be considered. The racial/ethnic president needs to be comfortable with the idea of having a mentor. The mentor probably needs to have had a long and successful tenure as president. Another important concern is the necessity that the mentor has a track record of relating well to racial/ethnic persons and a history of addressing racial/ethnic issues as a president. What a racial/ethnic president does not need is a mentor who is paternalistic or who forgets that he or she works for the president. While there are many other issues to be considered, before committing to a mentor the racial/ethnic president must have a face-to-face meeting with any potential mentor. No matter what the resume says, both parties need to feel a good personality match. Without this rapport, the mentoring relationship will not produce the desired results. One racial/ethnic president who has had a mentor states, "We began with a mutual respect that has developed into a true friendship." Mentoring will work when it reaches that level of trust.

Racial/ethnic presidents face unique challenges. These challenges emerge out of a painful history of racial relations in the United States and to a lesser degree in Canada. Nevertheless, these challenges can be overcome and theological education can be blessed by the perspectives racial/ethnic leaders bring to the table. Nurturing racial/ethnic presidents and giving them a chance to succeed is important for the future of theological education. May this chapter provide helpful information that enhances the opportunities for successful presidencies by persons who represent racial/ethnic communities.

Additional Resources

Aaron, Hank, with Lonnie Wheeler. *I Had a Hammer: The Hank Aaron Story.* New York: HarperCollins Publishers, 1991.

This book is a source of inspiration to any African American president (or a president from any racial/ethnic background) because it is the story of overcoming racism, prejudice, and one's own fears of inadequacy to achieve at the highest possible level and still maintain a humble spirit. Hank Aaron's challenges will be particularly familiar to African American presidents in predominantly white schools. While many of Aaron's challenges are less overt now, unfortunately they are still present and require the depth of character, commitment, and focus shown by Hank Aaron if African Americans are going to be successful in these relatively new leadership roles. Even persons who are not baseball fans will find it hard not to garner useful lessons from *I Had a Hammer.*

Benjamin, Lois. *Black Women in the Academy: Promises and Perils.* Gainesville: University Press of Florida, 1997.

This story presents the struggles and successes of women of color who have made exceptional contributions to the field of higher education. From the discussion of black women faculty to black women who have become exceptional college and university presidents, Dr. Benjamin recounts these amazing stories in first-person style and voice. The road to leadership in the academy for women in general has been difficult, but for African American women there have been the special challenges of race as well as gender. These stories are significant for men and women and are a must-read for young faculty who look toward academic leadership.

Benjamin, Lois. *Dreaming No Small Dreams: William R. Harvey's Visionary Leadership.* Irving, TX: Tapestry Press, 2004.

This story of visionary leadership provided by Dr. William R. Harvey, president of Hampton University in Hampton, Virginia, discusses the remarkable style and substance of leadership character. His gifted leadership allowed Hampton University to evolve from Hampton Institute, a college of fewer than 3,000 students with no doctoral degree offerings, to a university of nearly 7,000 with a host of PhD programs and major scientific research. During his tenure, Hampton's endowment has grown significantly, and its fiscal and physical plant have expanded dramatically.

Lewis, Reginald F., and Blair S. Walker. *"Why Should White Guys Have All the Fun?" How Reginald Lewis Created a Billion-Dollar Business Empire.* New York: John Wiley and Sons, 1995.

In some ways this book is about the "ins and outs" of high stakes business maneuvers. On another level, however, this book is about the ability of intelligent, hard-working African Americans to overcome the obstacles and challenges posed by racism and a lack of access to the power brokers in this society. Lewis's story is about the power inherent in visionary leadership. That power is applicable to the educational enterprise as well as to the business sector.

Mays, Benjamin E. *Born to Rebel: Autobiography of Benjamin E. Mays.* New York: Scribner's Sons, 1971.

This old classic is the autobiography of one of the twentieth century's greatest educators. Born in the racist, segregated South at a time when life was hard and the odds against the successful entrance of people of color into the mainstream of American life were overwhelming, Mays's book tells the story of how he beat the odds. While the entire book is of inestimable value to the reader, of particular interest and value to African American presidents and educational leaders is the book's focus on the years Dr. Mays served as president of Morehouse College. This section demonstrates how effective leaders make tough decisions, garner support for new and challenging visions, and bring those visions to reality. Dr. Mays's character and integrity can be seen throughout the book and help the reader realize once again that style without substance will not endure the pressures associated with presidential leadership.

Nelms, Charlie. "From Cotton Picker to University CEO." In *Grass Roots and Glass Ceilings,* edited by William B. Harvey. Albany: State University of New York Press, 1999.

Charlie Nelms was chancellor of Indiana University East when he wrote this chapter. His remarkable and unique story provides insights that are extremely valuable for those who are interested in or leading educational institutions. From his description of the importance of networking to the kinds of opposition he faced upon becoming chancellor of a predominantly white campus of a major university, Nelms's perspectives are relevant to all those in higher education leadership. His insightful analysis of the nature of racism on university campuses focuses on resolution rather than on finger pointing. While some of the specifics of Nelms's chapter do not fit the context of most theological seminaries, for African American presidents the chapter will, nevertheless, provide many moments of identification and reflection.

The resources identified in this handbook are listed on the ATS Website where the list will continue to be updated as new resources become available: www.ats.edu > Leadership Education > Presidents.

CHAPTER 14

The Unique Issues for Women Presidents

MARTHA HORNE, Protestant Episcopal
Theological Seminary in Virginia
HEIDI HADSELL, Hartford Seminary
LAURA MENDENHALL, Columbia Theological Seminary

The Joys of Being a Seminary President
Additional Resources

Introduction

In 1991, Barbara Brown Zikmund conducted a research project to identify and explore the needs and concerns of women in executive leadership positions in theological schools.[1] At that time, fewer than 3 percent
of the 211 schools listed in the Association of Theological Seminaries
(ATS) Membership List were headed by women. Six women served as
president or chief executive of ATS schools: four served in accredited
schools, while two others headed schools with associate status within
ATS. A higher percentage of women served as chief academic officers,
with fifteen women representing slightly more than 7 percent of ATS
schools.

As of January 1, 2005, the number of women serving as presidents
of theological schools listed in the ATS Membership List had grown to
sixteen, or 6.3 percent of 251 schools. The number of women serving as
chief academic officer had risen to thirty-six, representing 14 percent of
the total.

Despite the growth in the number of women in chief administrative positions in theological schools, they remain a distinct minority
within the ATS. As the number of women teaching in theological
schools has increased substantially in recent years, the number of
women presidents has grown at a much slower rate.

Do Women Presidents Face Unique Challenges?

This chapter is predicated on the assumption that women who serve as
presidents of theological schools face unique challenges that are not experienced by their male counterparts. This assumption has been the
subject of some thoughtful reflection and lively conversation among
nine women presidents who responded to inquiries during the writing

1. Barbara Brown Zikmund, "Walking the Narrow Path: Female Administrators in
ATS Schools," in *Theological Education,* Autumn 1992, pp. 55-65.

of this chapter. Most conclude that they have, indeed, faced issues and challenges that are unique to them as women. At the same time, as will be seen, they are wary of assuming that many of the challenges they have faced are not also experienced by men. At least one woman president is reluctant to say that the challenges of the seminary presidency are different for her as a woman.

The Challenge of History: Women's Traditional Roles in Religious Institutions

Unlike their male colleagues, women presidents must overcome centuries of historical precedence in which women were not afforded access to positions of leadership within religious organizations and institutions. Although often acknowledged as possessing gifts for pastoral care and spiritual discernment, women have traditionally been excluded from significant leadership roles in the official structures of the world's major religions. It has only been within the last century, and within only some religious communities, that women have begun to assume roles that traditionally belonged solely to men — hence the appearance of women clergy and rabbis within some Protestant Christian and Jewish communities. Even as some churches and denominations have moved to ordain women, acceptance of women in the upper echelons of religious leadership has been slow to evolve. Within some churches, for example, women can serve as pastors or ministers within a congregation, but not as bishops with vested authority for ecclesiastical oversight and governance. In many religious organizations and institutions, the privileged place of males in the highest positions of leadership is still very much intact.

In seminaries, as in congregations, certain leadership roles were long understood to be suitable for men, but not women. Participation in the decision-making functions of the seminary has been heavily weighted toward men, with males holding senior administrative positions and filling the majority of seats on boards of trustees. The fact that the number of women serving as presidents or academic deans has remained small while the number of women teaching in seminaries has grown steadily attests to the challenge women still face to "prove themselves worthy" of senior administrative posts. Men move into the office of the seminary presidency with challenges of their own, but without the need to prove that they, as male human beings, are up to the demands of the job.

Challenges in Relationships with Other Religious Groups

A second and related challenge identified by women presidents occurs within the context of interfaith or ecumenical circles in which women are still not accepted as religious leaders. One woman tells of hosting a meeting at her school where the guest of honor was a prominent Iranian imam. As he was introduced to her, she instinctively reached forward to shake his hand in welcome. He quickly withdrew his hand, nodded to acknowledge her, and walked past her to a group of male faculty. A member of his entourage whispered to her that "Imams of his stature do not touch women," leaving her both embarrassed and concerned that she had offended an honored guest. When she later wondered aloud to her staff why no one had alerted her in advance, she was met with a shrug of the shoulders, and the response, "Well, it probably just didn't occur to anyone that the president would be a woman."

Similar experiences occur within theological consortia where member schools include Roman Catholic and Protestant seminaries. Although women report a high level of collegiality among the chief administrators of schools within their consortium, tensions occasionally arise around shared leadership in worship events. The same can be true within some denominational settings. One woman, the only woman president among several seminaries in her denomination, never takes a turn presiding at the Eucharist during the annual meeting of denominational presidents, despite her seniority, because her ordination is not recognized as valid by one of her colleagues and the seminary he represents.

Challenges to Authority

It is not uncommon, particularly within institutions where women have not previously served at a senior administrative level, for female presidents to find their authority challenged by members of the community.

Several women speak of awkwardness in their relationships with women who serve as support staff. They may find themselves reluctant to ask women staffers, particularly if they are older, to make coffee or clean up after a meeting. At the same time, women staff members who are accustomed to working primarily with men may defer to senior male administrators in meetings while challenging the authority of the female president. The burden of proof falls on women to demonstrate that they are able to perform the duties of their office.

The Challenge of Being "the First"

As of this writing, most women serving as seminary presidents are the first to hold that office in the history of their schools. Many are also the first woman to head a theological school within her denomination, and some are still the only woman president among the seminaries of her denomination. These women often report a persistent undercurrent of performance anxiety during the early months and years of their presidencies, accompanied by a fear of failing at the job and thereby making it more difficult for women to be considered for future executive positions.

This concern, which was raised by nearly all the women interviewed for this chapter, is perhaps a natural outgrowth of the continuing assumptions many people have about the appropriateness of women's leadership in certain roles, as discussed above. In demonstrating competence for their job, many women feel that they were scrutinized more carefully than men, especially around the "hard decisions" involved in management of budgets, endowments, and property. They believe that they were closely watched until they had proven themselves to be competent and effective leaders. Some worried that any inadequacies or weaknesses in their job performance would be seen as a reason to deny other women opportunities to fill senior leadership roles.

This is not to say, of course, that male presidents do not worry about failing or being perceived as inadequate in their work as presidents. What is perceived as different for women, particularly those who are "firsts" in their schools or their denominations, is the strong sense of responsibility they feel, not only to their own institutions, but to other women. Women often speak of a desire to succeed not only for themselves and their schools, but also for the sake of women who will come after them.

It should be noted that some women presidents who are ordained recognize this challenge as a familiar one, having felt the same pressure to succeed as the first ordained woman to serve in one or more congregations, or the first woman to be a senior pastor within her judicatory. It would be surprising if a similar challenge is not also identified by men who are the first of their racial or ethnic identity to occupy the presidency within their institutions.

Challenges of Family

Many women become seminary presidents after their children are grown and have left home. For those with children at home, however, challenges of balancing family life with the demands of the job, including travel and frequent evening events, are great. This is certainly true for men, as well, as it is for women in other high-profile or demanding positions. A woman chief executive, who is a single parent with children at home, cites family issues as one of the greatest challenges she has faced as a woman. Although traditional roles of women and men have been undergoing change in recent years, with fathers assuming a larger role in the care of children and home, in many places the expectation remains that the mother will be the one to rearrange her schedule to care for children who are ill or unexpectedly at home because of inclement weather. Women find themselves torn in such situations: they want to put the welfare of their children first, but they fear that they will be regarded as unable to fulfill the responsibilities of their job or relegated to the dreaded "mommy track." Similarly, they are more likely to be criticized for working at night or on weekends when there are children at home, even as their male colleagues may be lauded for working long hours on behalf of the school.

Despite the difficulty many women report in achieving balance in their lives, one has found in her new status as chief executive an "opportunity for modeling a new understanding of time off and of putting family first. I have well-established boundaries and try to witness to a balanced life," she says. Her success in this goal offers hope and promise to other women who have yet to achieve the elusive balance.

It is interesting to note that men who are married to women presidents tend to have far fewer expectations placed upon them for participation in the life of the seminary community. Husbands of women presidents who are engaged in the practice of ministry or in other professions may be praised and commended for their support of their wives' vocations when they simply show up for community events. Wives of male seminary presidents, on the other hand, often find that their institutions expect them to entertain frequently and to engage in a range of other activities. They may be expected to sing in the choir, to serve as advisor for student spouses' groups, or even, in one case, to wash and iron the linens used in the seminary worship services. This experience is not unlike that of many male spouses of female clergy, who usually find themselves able to live their own lives free of congregational expectations about their proper role in the community.

Questions to Ask

Would This Be Happening If I Were a Man?

When faced with a challenge to her authority, or with a range of other issues, a female president may be tempted to assume that the problem exists because she is a woman, or that it is more complicated because she is a woman. Sometimes this question cannot be answered; there simply is no way of knowing. In the majority of cases, however, it is likely that the difficulty at hand would pose a challenge for a man as well as for a woman. It is important for women to remember that not all issues are gender-related and to consider other factors that may be contributing to the problem. As an example of this, a woman related an incident that occurred when she, as a newly ordained and first woman assistant minister in a congregation, accused the senior pastor of "having a problem with women." After much conversation and exploration of the precipitating incident, she came to agree with her supervisor that the issue was not so much a "male-female" issue as it was a "senior pastor–assistant pastor" matter.

What Have I Learned from Similar Challenges in Other Contexts?

In thinking about specific challenges, women often realize that they have dealt with similar issues in other arenas or different stages of their life. One woman observed that nearly all the challenges identified by other women presidents are challenges she encountered and success-fully addressed in her work as a pastor. The same set of skills that made her an effective pastor serves her well as a seminary president. Women presidents who were members of a seminary faculty bring valuable ex-perience as teachers, as well as insights about the unique culture of a theological school and the particular needs and idiosyncrasies of facul-ties. Mothers of two-year-olds and teenagers have plenty of experience with having their authority challenged! All of these prior experiences are helpful in analyzing a situation, identifying what is at stake for whom, and deciding how best to respond.

Where Can I Find Support in Doing My Job?

This question, certainly not unique to women, is still a critical one to ask. Women may find it harder to ask for support, either because they don't want to appear that they are not up to the task or because they are not sure where to turn for support. Those who have moved from a fac-ulty position to the president's office often find that their relationships with women faculty have changed; once colleagues on a "level playing field," they may now have a supervisory or evaluative role in annual and tenure review processes. Women who are new to the institution may not have had time to develop relationships of trust. While it is important for all leaders to develop a network of support and counsel, such net-works are particularly important for women who are moving into new levels of leadership within institutions still dominated by men. Estab-lishing a reliable network of support is one of the "best practices" any seminary president can adopt.

Signs of Change

As women think and speak about their experiences as presidents, they almost always express a conviction that many of the challenges faced by women in recent years will diminish or disappear as more women head theological schools. For those who are "firsts" in their schools and/or denominations, certain challenges are rooted in their institution's lack of experience with women in positions of leadership. As more women serve at senior administrative levels, and as board members, students, faculty, staff, and alumni experience them as effective institutional leaders, there will be less pressure on women to prove that they are equal to the task. Women presidents and academic deans in schools where women have already served as effective senior administrators report fewer challenges to their authority and note that their gender is less an issue than it appears to be for those who are "first."

Do Women Exercise a Different Style of Presidential Leadership?

Perhaps no question is more hotly debated than this, not only about women who hold senior positions in theological schools but also about women who have risen to top positions in business, management, and a wide range of professions. A growing field of literature has examined the question over the past twenty years or so, with a proliferation of books and articles in scholarly journals. The question inevitably arises when groups of senior women administrators in theological schools gather to compare notes about their experiences.

Women leaders frequently offer anecdotes to illustrate a style of leadership that is more collaborative and consultative than that of their male colleagues or predecessors. It has become an oft-repeated maxim that women are more collaborative in the workplace and more concerned about maintaining good personal relationships among colleagues and staff members. When asked to comment on their leadership styles, a number of women also noted their attentiveness to matters of hospitality within their schools. Examples may range from greater attention to the upkeep of buildings and grounds in order to make the campus a more welcoming place, to a comprehensive plan for including and welcoming a diverse population of students, faculty, and staff.

Even as many women cite collegiality, collaboration, and hospitality as characteristics of their own style, they are quick to acknowledge that they have known and worked with men who exhibit similar values and styles of leadership. They note that differences in style that may seem very pronounced or obvious to some are more likely a result of the socialization of women than of any inherent gender-related aptitudes or abilities.

A recent article in the *Chronicle of Higher Education* challenges unsubstantiated assertions that women are, by nature, more nurturing, more collaborative, more hospitable, and more concerned about relationships in the workplace. "Findings from a handful of small studies with nonrepresentative samples have often reported wildly over generalized but headline-grabbing findings about gender differences," according to Rosalind C. Barnett and Caryl Rivers. "Those findings have been picked up by the news media — and found their way back into the academy, where they are taught as fact."[2]

More research is needed in carefully designed studies, they contend, to show the degree of overlap that actually exists among the leadership styles of men and women.

Barnett and Rivers remind us of the need to be wary of accepting stereotypical notions of male and female behavior in the workplace. Such unexamined stereotypes are damaging both to men and to women. Cultural and environmental factors are likely to shape the leadership style of individuals to a greater extent than biological or genetic ones. Yet, at the present time, many of the students, faculties, and staff within our seminaries, as in our society, have been powerfully shaped and formed by those cultural factors. These factors affect not only the way in which women exercise their leadership but also the ways in which their leadership is perceived and received by members of the community. Hence, a woman who makes the hard decision to terminate an employee who is not meeting the requirements of the job may be perceived

---

2. Rosalind C. Barnett and Caryl Rivers, "Men Are from Earth, and So Are Women; It's Faulty Research That Sets Them Apart," *Chronicle of Higher Education,* September 3, 2004.

as harsh and unfeeling while a man making the same decision may be regarded as strong and decisive.

The Joys of Being a Seminary President

Despite the challenges many women have encountered as they assume the role of president, most are quick to name particular satisfactions and joys they experience in their work. Several point to the ability to make decisions and to help effect change within their institutions. With that comes the realization of the responsibility they bear: "I have this ongoing conversation with senior women faculty," said one woman, "as we look around and realize that we can now make change instead of sitting around and complaining about the ones in charge. We don't want to blow it, and yet there is a new responsibility in realizing that there is no one else to blame."

In the role of president, many women find the ability to integrate a variety of skills and past experiences. "The work of a seminary president requires the ability to multi-task," one woman observed, and "as a woman I had learned to do that well, balancing the demands of graduate school, family, and job, and dealing with constant interruptions to my schedule."

Others note the web of relationships that must be tended in the seminary community, appreciating the ability to move among students, faculty, staff, board members, alumni, donors, and friends of the seminary, as well as the external relationships within the denomination and the local community. One speaks with satisfaction about the improved patterns of communication and collaboration that have developed as a result of her intentional decision to model a new way of sharing information in a clear and consistent manner. Another speaks of the "safe place" she provides for members of the community to deal with mistreatment or abuse they may have experienced.

"I actually love it," one woman said of her vocation as chief executive officer of a theological school, speaking not only for herself but for other women who have had the privilege of sharing that vocation. The challenges are real, but so are the satisfactions and rewards of leadership.

Additional Resources

One of the most valuable resources available to seminary presidents, whether male or female, is the Association of Theological Schools in the United States and Canada (ATS). ATS offers a variety of leadership development opportunities, including an annual, three-day seminar for new seminary presidents and a more intensive, week-long presidential leadership event each year. In recent years, there has been an annual retreat in March for women who are presidents or academic deans of theological schools. In addition, opportunities are available for ATS-sponsored workshops for presidents and their development directors or chief financial officers. These events provide not only resources for dealing with specific topics, such as the ones addressed in this volume, but also opportunities for developing networks of collegial support with other presidents. For more information about these events, please visit the ATS Website at www.ats.edu.

Barnett, Rosalind C., and Caryl Rivers. "Men Are from Earth, and So Are Women; It's Faulty Research That Sets Them Apart." *Chronicle of Higher Education,* September 3, 2004.

This article questions some of the generalizations commonly made about differences in the leadership styles of men and women and encourages more careful research into whether such perceived differences actually exist and, if so, whether they are genetically or culturally determined.

Becker, Carol E. *Leading Women: How Church Women Can Avoid Leadership Traps and Negotiate the Gender Maze.* Nashville: Abingdon Press, 1996.

This volume provides a look at the rapidly growing number of ordained women serving Protestant congregations and recounts the experiences of women working in churches where patriarchal structures, theology, and language are still prevalent.

Buchanan, Constance H. *Choosing to Lead: Women and the Crisis of American Values.* Boston: Beacon Press, 1996.

The author examines the role of women as moral leaders in society and cites examples of such leadership by black and white women during the nineteenth and twentieth centuries. She reminds readers of the important role of women in fostering public debate and attention to social welfare issues.

Chopp, Rebecca S. *Saving Work: Feminist Practices of Theological Education.* Louisville: Westminster John Knox Press, 1995.

The former dean of the faculty of Candler School of Theology and provost of Emory University, now president of Colgate College, examines the ways in which feminist practices are changing the nature of theological education.

Helgesen, Sally. *The Female Advantage: Women's Ways of Leadership.* New York: Doubleday, 1990.

A case-study approach to observing women leaders at work in a variety of corporate and not-for-profit contexts, this book was an early entry into the study of the characteristics and qualities of women who worked their way up through business environments to become chief executives. Although somewhat dated, the experiences recorded in this book still have a familiar ring to many women.

Liswood, Laura A. *Women World Leaders: Fifteen Great Politicians Tell Their Stories.* San Francisco: Pandora, 1995.

Laura Liswood interviewed fifteen women who are or have been presidents or leaders of their countries. Because they represent very different cultures — from Great Britain to Bangladesh, from Norway to Sri Lanka, from Ireland to Poland — this volume offers interesting insights about the ways in which one's cultural context shapes the actions taken and decisions made by the president.

Morrison, Ann M., Randall P. White, Ellen Van Velsor, and the Center for Creative Leadership. *Breaking the Glass Ceiling: Can Women Reach the Top of America's Largest Corporations?* Reading: Addison-Wesley, 1987. Updated edition, Addison Wesley Publishing, 1994.

Research conducted by the Center for Creative Leadership is the basis of this book that examines issues facing women trying to break through the "glass ceiling." Although the book may seem dated in relationship to corporate America, many women in religious leadership still find it difficult to break through the barriers to the upper echelons of leadership within the church.

Tannen, Deborah. *Talking from 9 to 5 — Women and Men in the Workplace: Language, Sex and Power.* New York: Avon Books, 1994.

A fascinating look at the different ways in which men and women often communicate in the workplace, with specific examples drawn from a variety of workplace environments. Tannen explores the ways in which men and women often have different conversational rituals that structure the ways in which feedback is given to colleagues or staff members, and how feedback may be received and understood differently by women and men.

Zikmund, Barbara Brown. "Walking the Narrow Path: Female Administrators in ATS Schools," in *Theological Education,* Autumn 1992, pp. 55-65.

In this research project sponsored by ATS, one of the first women to head a theological school in North America identifies and explores "issues related to the special needs of women in leadership positions in theological schools in the nineties."

The resources identified in this handbook are listed on the ATS Website where the list will continue to be updated as new resources become available: www.ats.edu > Leadership Education > Presidents.

CHAPTER 15

The Unique Issues for CEOs
of University-based Theological Schools

JAMES HUDNUT-BEUMLER, Vanderbilt University Divinity
HAROLD W. ATTRIDGE, Yale University Divinity School
FREDERICK J. FINKS, Ashland Theological Seminary

Introduction

Theological schools in general are complex institutions. When a theological school is located within a larger university, the level of complexity intensifies. For those who would lead such institutions, the role and responsibilities of the chief administrative officer are likewise complex. The president, dean, or rector of such a school must contend effectively with both the strengths and the limitations of being the leader of a school bonded to a larger institution. This chapter seeks to offer guidance to those who might lead these institutions, stressing the interrelated nature of leadership in a university setting, relations with multiple constituencies, and practices that make for more successful and satisfying tenures in office.

One of the important things to recognize about leading a theological school that is a part of another larger institution is that one will be working in a unique structure of university governance. As such, a seminary president might work relatively independently within the broad regulation of the larger institution, and a divinity school dean might work within a structure that regiments faculty hiring and promotion according to the same procedures and standards used for the law school or arts and sciences school. One of the first tasks of leadership in this kind of setting is to understand the formal and informal governance structures of the particular institution.[1]

In every instance, no matter what kind of institutional structure is in place, there are some givens of leading a university-based theological school. Communication in all directions is the key responsibility of the dean of a school. It takes a wise and discerning leader to build proper lines of communication and to keep all parties apprised of the work and mission of the theological school. The president or dean must embody the mission and vision of the school and must advocate the mission of the school within and beyond the campus. Issues of development, faculty hiring, administrative staffing, budget control, and academic integ-

---

1. Granting the particularity of university-based theological schools and the many titles given to their CEOs, the balance of this essay will employ the term "dean," the most common designation used within ATS (Association of Theological Schools) schools of this kind, when referring to the head of the school. It will, likewise, use the term "school" to denote the theological school within the university.

rity are all central to the character of the school, even when the university provides support or controls in these areas.

The Question of Relationships

As in the leadership of any other kind of theological school — or any leadership position, for that matter — the considerations that go into being a good and effective leader at a university-based theological school are four in number. These considerations can be put succinctly into question form: For whom do you work? With whom do you work? What is the nature of the work? How does it work operationally? Four simple questions. What makes leadership of a university-based theological school especially challenging is that the answers to the four basic questions are anything but simple.

For Whom Do You Work?

Take the first question, for example: For whom do you work? The answer to this question generally has an easy formal answer. The dean of such a school almost invariably answers to a provost or chief academic officer of the university or to the president of the university. However, the dean is also accountable to a wider range of groups and individuals. In addition to the provost and president, the dean may be accountable to a board of trustees (sometimes with much greater accountability than access to the board). Where there are multiple schools in a university, deans will find that they have a web of bilateral associations of accountability with other deans, not to mention other general officers at the university who may oversee the school's budget, fundraising, and business practices. It is not uncommon for theological schools related to universities also to have visiting or advisory committees or councils that provide advice and sometimes support to the school. Theological schools related to universities also have accountability relationships to the church. Sometimes this is direct accountability, such as in instances where a church or denomination actually owns and operates the larger university and takes a strong interest in the affairs of the theological school, its faculty, and its students. Even supposedly freestanding, independent theological schools, however, can find that they are accountable to churches and supported by churches, with claims placed upon them by the churches in various forms: expectations as to how students will be educated and formed, requests for referrals as candidates for ministry positions, field education placements, and so on.

Deans of university-related theological schools find, in ways uniquely applicable to their particular schools, that they are accountable to a wide range of persons and publics. It is important to understand the nature of all of these forms of accountability in order to be effective. Another way to describe the level of accountability is to see the chief executive of a university-based theological school as relating to four public constituencies: the church, the academy, the university, and the community. A wise leader will discern early which of these constituencies is most important for his or her work with a particular school *and* decide what to do to meet the legitimate expectations of the other constituencies. In the setting of the university-based theological school, the university itself and the academy compete for the most attention, but, as we will argue later, what a president or dean does about relations with the church and community will often be important for the school's reputation and identity.

Not infrequently a senior university officer will turn to the leader of the theological school and admit that he or she knows next to nothing about running a theological school and will give the divinity school dean a free hand to run the school. At first blush this looks like a gift of autonomy. Deans should beware, however, for being ignored is not a prescription to power within a university. One of the essential job challenges is educating the dean's boss(es) as to the nature of the school and the challenges it faces. Deans will be successful, in part, to the extent that senior university leaders take interest in the mission and success of their divinity schools. These university leaders are often gatekeepers to board members, development prospects, and university resources. As powerful as they are in these gatekeeping roles, their support can best be leveraged when the dean, the faculty, and the staff are doing a good job *and* when what the school needs to do a better job is something the university's leaders can access. Senior university officers are like people in any other management role; they are human beings who love to provide a little extra — even critical — assistance to achieve success. On the other hand, as a rule, such managers do not like to be told about problems about which nothing can be done. They do not possess magic wands any more than deans do. So a key to leadership, given the fact that the school will have problems and challenges, is to redescribe institutional challenges so that the dean and other university officers can collaborate in surmounting them.

With Whom Do You Work?

Within the Larger University

One of the unique aspects of heading a theological school within a larger university is that one is not merely a school leader but also a leader in the broader university. The dean of the school may serve on a university cabinet or other governing council. He or she may have a dual role or title that indicates connectivity. In these capacities, the dean is called upon to walk a delicate line so as to maintain trust and integrity. The school's dean must be careful to support the overall goals and objectives of the university while at the same time remaining committed to the goals and objectives of the divinity school. Without mutual trust and respect, effective leadership is impossible.

The theological school dean must work closely with other administrative members of the larger university in areas of budget, marketing, development, and rules and regulations. The head of a school must also be able to operate under clearly defined rules for interaction with the board of trustees. Some institutions allow extensive interaction between boards and the deans of their theological schools. Others allow virtually no interaction that is not mediated by the president of the university. Any model of governance within this range can work effectively, provided the board makes and delegates decisions in appropriate relation to where the information for those decisions resides. Because of their special missions, however, theological schools are typically not served well by governance structures that assume that such schools are just like the undergraduate college, only smaller.

With the Church Constituency

As the head of a theological school, the dean is a public symbol of whether the theological school "really cares" about the church. But note that "church" takes on very specific meanings depending upon the tradition(s) the school serves. For a school with a dominant tradition, being visible at denominational meetings may be essential. At an ecumenical school, local ministerial gatherings, installations of bishops outside one's own tradition, and preaching at different congregations of varying denominations may be extremely valuable. Still, it is good to remember that no good deed goes unpunished and to learn that, if the dean does something that others find supportive to the church, they will expect the dean to do it again. There is never enough of the dean to go around, but it is best to make sure that he or she does get around.

With the Local Community

In a similar vein, various community causes will hope to enlist the dean as a leader. Our advice to deans is to try to contribute where possible and where they believe that what they can do is consistent with the mission of the school. On the other hand, deans should avoid associations with causes that are hard to explain as part of their role to donors, colleagues, and superiors. To do nothing for the community as a religious leader is to fail to use the office to which one is appointed. To use it unwisely undermines the essential nature of most schools, which is to be value-laden places of free inquiry and learning with an end in service.

With the Faculty and Staff

Inside the school, the dean encounters the delightful challenge of working with highly intelligent and motivated people (most of the time) in the field of theological education. For most heads of schools this is the aspect of the work that drew them to become a dean. It can be the most rewarding aspect of the work of an educator, but it is often also a working relationship fraught with ambiguities.

Faculty members appreciate the dean working on behalf of the institution as well as equipping faculty to do their work. Longtime deans also observe, however, that a "distance" or "separation" often develops, sometimes without thought or planning. It is key that the dean of a school think of himself or herself as a faculty member to do the job, but there will also be ways in which he or she will be expected to be "something more." Deans are in a unique relationship with faculty. Deans are members of the faculty in some ways and are not so in others. In many schools there is a strong tradition of faculty governance, particularly on matters of faculty appointments. A university dean who came from within his faculty says, "I understand that tradition and the sensitivities that go with it. I maintain my position in the faculty by continuing to teach (one course a term) and I continue with supervision of doctoral students as well." In other words, he maintains his credibility as a faculty member by doing faculty work.

Yet the dean's job requires clear recognition of duties and concerns that go well beyond ordinary faculty concerns: budget, external relations, and issues with facilities and support staff. Faculty have only the vaguest idea about budgets and financial affairs, fleeting glimpses of the development and external relations operations, and a passing acquaintance with some of the university's policies and procedures on most administrative matters. It is clear that the dean has to take responsibility for crucial big-picture issues, such as assessment, development, and long-range planning. Marshaling the faculty and staff resources to deal with such issues is the heart of the job. Yet even in the core areas of faculty responsibility, such as appointments and promotions, the school's chief executive plays a significant leadership role in establishing priorities and shaping positions and programs.

Dealing with the Shadow of One's Predecessor

One way in which the dean ends up exercising the greatest stewardship of faculty and staff is in responding to their perspectives as a long-term stakeholder. To have virtually any job in theological education is to have a predecessor. It will perhaps surprise new deans when their predecessor's name, leadership, or example is invoked and by whom. New deans should usually respond to these conversational gambits in two ways. First, they should be careful not to speak ill of the departed, and second, they should listen carefully to what their conversation partners may be trying to communicate between the lines.

The first piece of advice probably goes without saying, but it might be reinforced with a simple observation that the newest dean will someday be a former chief executive; charity on that dean's part now may not be fully returned, but a generosity of spirit is remembered better than vindictiveness. No matter what childish games the dean may see worked by others in the school, it is important not to let those displaying childish behavior pull him or her down to their level. The dean must remain the adult in the situation.

The guidance to listen between the lines is something that may take even more practice to observe than refraining from negative comments. It is not uncommon for faculty members to disclose something that the former head of the school did that irritated, hurt, or offended them. Or they may talk about a lack of some quality. What they are saying in these instances is usually not about the dean's predecessor, but about themselves and about their hopes for a relationship with the current dean. They may be saying, in effect, "When the dean did this I was deeply hurt because I was embarrassed before my colleagues, [or felt used for a task without any thanks,] and I hope you will never do that to me." Nine times out of ten this is about their vulnerabilities to someone in the dean's position. What can be said in response? While it is tempting to say, "That's terrible, I would never do [whatever it is]," deans must be careful not to promise more than they can deliver. Rather, it is preferable to say, "I will try never to do that, but if I ever disappoint you like that, I want you to let me know so that I can work to repair the breach." If a dean values a faculty or staff member's contribution, the dean should say so. After all, such contributions are basically all any of us have out of which to build a school. There are, of course, things deans will learn from these conversations that tell them what they should never do. Whether these insights are about delegating things that should not be delegated, spending too freely (or too penuriously), or handling bishops or pastors, it is a good practice to make mental notes to guide one's future actions. Deans are sure to make enough of their own mistakes. It is a wise dean who manages not to repeat his or her predecessor's clear mistakes as well.

Somewhat harder to handle are the positive contributions of predecessors that are brought to one's attention. Here the messages are once again about the dean and his or her conversation partner. The person who is telling the dean something the former dean did is probably conveying that they would like the current dean to continue or replicate that course of action. One should be careful not to dismiss ideas merely because the former dean acted on them. Even if deans choose to cut a divergent path, it will probably not help them at all to draw leadership lines in the sand with respect to someone's past success.

One more issue involving the dean and his or her faculty and staff is important to bear in mind: when parties outside the faculty or staff come to tell the dean about the faculty and staff. If the dean comes from inside the faculty, he or she may be all too likely to dismiss the complaints of those who gripe about long-time colleagues and friends. If the dean is appointed from outside the school, he or she may be too likely to believe all the terrible things said about the staff and faculty. Again, it is wise to work toward careful discernment of what the school's constituencies are really saying. Sometimes schools have bad apples in their faculty or staff ranks. But far more often, outside constituencies are trying to realize unmet desires through lobbying the new leader, and they are really not so far apart in their desires for the work of the school from the very same faculty or staff they target with criticism. An extraordinary amount of the stewardship of the job is explaining the faculty to the constituency and the constituency to the faculty. The dean has unparalleled access to both, but this means that the dean is the conduit to improve perennial misunderstandings and to promote realistic expectations for all the people who love and serve the school.

What Is the Nature of the Work?

The nature of work in a theological school attached to a larger university is much like the work of freestanding schools, with the addition of an extra few considerations that deserve to be noted. Some of the university-based schools are clearly in service to a single Christian tradition, while others try to serve the church universal by working with students, congregations, and churches of a wide variety of Christian traditions. To state the obvious, the dean of a school must know which model applies to his or her school. And not so obviously, the dean ought to accept the school for what it is and is not. It is hard enough to lead a

228

school one essentially accepts. Heading a school to change its basic type is like marrying a spouse to change him or her.

A similar question to face is whether the school is engaged in professional education, graduate education, or both. University-based schools are more likely to have a blend of these two forms of theological education, and having a mix sometimes increases the tension between ecclesial and academic values in a school.

Finally, in many universities it is customary to credit the theological school with being the conscience of the university. While this is complimentary to the school, it might also raise the question of whether the university should get or possess its own conscience. This in turn fosters the further question of what should be the theological school leader's role in matters of religious understanding, mission, and conscience in the larger university.

How Does it Work Operationally?

If the nature of the work of a theological school in a university setting is recognizably similar to that of a freestanding seminary, the way the school operates can be quite different. When asked, "What was the greatest surprise you've encountered in your work as head of your school?" one long-time leader replied that he encountered something akin to culture shock. "Because [the school] is part of the larger university," he said, "we are restricted from contacting area vendors, business leaders, etc., for development purposes since the university contacts them first. This makes both developing community donors and developing our ministry information difficult." Another leader who had spent years working as a faculty member on long-range issues was nevertheless also surprised "at how much time would be spent sorting out personnel issues on the staff" once he became his school's dean. Whether it be working with personnel, getting a check cut, getting clearance to contact a donor, or even having a publication's design centrally approved prior to printing, the consensus is that working within a larger university structure takes longer.

Universities are fluid operations. A good part of the complexity of the theological school leader's work arises out of the fact that the university does not stand still while the dean and his or her colleagues are attempting to move in a positive direction. As one experienced dean has said, "At any given point, the university seems resolute on centralizing activities that the dean would just as soon be left alone and decentralizing other functions that one would be happier to avoid." There are myriad fronts on which change may be taking place in university systems simultaneously. University fundraising procedures require close and constant scrutiny lest one be left out in the cold. Often relations with religion departments and with religious studies perspectives require extraordinary diplomacy on the part of the dean. The tenure process at many institutions involves people from outside the theological academy passing judgment on the intellectual accomplishments of those within the theological school. There is space to be shared (or fought over). There are housing policies and budgets that involve more than one kind of student and sometimes seem to be developed around a different set of ideals than would apply to adults attending a professional school aimed toward ministry or the professoriate. At universities where research is crucial, graduate education is often done in collaboration with other schools and entities (and other systems of budgeting). On these and a variety of fronts, in some matters the theological school's dean works relatively independently and on others proceeds only through elaborate permission processes.

Personnel and Student Problems

Personnel problems and problems having to do with student conduct are always painful, but they may be even worse in a university-based theological school insofar as such schools are caught between the norms of the university and those of sponsoring churches (or churches that have some accountability claims on the school). It is possible in today's climate to be asked to disclose to a church a student's progress in field education *and* to be prohibited from doing so by one's university's implementation of the Buckley Amendment (FERPA). Federal law places real limits on the disclosure of students' records to third parties without explicit permission from the student. Or churches may wish to know more about the sex lives of one's students and clergy members of the faculty than the institution as a whole is willing to divulge. It is also true that people in power in the classroom and elsewhere will sometimes abuse their authority. The trick to good leadership, especially when things go badly, is knowing the applicable policies and acting as a team within the institution both to respond with respect for the individuals involved in the given situation and to hold people appropriately accountable for their actions.

With all the difficulties that attend leading a theological school situated within a larger educational institution, it might be easy to miss the genius that drives these schools. Alongside the hassles of raising money the hard way (by sharing donors) and working with people who do not answer directly to the dean of the school come opportunities. Working a school's finances with someone looking over one's shoulder often means working with greater depth of available expertise. Sharing resources (and problems) with dissimilar educational units often means better libraries, health services for students, and benefits structures for employees. Deans of theological schools within larger universities often find a remarkable level of support from other senior leaders in the university and their respective staffs that makes it possible to concentrate more on issues of educational mission than would be the case in a smaller institution.

Key Points to Remember

- Good relationships with senior leaders in the broader university are essential for good leadership by the theological school CEO.
- Theological school CEOs must always articulate the mission of their schools within and beyond the bounds of the university.
- Faculty and staff expect the head of their school to protect and advance their welfare almost the way good parents do in families.
- Getting things done in a university setting often takes more time, but highly competent help to do those things is usually available.

Additional Resources

Ehrle, Elwood B., and John B. Bennett. *Managing the Academic Enterprise: Case Studies for Deans and Provosts.* New York: American Council on Education/Macmillan Series in Higher Education, 1988.

A useful series of case studies for people who must lead schools within the structures of a larger university.

Toma, J. Douglas, and Richard L. Palm. *The Academic Administrator and the Law: What Every Dean and Department Chair Needs to Know.* San Francisco: Jossey-Bass, 2000.

While state law governs employment in some church-related schools, a remarkable amount of employment, student, discrimination, and harassment law is federally based. This volume is an essential guide without being overly technical.

Wolverton, Mimi, and Walter H. Gmelch. *College Deans: Leading from Within.* Westport, CT: Oryx Press, 2002.

Much in this well-researched study is transferable to theological school deans and presidents. The authors are particularly good on the changing power dynamics in higher education and the ways in which various "markets" affect the outlook of leaders of institutions above the high school level.

The resources identified in this handbook are listed on the ATS Website where the list will continue to be updated as new resources become available: www.ats.edu > Leadership Education > Presidents.

CHAPTER 16

The Unique Issues for Presidents
of Canadian Theological Schools

DORCAS GORDON, Knox College
MARVIN DEWEY, Taylor Seminary
RON MERCIER, Regis College

Conclusion

Additional Resources

Introduction

We will begin this chapter on Canadian theological school presidents by noting that the title of "president" is not universally used. Within the Roman Catholic tradition, the title "rector" is common, while "dean" is also used, particularly within denominational schools that are part of a public university. In some schools the title "principal" indicates the equivalent of the president. Hence, when advice from a colleague would be helpful, remember that the colleague most knowledgeable may have a different title. For purposes of this chapter, the term "president" will be used to refer to the Chief Executive Officer of a seminary.

The president of a Canadian theological school, in addition to consulting the valuable information in the previous chapters, needs to be aware of the ways in which some of the issues identified translate into the Canadian context. In an effort to provide easy access to things specifically Canadian, this chapter is divided into three broad headings: regional issues, federal issues, and issues that have both regional and federal implications. The issues identified are not exhaustive but are ones that colleagues within Canada emphasized as most critical for their work. In fact, it is suggested that Canadian presidents using this handbook for any issue regularly ask themselves the question: Are there Canadian particulars that I need to consider?

Regional Issues

Canadian regional dynamics make university and governmental relations of great importance to the seminary president. The primacy of the university system; the propensity for seminaries to be invisible; changing governmental regulations regarding oversight of educational programs; laws concerning employment, privacy, and reporting; and the potential of some provinces to provide funding are some of the reasons for presidents to be intentional about these relationships. In this section two issues will be addressed in detail: provincial accreditation, and fundraising and provincial funding.

Provincial Accreditation

Because education is provincially regulated in Canada, presidents should become acquainted with provincial requirements and with personnel who oversee higher education. Some provinces regulate divinity programs while others do not. Nomenclature may be legally regulated even if programs are not (e.g., the MA degree).

Accredited seminaries tend to fall into two primary categories: theological schools that are part of the public university system, and stand-alone seminaries. The second category primarily includes evangelical seminaries. Depending on the province, the programs of stand-alone seminaries often are neither recognized nor accredited by the government. This lack of recognition poses challenges for students who may want to continue their education in the Canadian university system. Graduates are often evaluated on a case-by-case basis, with the reputation of the institution playing a substantial part in the consideration. Seminary presidents would do well to cultivate relationships with university faculties for the benefit of their graduates and reputation.

On the broader Canadian scene, the ubiquitous unaccredited Bible institutes and Bible colleges have affected adversely the university community's perception of seminaries. The educational quality of these schools has varied greatly, and the focus of many on practical living has not met the rigors of academic review. The lack of provincial regulation and recognition has further contributed to the hesitancy of universities to recognize the quality of education offered at seminaries.

The lack of government recognition of seminaries in some provinces may pose problems for international students who return home and want their country's government to recognize their degree. In one situation a European official contacted the Canadian government to see if a stand-alone seminary was accredited. Because this institution was not on the provincial government Website, the Canadian official contacted the president prior to responding to the request. The president directed him to Association of Theological Schools (ATS) personnel who were helpful in verifying the institution's accreditation, and as a result the student's degree was recognized by the European country. Through intentional contacts with federal government ministries and with church officials, seminary presidents can raise the profile of Canadian seminaries and assist others to understand better the role seminaries play in the post-secondary sector and the quality assurance/control that the Association of Theological Schools provides.

There continue to be changes in the recognition and regulation of divinity programs by provincial governments. The British Columbia government now controls the offering of degree programs. Ontario Council on Graduate Studies (OCGS) evaluation may be possible for ministerial degrees in Ontario, in addition to the current accreditation of certain master's and doctoral degrees. It has only been since 1980 that private church-related undergraduate institutions have been recognized by provincial governments to offer university degrees (e.g., Trinity Western University, Taylor University College, Alliance University College, and Tyndale University College). Alberta has been a leader in establishing rigorous accreditation/quality control standards and a review process for these university colleges.

Fundraising and Provincial Funding

Canada has a strong history of public education. Provision has been made for Catholic and charter schools to be part of this public system (e.g., in Alberta); Ontario has a fully funded Catholic system paralleling the public one. These schools receive public funds just as traditional public schools do, though recent changes in Newfoundland and Labrador and Quebec point to the tenuous reality of such funding.

Public universities have dominated the higher education arena. Divinity schools/seminaries under the umbrella of public universities have benefited financially from their participation in that system. Most stand-alone seminaries have chosen not to become part of a public university system and therefore do not normally benefit from such funding. Through maintaining good relationships with their provincial education minister, presidents may be able to influence funding decisions as they come up for review periodically. At the very least a president should explore the openness of provincial officials to such funding.

All Canadian seminaries, by necessity, have to be involved in fundraising to meet current and long-term financial challenges. The decline in denominational funding has increased this need. The more socialized cultural milieu (public funding of education), along with the late development of fundraising within the Canadian context, can make fundraising difficult. One president recently commented, "Many Christians are puzzled as to why we don't get government assistance. This puzzlement increases a kind of apathy that does not exist in the U.S., where people can be horrified by the thought of state funding and therefore are highly motivated to give." Another president concurs: "Canadian presidents are often operating in a culture that is far less supportive of private funding for postsecondary education."

Fundraising is further influenced by the regionalism that pervades the Canadian context. Many Canadians tend to think provincially. Thus persons in one province question why they should support private education in another province; they prefer doing so within their own context. Regional perspectives and rivalry also affect giving (e.g., eastern and western Canadians are at times less likely to give to a school outside of their perceived region; some donors are hesitant where the province is perceived to be wealthy). Denominational support does reduce provincialism, but not entirely so. Further, Canadian seminaries tend to have smaller enrollments than U.S. seminaries, which affects both their influence and their profile. This small enrollment, along with smaller fundraising capacity, increases the operating challenge for Canadian seminaries.

The availability of foundation money is significantly less than in the United States. In Canada, foundations are fewer and smaller than their U.S. counterparts. In our research one seminary president referred to a "de facto imbalance that occurs when the U.S.-based foundations grant to the U.S. schools but generally do not provide the same support to the Canadian schools; this puts Canadian schools at a disadvantage even though they are part of the same association."

Corporate giving for seminaries is almost nonexistent in Canada. Stand-alone seminaries are not eligible for most corporate matching gifts, nor are private university colleges associated with seminaries unless they are members of the Association of Universities and Colleges of Canada (AUCC). The Canadian milieu is generally less predisposed to supporting seminaries.

Federal Issues

The Canadian context as a whole offers a number of distinctive challenges to any academic leader, especially a president. While any number of challenges span the nation as a whole, four will be emphasized, each important in its own right. Here the focus will be on distance and the attraction of faculty, diversity, and a "scissors effect" of the relationship between tuition and costs. Attention to these would be important to the success of any school.

Distance

It may seem obvious, but it still needs to be stated that the size of Canada presents challenges to any school and therefore to any president. Distance impacts not only delivery systems for education but also the recruitment of faculty, staff, and students. The significant difference between the United States and its schools (with its far greater population spread over a smaller land mass) and the Canadian context can help to highlight the challenges.

Regions within the United States tend to have populations great enough to support a number of theological institutions representing a variety of perspectives. Canadians, however, have to think nationally and internationally to achieve similar population densities, especially when one focuses on each distinctive faith tradition. This will have an impact in two areas of importance to the president: recruitment and delivery systems.

The first area of challenge is recruitment. Recruitment will require creativity in any institutional leader. This will be true with respect to students; but even more challenging, and often overlooked, is the need to recruit — and maintain — excellent faculty and staff given the geographical challenges, especially for schools not located within the population centers of Canada. Relocation costs, finding an attractive pool of dialogue partners within one's academic discipline, finding research resources with which to continue one's research — all of these can be quite daunting for the prospective member of faculty or staff, especially when the school is competing with other theological centers from within one's own faith tradition. The recruitment pool for qualified faculty is also small, especially because Canadian citizens and permanent residents of Canada must be given first priority when conducting searches. Presidents may want to check provisions that allow for teachers in colleges, seminaries, and universities to be hired on a temporary basis that does not require priority to be given to Canadians. Information may be found on the North American Free Trade Agreement Website (http://www.nafta-sec-alena.org).

Denominational seminaries, which have denominational membership requirements, face further limits with respect to the available pool of potential faculty members. Cultural differences and salary differentials, in part due to exchange rates, size of school, and smaller budgets, make the issues of salary and benefits important ones for the recruitment of faculty. The Canadian president needs to devote a great amount of creativity to developing incentives for faculty, especially as the viability of a theological school depends upon the quality of its faculty. For example, a number of ATS schools in Canada have sought to foster the academic studies of doctoral candidates from their own faith tradition as one way of both expanding the pool of qualified Canadian theologians and ensuring their own academic futures.

The president needs to be aware of another challenge — that of guaranteeing the diversity of one's faculty and staff — because competition for persons from a variety of ethnic, gender, and racial constituencies is acute. Here ATS has resources for developing racial, ethnic, and gender diversity (the Committee on Race and Ethnicity and Women in Leadership), which can provide an incoming president with invaluable support.

At the same time, even as a Canadian president seeks to ensure the future of a faculty in recruiting Canadian scholars, the reality is that one is often required to turn to scholars from other nations. It is critical for any president to become very familiar with the immigration rules and procedures set in place by both Human Resources Development Canada and Citizenship and Immigration Canada; both of these governmental agencies need to be consulted, because one is dealing with both recruitment and immigration. Rules have been significantly tightened in recent years, despite the relative openness promised by the North American Free Trade Agreement. Absolute clarity with respect to both proper procedure and regulations must be a priority for any president who is ultimately responsible for relationships with the federal government.

The second challenge to be addressed when speaking of distance within Canada concerns the need for Canadian theological faculties to be at the forefront of innovation in the use of educational technologies. Differing faith traditions have communities spread over a vast area in Canada, with few local resources for the development of clergy and laity. Canadian ATS schools now find themselves faced with requests from their faith communities for courses from far afield, attending to people who are for the most part unable to relocate to take such courses. Investment and expertise in technology, coupled with curricular flexibility, are increasingly significant concerns for all Canadian ATS schools. Presidents need to ensure that there are persons on the staff and faculty who can meet these needs. Especially as faith communities make increasing demands on Canadian schools, the viability and church support for schools could be at stake.

A response to these challenges has led, among other initiatives, to the development of institutional partnerships and creative delivery systems. For example, a western Canadian network emerged among evangelical seminaries to facilitate greater seamlessness in transferring courses and completing programs for students moving to a different province. This partnership also facilitates awareness of on-line courses offered among its members. Other seminaries offer modular classes in a variety of locations, accepting the fact that ongoing attention to delivery systems is essential.

Diversity

One does not need to consult the works of Reginald Bibby to recognize a second shift that is dramatically affecting the work of presidents in Canada. At a pace far greater than in the United States, Canada is being forced to come to terms with dramatic demographic changes, and not only within its principal population centers. As 250,000 immigrants from all over the world enter Canada each year, theological schools must adapt to a new environment.

Part of this will necessarily relate to the shift in the demographic make-up of our various faith communities. Most Canadian churches, for a variety of reasons, have begun to come to terms with a relative loss of membership from their traditional ethnic bases. This has in part been balanced by an increase in membership from immigrant communities. As the racial and ethnic mix in the church changes, however, ATS schools in Canada have had to struggle to adapt to this new reality with changes to faculty, curriculum, and general ethos. This has been accentuated in Canada by a major difference from our U.S. counterparts. The United States has witnessed a surge in theological schools dedicated to meeting the needs of particular ethnic constituencies, notably on the West Coast. In Canada, however, adaptation has been located within existing schools, which have drawn traditionally from groups of European origin. This has a direct impact upon the need to develop a very different kind of faculty for schools, one which addresses the change in the student body; this will have to be a priority within all Canadian ATS schools. The new president would be well advised to develop personal skills or to seek out support from others with expertise in matters of cultural diversification. Globalization is increasingly a matter of fact within the student bodies of every Canadian ATS school.

ATS schools must also face vastly different ethnic and racial landscapes in their own regions. The interfaith reality will have an impact on fundraising and on all other aspects of the life of ATS schools in Canada, especially as donors and others ask why funding should be dedicated to schools serving just one faith tradition. The cultural assumptions concerning religious pluralism will no doubt change at an increasing pace as Canada's population — and faith — mix continues to undergo such rapid diversification.

At the same time, Canadian presidents will have to cope with faith communities demanding pastors who are adept at coping with such a new and diverse environment. The precise nature of such a demand will be church-specific, perhaps with a focus on interfaith dialogue, or on sensitivity, or on mission. Nevertheless, the pastor of the future will need a greatly different tool set to meet such changes. While no doubt the president of a given school will focus more directly on academic matters, this demographic shift will make significant demands on the president as well. Attention to the rapidly changing socio-cultural mosaic in Canada will be unavoidable.

The "Scissors Challenge" and Its Effect on Fundraising

Across Canada, a pattern first noticed a decade ago has now become a standard expectation for presidents of Canadian ATS schools. The budget assumptions of the 1980s have now been replaced by a dual pressure that complicates any forecast: limitations in revenues and increasing expenditures. In addition to this scissors effect, Canadian presidents face the added challenge of fundraising.

Limitation in Revenues

Most ATS schools depend heavily on tuition revenue in projecting their budgets. The emphasis on fundraising and on endowment is a relatively recent phenomenon within the Canadian context. Yet tuition fees do not represent a profoundly elastic variable for most Canadian schools. Within schools (and degree programs) governed by provincial regulations, there has been a regular pattern across most provinces of limiting tuition increases by government fiat. In Ontario, for example, years of limiting increases have given way to a tuition freeze for two years. While such limits are occasionally cushioned by some increased government funding, schools now have become accustomed to realizing that increases are dictated less by market than by political forces.

The tuition ceiling in most Canadian schools is considerably lower than in their U.S. counterparts, while operating costs are not. Although this is advantageous for students, who end up with fewer debts, it adds to the operating challenges for seminaries. The effect is exaggerated for stand-alone seminaries that receive no government funding and reduced or no denominational funding. Smaller enrollment, endowment, and traditions of giving in the Canadian context add to the challenge for seminaries.

Increases in Expenditures

The expense side of the ATS school ledger has no such restrictions, of course. Costs of providing education have increased at more than the rate of increase in cost of living. The difference between the slow increase in revenues and the rapid increase in costs has placed most Canadian ATS schools in a financial crunch, one that shows no sign of abating in the near future and that will shape the ground for any new president.

Fundraising

Traditionally in the United States the gap would be filled by fundraising from one's various constituencies. A new president of a Canadian theological school would need to realize that there is a lack of such a history of giving in Canada. The fiscal viability of all ATS schools in Canada will rely on the skills of presidents in fostering a culture of giving within their constituencies and in reaching out to new support bases, often outside one's faith tradition.

Issues Regional and Federal

It is clear that a variety of regional and federal issues will challenge a new president. Their complexity, however, is increased by the ways in which some of these issues relate to both provincial and federal authority.

Human Rights and Employment Standards

Not only are human rights and employment standards regulated federally but also the regulations vary from province to province (e.g., retirement, maternity, paternity, severance, privacy laws, etc.). A president needs to ensure that someone at the institution is accountable for monitoring the school's compliance with these requirements. In Canada, among other things this means awareness of the recent changes to legislation concerning sexual orientation and ongoing attention to issues such as maintenance of pay equity. Presently, discussions within the federal government and in some provincial legislatures concerning the removal of 65 as the mandatory retirement age are being watched closely. The University of Alberta won a legal suit allowing institutions to require a mandatory retirement at 65 years of age. Other provinces vary on this requirement. There are a number of Websites where information can be obtained. In the case of the issue of maintenance of pay equity, information sources vary. In some provinces information may be found at a provincial Employment Standards Office, Status of Women Office, or Labour Board. In the case of the federal government, similar information is found at the Canadian Human Rights Commission, and information concerning sexual orientation and legal rights can be found on Websites listed at the end of this chapter under Additional Resources.

In some schools a committee of the board assumes responsibility for ensuring annually that the institution is compliant with any changes in human rights legislation and that appropriate policies are developed and approved by the board. In other situations the school lawyer might perform that function. The fact that the definition or legal requirements associated with such rights may vary from province to province necessitates a proactive stance. One example might be the need to make a change in a school's pension policy or sick leave benefits because of the recent decision of the Canadian government to permit gay and lesbian people to marry. Presidents of Canadian denominational schools need to be aware of all such requirements, especially the coherence or potential lack of coherence between denominational and governmental regulations.

Privacy Legislation

In Canada a number of provinces as well as the federal government have developed privacy legislation. The federal legislation refers to a list of ten principles (e.g., accountability, consent, openness, safeguards, complaints, etc.) that are critical aspects of a school's commitment to privacy. These principles are based on the values set by the Canadian Standards Association's *Model Code for the Protection of Personal Information* and Canada's *Personal Information Protection and Electronics Documents Act* (see Additional Resources). It is essential that a Canadian president also be familiar with requirements specific to his or her province if such exist. At the very least, privacy legislation has implications for how a school handles donor lists and for the confidentiality of student, academic, and staff personnel records. At the present time many Canadian schools are in the process of developing a privacy policy and appointing privacy officers whose responsibility it is to keep the institution aware of growing requirements in this area (see Additional Resources for further details).

Financial and Statistical Reporting

While a president may not be directly involved in preparing such reports, the president does need to be aware of the forms that are required from Canadian schools, some of which are generated by the federal government and some by provincial authorities. The following examples reflect the experience of many Ontario schools.

1. T3010 Charitable Tax Return is prepared for the Canadian Federal Government and must be submitted six months after the fiscal year end.
2. Statistics Canada requires annual reports on full-time and part-time faculty and staff. For part-time faculty and staff this report is due by the end of summer, for full-time faculty and staff by October 15.
3. Reporting to the provincial government on a Facilities Renewal Grant is required four times each year, with a final report due September 30. Through this report, schools justify to the government their disbursement of this grant.
4. Each year a school is required to report to the provincial government as to its appropriate disbursement of a provincially funded matching grant bursary program. The government requires that the financial statements of a school be submitted at the end of each academic year.
5. The Council of Ontario Universities (COU) requires any school associated with a university to summarize and report by mid-September annually on its various educational programs, student enrollment, etc. These statistics are submitted by the university and used in the MacLean's Magazine survey, which ranks universities across Canada for high school graduates and their parents.
6. An annual financial audit is required for the maintenance of the school's charitable status and ATS accreditation. In Canada this is governed by rules for not-for-profit organizations as required by the Canadian Institute of Chartered Accountants (CICA). In light of recent scandals, the president needs to be aware that, although the rules for audits have not changed in any substantial way, the way in which auditors provide for verification has.
7. For any schools in a consortium there are the added financial and

statistical reports needed to facilitate the development of a formula for the fair assessment of shared costs and/or for the allocation of government funding.
8. And, of course, there is the annual required reporting to the Association of Theological Schools.

At times it feels like death by a thousand reports!

Conclusion

As indicated at the outset, this presentation of unique issues for presidents of Canadian schools is meant to be suggestive and not exhaustive.
Within Canada there are many regional and national challenges to a
president's work. The material included in this chapter seeks primarily
to alert a new president to issues identified as critical by a number of his
or her Canadian colleagues so that new presidents may avoid many of
the pitfalls that seem ever present in the work of a president.

Additional Resources

General

Brown, Graham, ed. *Theological Education in Canada.* Toronto: UCC Publishing House, 1998.
A series of articles, both practical and theoretical, that discuss the ideas,
concerns, and practical problems within theological education in Canada over a forty-year period (1960-1998). This work, celebrating the
contribution of the Rev. Dr. Douglas Jay to Canadian theological education, includes essays on ecumenical theological education, religious diversity, biblical exegesis, and theological education, among others.

Government Documents

Federal

Human Rights Code (http://www.ohrc.ofcda.ca)

Privacy Act (Canada), 1985 chapter P-21, updated April 2004 (http://privcom.gc.ca)

Canadian Charter of Rights and Freedoms, Constitution Act, 1982 (79) (http://laws.justice.gc.ca/en/charter/)

Canadian Standards Association's *Model Code for the Protection of Personal Information* (www.csa.ca/standards/privacy)

Canada's *Personal Information Protection and Electronics Documents Act* (www.privcom.gc.ca)

The Canadian Human Rights Commission (http://www.chrc-ccdp.ca/)

A document concerning sexual orientation and legal rights can be found at http://www.parl.gc.ca/information/library/PRBpubs/921-e.htm.

Regional

These need to be accessed individually by province.

ONTARIO EXAMPLES

Employment Standards Act (Ontario). Statutes of Ontario, 2000, chapter 41 (http://www.gov.on.ca/LAB/english/es/index.html)

Ontarians with Disabilities Act, 2001, chapter 32 (http://www.e-laws.gov.on.ca/DBLaws/Statutes/English/)

Ontario Building Code, 1997 (http://www.obc.mah.gov.on.ca/)

Occupational Health and Safety Act (Ontario). Revised Statutes of Ontario, 1990, chapter 0.1 (http://www.gov.on.ca/LAB/english/hs)

Government of Ontario Pay Equity Commission (http://www.gov.on.ca/lab/pec/index_pec.html)

ALBERTA EXAMPLES

Employment Standards Act (http://www3.gov.ab.ca/hre/employmentstandards/index.asp)

Disability Related Information
  (http://www3.gov.ab.ca/hre/dres/index.asp)
  (http://www.wcb.ab.ca/policy/legislation.asp; look at Queen's Printer
    Part 4.56-69)
Occupational Health and Safety Act (Alberta)
  (http://www.qp.gov.ab.ca/documents/acts/O02.cfm)
  (http://www3.gov.ab.ca/hre/whs/law/ohs.asp#ohsact)
Employment Standards Act — Payment of Earnings
  (http://www3.gov.ab.ca/hre/employmentstandards/about/earnings.asp)
  (http://www.qp.gov.ab.ca/documents/acts/W15.cfm; look at Part 4.24-
    55)

The resources identified in this handbook are listed on the ATS Website
where the list will continue to be updated as new resources become
available: www.ats.edu > Leadership Education > Presidents.

Contributors

Daniel Aleshire, The Association of Theological Schools
Harold W. Attridge, Yale University Divinity School
Albert Aymer, Hood Theological Seminary
Rebekah Burch Basinger, In Trust, Inc.
Michael Battle, Interdenominational Theological Center
Maxine Beach, Drew Theological Seminary
Charles E. Bouchard, Aquinas Institute of Theology
C. Samuel Calian, Pittsburgh Theological Seminary
Cynthia Campbell, McCormick Theological Seminary
John Canary, University of St. Mary of the Lake, Mundelein Seminary
Robert Cooley, Gordon-Conwell Theological Seminary
Vincent Cushing, Washington Theological Union
Marvin Dewey, Taylor Seminary
David Draper, Winebrenner Theological Seminary
Ward Ewing, General Theological Seminary
Frederick J. Finks, Ashland Theological Seminary
Dorcas Gordon, Knox College
Thomas Graves, Baptist Theological Seminary at Richmond

Heidi Hadsell, Hartford Seminary

Adolf Hansen, Garrett-Evangelical Theological Seminary

Martha Horne, Protestant Episcopal Theological Seminary in Virginia

James Hudnut-Beumler, Vanderbilt University Divinity School

Byron Klaus, Assemblies of God Theological Seminary

Christa Klein, In Trust, Inc.

Steven Land, Church of God Theological Seminary

Robert Landrebe, Gordon-Conwell Theological Seminary

Robert F. Leavitt, St. Mary's Seminary and University

G. Douglass Lewis, Wesley Theological Seminary

David Maldonado, Iliff School of Theology

Kevin Mannoia, Azusa Pacific University

David McAllister-Wilson, Wesley Theological Seminary

William McKinney, Pacific School of Religion

Laura Mendenhall, Columbia Theological Seminary

Ron Mercier, Regis College

Donn Morgan, Church Divinity School of the Pacific

Richard J. Mouw, Fuller Theological Seminary

David Neelands, Trinity College Faculty of Divinity

Anthony Ruger, Auburn Theological Seminary

Donald Senior, Chicago Theological Union

Jean Stairs, Queen's Theological College

Brian Stiller, Tyndale University College and Seminary

Susan Thistlethwaite, Chicago Theological Seminary

David L. Tiede, Luther Seminary

Timothy Weber, Memphis Theological Seminary

Kent M. Weeks, Senior Attorney, Weeks, Anderson, and Baker

Louis Weeks, Union Theological Seminary and Presbyterian School of
    Christian Education

Lovett H. Weems Jr., Wesley Theological Seminary

Edward Wheeler, Christian Theological Seminary

Craig Williford, Denver Seminary

Wilson Yates, United Theological Seminary of the Twin Cities